Hannah Arendt

Hannah Arendt
An Introduction

John McGowan

 University of Minnesota Press

Minneapolis

London

Copyright 1998 by the Regents of the University of Minnesota

All rights reserved. No part of this publication may be reproduced, stored in a retrieval system, or transmitted, in any form or by any means, electronic, mechanical, photocopying, recording, or otherwise, without the prior written permission of the publisher.

Published by the University of Minnesota Press
111 Third Avenue South, Suite 290
Minneapolis, MN 55401-2520

http://www.upress.umn.edu

Printed in the United States of America on acid-free paper

Library of Congress Cataloging-in-Publication Data

McGowan, John, 1953–
    Hannah Arendt : an introduction / John McGowan.
        p.   cm.
    Includes bibliographical references and index.
    ISBN 0-8166-3069-0 (hardcover : alk. paper). — ISBN 0-8166-3070-4 (pbk. : alk. paper)
        1. Arendt, Hannah—Contributions in political science.   I. Title.
JC251.A74M395   1997
320.5′092—dc21   97-15017
                                                                                              CIP

The University of Minnesota is an equal-opportunity educator and employer.

10 09 08 07 06 05 04 03 02 01 00 99 98   10 9 8 7 6 5 4 3 2 1

For Jane
finally

Contents

Acknowledgments   ix

A Note on Usage and References   xi

1. Origins: Arendt's Life and Coming to Terms with Totalitarianism   1
    Biography   1
    Arendt on Totalitarianism   15

2. Politics as Identity-Disclosing Action   34
    The Political and the Public   38
    Labor and Work   42
    Behavior and the Social   45
    Explaining the Rise of the Social   52
    Action, Freedom, and Identity in the Space of
        Appearances   60
    A Pickup Basketball Game   70
    Participatory Democracy   81
    Conclusion: Recovering Citizenship   94

3. Understanding and Judging the Reality of Evil   96
    The Reality of Evil   100
    Thinking   108
    Judging   120
    Storytelling   137
    Conclusion: Are We Being Political Yet?   147

4. Arendt Now   150
    The Meaning of Democracy   154
    A Democratic Ethos   166

Notes   181

References   185

For Further Reading   187

Index   189

Acknowledgments

That I have compiled so many debts in writing so short a book testifies to my membership in the vibrant intellectual community that is the University of North Carolina at Chapel Hill. This book would not exist if it were not for two people I did not even know five years ago: Craig Calhoun and Susan Bickford. Craig asked me to team-teach a graduate seminar on Arendt with him; initiated and found the funds for a conference on Arendt, "Hannah Arendt and the Meaning of Politics," that we ran together; and suggested that I complement the volume of essays we compiled from that conference with an introduction to Arendt's thought. Through the Program in Social Theory and Cross-Cultural Studies (which he founded), Craig created an intellectual space of appearances for a whole generation of UNC faculty and students. I, a latecomer, am only one among many who benefited from Craig's generosity, vision, energy, and (not least) breathtaking brilliance. Susan was the reader perched on my shoulder as I wrote this book. I think she has memorized every word Arendt ever wrote. She read each draft as I produced it, saved me from countless errors, talked me through any number of difficult points, and buoyed me with what I flatter myself was judicious praise. I can only hope that her theoretical acuity, political commitment, and intellectual courage enliven these pages as they do all those who are lucky enough to be her colleagues, students, and friends.

My thanks to Laurence Avery and the Department of English for a study leave, and to Ruel Tyson, Lloyd Kramer, and the Institute of Arts and Humanities both for a faculty fellowship and for financial support of the Arendt conference. No work coming out of the Program in Social Theory is complete without mention of Leah Florence, whose unfailing cheerfulness and characteristic wisdom made all the activities of the program possible. Of the students in the Arendt seminar, I particularly thank Jill Craven, Joe Gerteis, Jay Murray, and auditor–research assistant Paul Price. Jim Moody read the entire book in manuscript, and I have taken many of his suggestions for improving it. Among the participants in the Arendt conference, I must single out Lisa Disch and Kim Curtis, not least because much of what I say about Arendt's storytelling and her ontology in this book derives from their work. I do not mean, of course, to slight the other students and conference participants, all of whom contributed to my ongoing education in matters Arendtian.

One of the conference participants, Tony Cascardi, read the manuscript for Minnesota. I have incorporated his suggested revisions—along with those of a second, admirably conscientious, anonymous reader—to the best of my ability. My editor, Micah Kleit, conceived this project, supported me throughout its execution (including supplying me with hard-to-get Arendtian texts), and—miracles never cease—read the manuscript from start to finish. Thanks also to fearless and competent copy editor Tammy Zambo, who undoubtedly tampered with this sentence as with so many others—and made it better.

Of friends old and new who have encouraged my intellectual wanderings over the years, I think especially (this time around) of Charlie Altieri, Reid Barbour, Doug Dempster, Allen Dunn, Judy Farquhar, Jessica Fields, Dan Hayes, Jim Hevia, Nancy Jesser, John Kucich, Laurie Langbauer, Megan Matchinske, Carol Mavor, Greg McAvoy, Jeff Nealon, Lee Quinby, Kevin Parker, Della Pollock, Alan Shapiro, and James Thompson.

Family debts, as Arendt tells us, are not matters of public appearance, and thus a nod in their direction must stand in for a gratitude I better express (I hope) elsewhere. Jane, Kiernan, and Siobhan bind me to this world, a world I can love because they exist, a world in which I can exist because they love me.

A Note on Usage and References

Hannah Arendt uses words distinctive to her, such as "plurality" and "natality," to designate certain specific concepts; and she uses various common words, such as "life" and "world," in highly specific, even technical, ways that should not be confused with our ordinary understanding of these words. My practice in this book is to define these specific Arendtian usages as early as possible and then to place the special term in quotation marks every time I think the reader will need help remembering that the special Arendtian sense is intended. But, in order not to proliferate quotation marks to the point of annoyance, I don't use them when it seems to me that the context or sheer repetition (after five times or so, I figure the reader has gotten the idea that "natality" is peculiar to Arendt and has a specific meaning) makes misunderstanding unlikely.

I use "she" and "he," "his" and "her" interchangeably when I need a third-person singular pronoun, somewhat preferring the feminine form but relying on context to use the form that will most aid comprehension. So, for example, I use "his" in a context where "her" might be mistaken as referring to Arendt.

All italics in quoted passages are Arendt's. All material in brackets in quoted passages is mine, except where noted otherwise. Dictionary definitions in the text come from *Webster's New World Dictionary of the American Language*, second college edition (New York, 1972).

References to works not by Arendt are marked in the text with the author's name, date of publication, and page number when the author is quoted directly. Full bibliographic information for these citations can be found under the heading "References" at the end of the book. Passages from works by Arendt, from Elisabeth Young-Bruehl's biography of Arendt, and from Melvyn A. Hill's compilation of a 1972 colloquium on Arendt's work (which Arendt attended) are marked in the text according to the abbreviations that follow, with the page number following the appropriate abbreviation. The date in brackets is the date of original publication if that differs from the publication date of the edition I use. This issue of dates is complicated by the fact that Arendt often added material when her books came out in a second edition. When two dates appear in brackets, the first indicates the first edition, the second an expanded or otherwise altered second edition.

Works by Hannah Arendt

BPF	*Between Past and Future: Eight Exercises in Political Thought* (New York: Penguin Books, 1977 [1961 and 1968]).
EJ	*Eichmann in Jerusalem: A Report on the Banality of Evil* (New York: Penguin Books, 1977 [1963 and 1965]).
EU	*Essays in Understanding, 1930–1954*, ed. Jerome Kohn (New York: Harcourt Brace, 1994).
HC	*The Human Condition* (Chicago: University of Chicago Press, 1958).
JP	*The Jew as Pariah: Jewish Identity and Politics in the Modern Age*, ed. Ron H. Feldman (New York: Grove Press, 1978).
L	*Hannah Arendt/Karl Jaspers Correspondence, 1926–1969*, ed. Lotte Kohler and Hans Saner (San Diego: Harcourt Brace, 1992).
LK	*Lectures on Kant's Political Philosophy*, ed. Ronald Beiner (Chicago: University of Chicago Press, 1982).
LOM	*The Life of the Mind* (New York: Harcourt Brace Jovanovich, 1981 [1978]).
MDT	*Men in Dark Times* (San Diego: Harcourt Brace Jovanovich, 1968).
OR	*On Revolution* (New York: Penguin Books, 1977 [1963 and 1965]).
OT	*The Origins of Totalitarianism* (San Diego: Harcourt Brace, 1966 [1951 and 1958]).
OV	*On Violence* (New York: Harcourt Brace Jovanovich, 1972).

RLR   "Reflections on Little Rock," *Dissent* 6, no. 1 (winter 1959): 45–56.

SQ   "Some Questions of Moral Philosophy," *Social Research* 61, no. 4 (winter 1994): 739–64.

T   *Thinking*, vol. 1 of *The Life of the Mind (LOM).*

W   *Willing*, vol. 2 of *The Life of the Mind (LOM).*

Other Works

Hill   *Hannah Arendt: The Recovery of the Public World*, ed. Melvyn A. Hill (New York: St. Martin's Press, 1979).

Y-B   Elisabeth Young-Bruehl, *Hannah Arendt: For Love of the World* (New Haven: Yale University Press, 1982).

1
Origins: Arendt's Life and Coming to Terms with Totalitarianism

Biography

Hannah Arendt was born in 1906 in Hanover, Germany.[1] Her parents were both natives of Königsberg, the capital of East Prussia and home of Immanuel Kant, the philosopher to whose work Arendt would return at the end of her life. After World War II, Königsberg passed into Russian hands, was renamed Kaliningrad, and was used as a military center (closed to all outside visitors) until 1989. Today Kaliningrad is still part of Russia, although it is separated from the rest of the country by the Baltic states.

Arendt's parents, Paul and Martha Arendt, came from prosperous, although not wealthy, members of Königsberg's five-thousand-member-strong Jewish community, many of whom (including Martha's family, the Cohns) were refugees from Alexander II's Russia. Paul and Martha were both members of the illegal Socialist Party. Neither was religious, but they sent Hannah to synagogue with her grandparents after the family returned to Königsberg when Hannah was four. The return was occasioned by Paul Arendt's illness: the syphilis he had contracted as a young man now entered its final phase. In the spring of 1911, he had to be institutionalized, and he died in 1913, when Hannah was eight. Six months earlier, Paul's father, Max, with whom Hannah spent much time, had also died.

Hannah and her mother fled Königsberg for Berlin for ten weeks in the early fall of 1914, when it was not clear whether Germany could stop the advancing Russian army as World War I began. The remainder of the war years passed uneventfully back in Königsberg, although Hannah was recurrently, albeit not dangerously, ill throughout 1915 and 1916. The Spartacist rebellion of 1919, led by socialists Rosa Luxemburg and Karl Liebknecht, made a profound impression on the young Hannah, if only because of her mother's excitement at the news. The murders of Luxemburg and Liebknecht by the rightist paramilitary Freikorps brought the rebellion to a swift halt—and was an unrecognized portent of things to come.

Hannah's mother remarried in 1920. Her new stepfather, Martin Berwald, was a widower with two daughters, and a businessman whose prosperity carried Hannah and her mother safely through the inflation years of the early and middle 1920s in Germany. The teenage Arendt was already reading Kierkegaard, Kant, and Karl Jaspers, and was planning to study theology when she went off to university. She arrived at Marburg in the fall of 1924 and almost immediately fell under the spell of thirty-five-year-old Martin Heidegger, whose lectures at the time were working through the material that was to become his masterpiece, *Being and Time* (published in 1927). Arendt was not only Heidegger's student. By the spring of 1925, the two were lovers, a fact kept strictly secret because Heidegger was married. The hopelessness of the situation played at least some role in Arendt's decision to leave Marburg in the summer of 1925 and go on to Heidelberg to study with Karl Jaspers. (It was common for German university students to move freely from one university to another to take courses of lectures from various famous professors.) In Jaspers, Arendt found a nurturing mentor who would later become her dearest friend. Under Jaspers's direction, she wrote her dissertation on the concept of love in Augustine (recently published in English for the first time).

The year 1929 found Arendt in Berlin, married to Günther Stern (a young Jewish intellectual and writer), and involved in various writing projects. Most significant among her Berlin acquaintances during this time was Karl Blumenfeld, an old family friend from Königsberg, who was executive secretary of the Zionist Organization of Germany. Arendt, then as later, had severe doubts about Zionism. She was, as she remained, deeply committed to a pluralist model of a polity in which all citizens learn to live amid differences. But despite her doubts—and this is typical of Arendt—she was drawn, both through personal loyalty to Blumenfeld and through the demands of the worsening situation for German Jews as the Nazis became more and more prominent, into helping the Zionists compile evidence of German anti-Semitism. Similarly, although not a Communist herself, Arendt offered her flat in Berlin as a refuge for Communists fleeing the increasingly violent police and paramilitary attacks on known leftists. In February 1933, her husband fled Berlin for Paris shortly after the Reichstag fire. (The Reichstag, the German Parliament building, was set on fire by Nazis, who then blamed the fire on the Communists and used the arson as a pretext for violent reprisals against leftists.) Stern was a member of leftist intellectual circles; he had worked with Bertolt Brecht on several projects.

Arendt stayed. As someone not affiliated with either the Zionists or the leftists, she felt a certain safety even as she aided both groups. But she was also motivated by her feeling of responsibility: "That is, I was no longer of the opinion that one can simply be a bystander. I tried to help in many ways" (*EU*, 5). She felt compelled to do what she could in Germany to resist the collapse of the world she knew. In the spring of 1933, Arendt was arrested (along with her mother) and held for eight days before being released. Shortly after, Arendt and her mother fled Germany without documents, making their way from Prague to Geneva and, finally, to Paris. Telling the story of these events for the first time publicly in 1965, Arendt found a "satisfaction" in knowing that she had been arrested, that she had "at least done something":

> I intended to emigrate anyhow. I thought immediately that Jews could not stay. I did not intend to run around Germany as a second-class citizen, so to speak, in whatever form. In addition, I thought that things would just get worse and worse. Nevertheless, in the end I did not leave in a peaceful way. And I must say that gives me a certain satisfaction. I was arrested, and had to leave the country illegally . . . and that was an instant gratification for me. I thought I had at least done something! At least I am not "innocent." No one could say that of me! (5)

There was work for Arendt in Geneva, where her mother had a friend who worked for the League of Nations, but Arendt insisted on going to Paris. Her decision stemmed from her belief that "if one is attacked as a Jew, one must defend oneself as a Jew. . . . I wasn't discussing my personal problems as a Jew. But now, belonging to Judaism had become my own problem, and my own problem was political. Purely political! I wanted to go into practical work, exclusively and only Jewish work. With this in mind I then looked for work in France" (*EU*, 12). Through Günther Stern's sister, Arendt went to work for a Zionist organization called Youth Aliyah, which helped provide education for the children of Jewish refugees from Germany and Eastern Europe while also arranging for emigration to Palestine for some refugees.

Arendt's actions as a Jew had also taken an intellectual form during the rise of Nazism and anti-Semitism in Germany. During 1931–32, her energies as a writer were chiefly devoted to a biography of Rahel Varnhagen (1771–1833), a wealthy Jewish woman of Berlin who held a salon to which various eminent intellectuals came during the German romantic period. Arendt's book, not published until 1958, is subtitled *The Life of a Jewish Woman* and tells the tale of a failed attempt to flee from Jewishness and a final reconciliation to the Jewish identity that Varnhagen at first tried to repudiate. The story hinges on words attributed to Varnhagen on her deathbed: "The thing which all my life seemed to me the greatest shame, which was the misery and misfortune of my life—having been born a Jewess—this I should on no account now wished to have missed" (*Y-B*, 87). Arendt's point, she claimed in looking back, was to dramatize the "Zionist critique of assimilation" (*L*, 197): the Jew cannot expect psychologically to shed her identity as Jew, although that demand should never be made politically. But this conclusion does not mean, for Arendt, that the political ideal is the complete consonance of ethnic and political identity in a racially or ethnically homogeneous nation. Rather, she looks toward a state in which citizenship and ethnicity are not tied to each other, are totally independent of each other. In her more optimistic moments, America seemed such a political entity to Arendt:

> In conditions of freedom every individual should be able to decide what he would like to be, German or Jew or whatever. In an a-national republic like the United States, in which nationality and state are not identical, this becomes more or less a question with only social and cultural meaning but no political meaning. (For example, so-called anti-Semitism here is purely social, and the same people who wouldn't dream of sharing the same hotel with Jews would be astonished and outraged if their fellow citizens who happened to be Jewish

were disenfranchised. This may change, but for now that's the way things are.) In the European system of nation-states it is all much more complicated. (90–91)

The republic here, which gives nationalities freedom and yet includes every citizen, indeed, treats even an immigrant as a future citizen. (99)

Where citizenship and ethnic identity are separate, the price exacted for becoming a full-fledged political subject will not be assimilation or, even more radically, repudiation of ethnic roots.

Hannah Arendt arrived in Paris alone, her mother having decided to return to Königsberg. Arendt shared an apartment with Günther Stern, but the two no longer thought of themselves as married and were officially divorced in 1936. In Paris, Arendt met Walter Benjamin and Heinrich Blücher. Benjamin, the Jewish literary critic–philosopher, became a close friend and entrusted his manuscripts to Arendt when both were trying to escape France after its fall to the Nazis in 1940. Arendt later oversaw the publication of Benjamin's work in English. Blücher, a non-Jewish German Marxist, became Arendt's second husband. They were married in January 1940, a short time after Martha Arendt fled Germany a second time (at just about the last possible moment).

I will not reconstruct here the torturous path these three (Hannah, Heinrich, and Martha) traveled to finally arrive in New York in May 1941. All three spent time in internment camps for enemy refugees, and only a combination of resourcefulness, luck, fortunate times, and a persistent, cold-eyed view that they could rely on no official authorities (whether French, Vichy-French, or American) to protect them enabled their escape. They got 1 of only 238 visas (out of 1,137 requests) granted by the U.S. Department of State to European refugees between August and December 1940. (Their luck was aided by the intercession of Günther Stern, already in New York, on their behalf.) And even possession of one of these precious visas did not save Walter Benjamin's life. The Vichy government was completely fickle on the matter of refugees, with no consistent policy on refusing or allowing exit from the country. Turned back by officials at the Spanish border because he lacked the proper exit visa, Benjamin committed suicide.

Although I have passed over the details quickly, I must emphasize how crucial this experience of "statelessness," of losing all the rights, privileges, and protections afforded to citizens, was to the formation of Arendt's subsequent political philosophy. The political and human catastrophes that resulted from the totalitarian regimes of Hitler and Stalin were the data, the facts with which Arendt's mature work struggled to come to terms. Terror, concentration camps, radical evil, and total war were the monstrous manifestations of an unprecedented reality—manifestations Arendt herself was lucky enough to know almost entirely by report alone. What she did know first-hand were anti-Semitism (which she would take pains to insist took a new, distinctive form in twentieth-century totalitarianism) and statelessness. Rights, Arendt insisted, are always legal, not natural; rights are created in the formation of a political entity and can be enjoyed only by those who are members of that entity and subject to its laws. Thus, "the first essential step on the road to total domination is to kill the juridical person in man" (*OT*, 447).[2] By placing certain persons outside the boundaries of any state, by stripping them of citizenship in any polity, totalitarianism creates persons upon whom it can unleash the most fearsome terror.

Her own experience of statelessness led to Arendt's focus on totalitarianism as the destruction of the political, thus leading further to her insistence that it was not too much politics that occasioned the "totality of the moral collapse" of Germany (and, subsequently, most of Europe) under the Nazis (*EJ*, 125), but not enough politics. The origins of Arendt's first great work, *The Origins of Totalitarianism*, lie in her having lived this collapse of the political in Europe from 1933 to 1941.

In New York, Arendt set about learning English with her characteristic energy, while she found work writing for *Aufbau*, the newsletter of the German Club, an organization founded in 1924 to provide new immigrants with a meeting place. She was soon deeply involved in Jewish debates about the desirability of a specifically Jewish army to fight Hitler (Arendt strongly favored one) and of the establishment of a Jewish state in Palestine. Arendt was not against the Zionist state, but she always insisted that it was not the only political goal for Jewish people and that it could never be the home of all Jews or of only Jews. Her attitude is best summed up by a comment in a 1947 letter to Jaspers: "For me and many others today it has become a matter of course that the first thing we do when we open a newspaper is to see what's going on in Palestine, even though I don't intend ever to go there and am almost totally convinced that things will not work out there" (*L*, 91). In a series of 1942 articles in *Aufbau*, Arendt offered her own hopes of a postwar European federation and of a Palestine aligned to that federation as part of the British Commonwealth. There were no takers—and Arendt had assumed for the first time the lonely position of presenting views aslant from those of prominent Jewish leaders and writers of all the recognizable factions, a position she would hold until the end of her life. In 1944, Arendt went to work for the Conference on Jewish Relations, producing (as the published report phrased it) a "Tentative List of Jewish Cultural Treasures in Axis-Occupied Countries." She subsequently worked from 1948 until 1952 directing an operation to recover such treasures, returning them to rightful owners where possible, and housing them in appropriate Jewish institutions where not. She also worked for Schocken Books during this time, most notably on a German edition of Franz Kafka's *Diaries*.

An essay on Kafka (1944) that grew out of that editorial work marked Arendt's first contribution to *Partisan Review*, the most prominent outlet for what we know today as the "New York Intellectuals." Arendt was soon a regular contributor to *Partisan Review* and other New York–based publications such as *Commentary* and the *Nation*. Her friendships with the poet Randall Jarrell and the novelist Mary McCarthy date from this time. Yet even as a new life began to take shape, Arendt was, along with the rest of the world, beginning to learn how completely the old world had disintegrated. "What was decisive," Arendt recalls in 1965, "was the day we learned about Auschwitz":

> That was in 1943. At first we didn't believe it—although my husband and I always said that we expected anything from that bunch. But we didn't believe this because militarily it was unnecessary and uncalled for. . . . And then a half-year later we believed it all, because we had the proof. That was the real shock. . . . It was really as if an abyss had opened. Because we had the idea that amends could somehow be made for everything else, as amends can be made for just about everything at some point in politics. But not for this. *This ought not to have happened.* And I don't mean just the number of victims. I mean the method, the fabrication of corpses and so on—I don't need to go into that. This should not have happened. Something happened there to which we cannot reconcile ourselves. None of us ever can. (*EU*, 13–14)

Arendt could only respond to her incredulity, her insistence that this should not have happened, with an attempt to understand how it did, after all, happen. The result was *The Origins of Totalitarianism*, begun in late 1945 and published in 1951. The book was immediately recognized as an ambitious effort to provide a comprehensive account of the dominance of totalitarianism in Europe after World War I, an effort that refused to focus on Germany as exceptional, instead linking Nazism with Stalin's Communism in Soviet Russia, and linking totalitarianism itself with "race-thinking," with imperialism, and with developments (especially toward "mass society") evident in Western (European and American) society as a whole.

Although reflections on Europe's fate in the twentieth century could only be grim, there was some happy news: Karl Jaspers and his Jewish wife, Gertrud, had survived the war in Heidelberg. "Ever since I've known that you both came through the whole hellish mess unharmed, I have felt somewhat more at home in the world again," Arendt tells them in a November 1945 letter (*L*, 23). On a 1948 trip to Europe (undertaken in her work to recover Jewish cultural treasures stolen by the Nazis), Arendt visited the Jasperses in their new home in Basel, Switzerland. She also saw Martin Heidegger again, in Freiburg, where Heidegger, as rector of the university there, had participated in the slander and dismissal of Jewish professors during the 1930s. (Heidegger was also a member of the Nazi party; for just how long is a matter of dispute.) Arendt had written a dismissive appraisal of Heidegger's work in a 1946 *Partisan Review* essay, "What Is Existential Philosophy?" (reprinted in *Essays in Understanding*). The essay also mentioned, in a footnote, Heidegger's membership in the Nazi party and that "in his capacity as rector of Freiburg University, he forbade Husserl, his teacher and friend, whose lecture chair he had inherited, to enter the faculty, because Husserl was a Jew" (*EU*, 187). The 1948 meeting with Heidegger was overwrought, with Heidegger full of memories of days long past and Arendt indignant about his failure to see that intervening events had changed everything (it was more than sixteen years since they had last met) yet attracted once more by this man she had loved at eighteen. Arendt and Heidegger corresponded sporadically for the next twenty-five years, and she visited him on trips to Europe, but the intensity of the 1948 visit was never repeated. The issue of Arendt's intellectual debt to Heidegger is a complex one; certain Heideggerian themes are prominent in her work (especially in *The Human Condition*), and she offers an explicit discussion of some parts of his work in her last work, *The Life of the Mind*.[3] If the relationship to Heidegger is more intriguing to us because of his shady past and because of the love affair of the 1920s, it was the relationship to Jaspers that proved more sustaining to Arendt. She tried to arrange her life so as to visit him at least once a year from 1948 on, and their correspondence pays testimony again and again to how much she trusted Jaspers's intellectual responses and treasured his friendship.

The Origins of Totalitarianism brought Arendt recognition in American academic circles. In 1952, she was the first woman to give the Christian Gauss lectures at Princeton. She received a Guggenheim Fellowship, and in 1956 she lectured, for the first of many times, at the University of Chicago. These lectures formed the basis of *The Human Condition* (1958), the book in which Arendt most fully sets out her political philosophy. That philosophy is also presented in the essays collected in *Between Past and Future* (1961; revised edition with two additional essays, 1968) and in her study of the French and American Revolutions, *On Revolution* (1963). This triptych constituted what might be called the "middle period" of Arendt's work, the development of an understanding of the political designed to stand against the deformations that led to totalitarianism.

In 1960, while Arendt was trying to finish *On Revolution*, Israeli secret service officers kidnapped Adolf Eichmann in Buenos Aires and brought him back to Israel to be tried for crimes against the Jewish people, crimes against humanity, and war crimes. Eichmann had been an SS officer whose task had been to arrange the deportations and evacuations of Jews in a number of Eastern European countries under Nazi rule. His trial would begin in Jerusalem in 1961. "To attend this trial is somehow, I feel, an obligation I owe my past," Arendt wrote (Y-B, 329), and she arranged to go as a special correspondent for the *New Yorker*. Her five-part report, published in February and March 1963 and subsequently as the book *Eichmann in Jerusalem: A Report on the Banality of Evil* (1963), made Arendt famous—and infamous. The phrase "the banality of evil" became a permanent part of the English language, whereas Arendt was widely vilified for her interpretation of Eichmann and her discussion of the ways in which the deportation of the Jews was organized. Arendt did not quite satirize the Jerusalem trial, but she did show her distaste for what she hinted were practically hysterical attempts (on the part of the prosecution) to see Eichmann as a criminal mastermind, as the architect of the Final Solution. (To be clear—and it is crucial to be clear on this matter that still inflames her readers—Arendt is pretty openly contemptuous of the prosecution, but she explicitly praises the three presiding judges and explicitly endorses both the judgment that Eichmann was guilty of crimes against humanity and the justice of his penalty, death by hanging.)

In Arendt's eyes, Eichmann was something much more terrifying than a master criminal or the architect of the Holocaust; he was a completely ordinary man, a functionary who did his job and was so enveloped in the ordinary, the banal, the chore at hand, that he lost all capacity to tell right from wrong. His sheer "thoughtlessness" is what struck Arendt most forcibly, and she thought she recognized how to-talitarianism managed to gain sway over such vast numbers of people: it exploited people who live in a world of daily demands and daily tasks that command their attention and obedience, leaving little, if any, room for reflection, for consideration of the possibility that the world might be otherwise, that they might act differently. In a January 1945 essay entitled "Organized Guilt and Universal Responsibility," Arendt was already pursuing the line of thought that would lead to the conclusion that Eichmann's evil was "banal," that it grew out of mundane considerations and anxieties. She argues that Himmler

> consciously built up his newest terror organization, covering the whole country, on the assumption that most people are not Bohemi-ans nor fanatics, nor adventurers, nor sex maniacs, nor sadists, but, first and foremost job-holders, and good family-men. . . . The docil-ity of this type was already manifest in the very early period of Nazi "gleichshaltung" [equal rule]. It became clear that for the sake of his pension, his life insurance, the security of his wife and children, such a man was ready to sacrifice his beliefs, his honor, and his human dignity. It needed only the satanic genius of Himmler to discover that after such degradation he was entirely prepared to do literally any-thing when the ante was raised and the bare existence of his family threatened. The only condition he put was that he should be fully ex-empted from responsibility for his acts. Thus that very person, the average German, whom the Nazis notwithstanding years of the most furious propaganda could not induce to kill Jews (not even when they made it quite clear that such a murder would go unpunished) now serves the machine of destruction without opposition. (*JP*, 232)

If her interpretation of Eichmann was controversial, Arendt's depiction of the Jewish response to the Nazis was infuriating. She described how the Nazis made use of local Jewish leaders and Jewish councils (even creating such councils in Jewish communities where they did not preexist the Nazi intervention) to organize deportation. The councils, in other words, handed the people over to their killers. It sounded as if Arendt were accusing the Jews, especially the Jewish leaders, of collaborating with the Nazis in the Holocaust. Her actual position was rather more complex than that. For starters, she did not believe that denial of the role played by the Jewish councils could be productive in any way. Not only was refusal to face the facts (and, even worse, the attempt to rewrite history) a salient feature of the very totalitarianism that Holocaust survivors should strive to combat, but Arendt also believed that Jewish cooperation demonstrated the way that totalitarian regimes can make the unthinkable part of everyday existence precisely by creating a daily reality that affords no alternatives. Arendt was not "blaming the victims" but was chronicling the immensity of the moral collapse precipitated by the Nazis. That "the prosecutor [in the Eichmann trial] ask[ed] witness after witness, 'Why did you not protest?,' 'Why did you board the train?,' 'Fifteen thousand people were standing there and hundreds of guards facing you— why didn't you revolt and charge and attack?'" (*EJ*, 11) angers Arendt because it "distorted the truth, even the Jewish truth" (12): "[T]he sad truth of the matter is that . . . no non-Jewish group or people had behaved differently. . . . There exist many things considerably worse than death, and the SS saw to it that none of them was ever very far from their victims' minds and imaginations" (11–12). Resistance, whether of functionaries such as Eichmann or of victims such as the Jews, proved well nigh impossible under such conditions, for reasons ranging from the sheer physical force commanded by the Nazis to "thoughtlessness" and the sheer, incontrovertible weight of daily reality. Questions of motive, opportunity, and emotion aside, there remains what was done, what happened—and Arendt (consistent with her ever present desire to lay the stress on action, on what appears in the world) felt that she, as a reporter, should state the facts:

> But the whole truth was that there existed Jewish community organizations and Jewish party and welfare organizations on both the local and international level. Wherever Jews lived, there were recognized Jewish leaders, and this leadership, almost without exception,

cooperated in one way or another, for one reason or another, with the Nazis. The whole truth was that if the Jewish people had really been unorganized and leaderless, there would have been chaos and plenty of misery but the total number of victims would hardly have been between four and a half and six million people. (125)

Such a statement, especially if read out of context, was bound to provoke howls of outrage.

The subtleties of Arendt's argument were not much heard in the storm of controversy that greeted Arendt's report on the banality of evil. She was widely attacked in the Jewish press and by Jewish organizations, and by non-Jewish intellectuals as well. As usual in such cases, many who attacked her had not read her book, and little that was intellectually or ethically worthwhile resulted. It was a good five years before Arendt was able to put the controversy behind her—and, in some ways, it dictated the whole course of her remaining work. The best that might be said of the whole affair is that it brought the topic of the Holocaust in all its various guises to the public's attention— where it has remained ever since. Of course, Eichmann's arrest and trial had already begun to do that work. But it is worth noting how little was known prior to 1963 about the Holocaust and how little its image dominated the general public's imagination. (The 1950s were lived under the shadow of the atom bomb and the cold war almost exclusively.) Almost everything we know about the Holocaust comes from historical research done after Arendt's book was written. Inevitably she got some facts wrong, but none crucial enough to discredit her argument. Disagreement with that argument must depend not on the facts of the case but on her understanding of the case's significance, on her account of the daily reality and the options facing people in their daily lives under the totalitarian rule of the Nazis. That those options were severely restricted—they were little more than different ways of facing death for millions of Jews—does not, in Arendt's view, absolve us, as the survivors who must remember this history in our chronicles, from the effort to understand the unthinkable and to judge those—both functionaries and victims—who acted under such extreme conditions. It was this insistence on the necessity of judgment that marked the most significant exchange that followed her book's publication—between Arendt and the Jewish religious scholar Gershom Scholem—and motivated Arendt's turn, in the last twelve years of her life, to questions of morality and of the nature of thinking, willing, and judging.

Arendt was no stranger to controversy on the American scene as well. Even before the Eichmann book, she had been attacked for an essay deploring President Eisenhower's use of federal troops to integrate the schools of Little Rock, Arkansas, in 1957. Such an action, she argued, both threatened the decentered multiplication of powers she favored in a federal republic (her ideal political entity) and did the young black children who served as guinea pigs for the social experiment no good at all. Later, Arendt was an early opponent of the war in Vietnam and a sympathetic, if not always approving, commentator on the student protests against the war. Her essay on Little Rock was never included in a book, but her various responses to the events of the 1960s are gathered in *Crises of the Republic* (1972). *Men in Dark Times* (1968) gathers essays on Karl Jaspers, Walter Benjamin, Pope John XXIII, Isak Dinesen, and other figures Arendt celebrates as exemplars.

As Karl Jaspers had done before her, Arendt dreamed of the day when she could abandon her political writing (called forth by the political disasters of the age) and return to philosophy. Her final work, *The Life of the Mind* (published posthumously in 1978), was an unfinished attempt to rethink the tripartite Kantian distinctions between pure reason (thinking), practical reason (willing), and judgment. Arendt managed to complete only the first two parts, *Thinking* and *Willing*, before her death on December 4, 1975. The first page of what was to become the third part of this work, "Judging," was found on her typewriter. In 1982, the lecture notes for a course on Kant that Arendt had taught at New York's New School for Social Research were published as *Lectures on Kant's Political Philosophy* (edited by Ronald Beiner). These lectures are concerned primarily with "judging" and have been the chief source for a lively and ongoing scholarly debate about just what the third volume of *The Life of the Mind* would have said and the relevance of Arendt's views of judgment to various controversies in political philosophy in our own day. Arendt's uncollected essays and reviews from the first part of her career have recently been collected in a volume edited by Jerome Kohn (1994) entitled *Essays in Understanding, 1930–1954*; a second volume covering the remainder of her life is promised. And her doctoral dissertation has just been published under the title *Love and St. Augustine* (1996) by the University of Chicago Press.

Rather than attempt in this introductory book to give a précis of Arendt's major works one by one or to provide one sweeping summary of her thought, I have chosen to focus on three broad themes and to consider how these themes develop, deepen, change, and remain touchstones in her work from *The Origins of Totalitarianism* through *The Life of the Mind*. The three themes are:

1. The constitution and public disclosure of identity. This topic includes the question of identity's relationship to citizenship, the exploration of motives of political agents, the analysis of the roles racism and nationalism have played in twentieth-century politics, and an emphasis on meaning-creating action on the part of human beings who interact with one another.
2. Ontological issues concerning what is real. This topic encompasses Arendt's concern with how we distinguish the limits to human action (the "necessary") from the possibilities afforded to humans by their freedom; it also includes Arendt's belief that modern societies are characterized by a diminishment of the "common world" shared by people living together. Arendt sees modern people as having lost a sense of reality, as exiled from a fully tangible, multitudinous world that provides a "space" for action. We find here also Arendt's departure from the predilection to assign reality to "depths" that are hidden from sight. She strives to establish the reality of appearances. (The dictionary defines "ontology" as "a particular theory about being or reality.")
3. The crisis in understanding precipitated by the experiences of totalitarianism and the Holocaust. Arendt insists that totalitarianism as a political form is unprecedented and that all our traditional ways of understanding are incapable of comprehending it. Thus, a major concern in her work is to develop new forms of understanding adequate to the horrific experiences of our century.

The rest of this chapter introduces these themes as they first appear in her book on totalitarianism. Chapter 2 presents the "mature" Arendt's political philosophy as found in the middle works, focusing primarily on my first theme: the centrality of "identity disclosure" to Arendt's concepts of action and the political. Chapter 3 takes up the last two themes, by examining how the Eichmann case and the controversy surrounding Arendt's report on it crystallize a set of concerns present in her earlier work but now developed more fully. Roughly, chapter 2 examines Arendt's political theory, whereas chapter 3 presents the ontological, epistemological, and moral positions she came to develop as the philosophical underpinnings of her political views. I do not want to make any chronological claim about Arendt's career in choosing this way to organize this book. The philosophical underpinnings are already indicated in *The Origins of Totalitarianism* and play an important role in the "middle works," even though I find it most convenient to present them here through *The Life of the Mind* and the *Lectures on Kant's Political Philosophy*. Almost every idea and theme Arendt developed during her career is indicated as an issue she is striving to understand in the essays and books she wrote before 1950. Finally, in the last chapter I suggest some ways that Arendt's work contributes to and intervenes in current debates about the possibilities of politics, especially of democratic politics, as we enter the twenty-first century.

Arendt has important, insightful things to say about an astounding range of issues. In focusing on three particular themes, I am hardly pretending to cover comprehensively Arendt's entire writings—and the reader will be ill served if he or she takes this book as an adequate substitute for reading Arendt's works themselves. My emphasis is on the startling, original, and helpful contributions that stem from Arendt's insistence on the specifically political dimensions and ramifications of issues of identity, reality, and understanding. Sticking to this insistence on the political, and striving to see how and why ontological, intellectual, and identity issues are primarily political issues for Arendt, is the thread this book follows in presenting an overview of Arendt's work.

Arendt on Totalitarianism

Totalitarianism, in Arendt's argument, is made possible by the development of mass society, with a helping hand from "race-thinking," nationalism, and imperialism.[4] For Arendt, mass society is most fundamentally a condition in which individuals (as distinct and unique) are "superfluous." Mass consumption, mass unemployment, mass employment in large corporate enterprises, the collapse of local communities and associations in the face of the centripetal force of large bureaucracies and the nation-sate, and the reliance on infrequently staged popular votes as the sole opportunity for political participation all contribute to the loss of individual distinctiveness. For Arendt, politics is a highly specific human activity that takes place in a specific realm ("the political") for a specific reason: freedom. And freedom, for her, is the freedom to act in ways that produce and manifest two crucial entities: the individual's unique identity and the "world" (the publicly shared "reality" of "common sense"). The proliferation of identities through action is what Arendt calls "plurality," the many-sided diversity in which we find ourselves and that constitutes the "world" in which humans can experience freedom. Totalitarianism represents the attempt to obliterate plurality and freedom—and, hence, to obliterate the "world" of human action itself. At its most extreme, this nonworld (or antiworld) of totalitarianism is manifest in the concentration camps. But in looking to the "origins" of totalitarianism, Arendt wants to consider the extent to which a taste for freedom, a striving for distinctive identity, has been lost in modern society—a loss which makes that society susceptible to the extremes of totalitarianism. For Arendt, Nazi Germany cannot be understood as some monstrous result of a sick German psyche. Rather, from her standpoint at mid-century, totalitarianism (found in various forms in Italy, Spain, Russia, and the Balkans as well as in Germany) appears to be *the* political form of choice of the twentieth century. Why has democracy proved so unattractive an alternative to the citizens of modern nation-states? Arendt's answer to this question is very complex; what I want to highlight here is how that answer follows from her argument that identity has been disconnected from citizenship in modern society, with the result that we moderns have lost our sense of what politics is for.

What characterizes the masses from whom totalitarian leaders derive their support is their lack of political commitment and, surprisingly, their "radical loss of self-interest" (*OT*, 316). Totalitarianism revealed the hitherto unrecognized fact "that democratic government had rested as much on the silent approbation and tolerance of the indifferent and inarticulate sections of the people as on the articulate and visible institutions and organizations of the country." Such a system can function "only where the citizens belong to and are represented by groups or form a social and political hierarchy" (312). Bourgeois individualism and the bourgeois location of all ambition, interest, and motives in economic activity had dissolved such group affiliation by emphasizing the competition of all against all, creating "a highly atomized society. . . . The chief characteristic of the mass man is not brutality and backwardness, but his isolation and lack of normal social relationships"(317). This isolation can only generate an identity crisis, because identity in Arendt is always an intersubjective product of the interaction among people, not something any single person can fashion or discover in isolation: "[W]e become one whole individual, through and only through the company of others. For our individuality, insofar as it is one—unchangeable and unmistakable— we depend entirely on other people" ("On the Nature of Totalitarianism," in *EU*, 358). Isolated, the person loses a sense of his or her individuality, of that uniqueness which constitutes what he or she alone can bring to the world; the loss of this sense breeds "the mass man's typical feeling of superfluousness" (*OT*, 311). This feeling of superfluousness arises in part from the senseless slaughter of millions in World War I and the mass unemployment of the postwar years, but it also stems from the collapse of intricate and varied local associations with others, the loss of relationships through which the individual is defined vis-à-vis particular others as a particular person cherished precisely because of her difference. In sum, bourgeois society, in focusing activity on the individual accumulation of wealth, paradoxically undermines identity (and distinctiveness), because identity is dependent on interaction with others. What the bourgeois scorns is the "public" world of politics and civic interaction in favor of "private" enterprise, but to lose the public world is to lose the realm where individuals are valued as individuals, for their difference from others.

The response to feeling superfluous is anger and a fatalistic selflessness. The anger tends to be inchoate and directed at any number of real or imagined enemies—hence, it is an anger just waiting to be tapped by totalitarian organizations. The selflessness grows out of "the feeling of being expendable" (*OT*, 315) and results in "such unexpected and unpredicted phenomena as the radical loss of self-interest, the cynical or bored indifference in the face of death or other personal catastrophes, the passionate inclination toward the most abstract notions as guides for life, and the general contempt for even the most obvious rules of common sense" (316).[5]

The substitution of the "abstract" for the concrete interactive relations and group memberships that have been lost provides the catalyst that transforms "race-thinking" (which Arendt argues dates from mid-eighteenth-century Europe) into full-scale racism. Racism is abstract precisely because it substitutes general characteristics (for example, "sly") supposedly true of whole groups (the Jews), for descriptions based on concrete encounters with particular people and applicable only to the particular people actually encountered. In Arendt's account, various sides in the internal (mostly class) struggles of European nations from 1750 to the late 1800s asserted racial superiority in an attempt to legitimate claims to monopolize political and/or social power. But such attempts were generally marginalized as the European nation-state recognized that "racism can stir up civil conflicts in every country, and is one of the most ingenious devices ever invented for preparing civil war." Because no geographically defined space will ever be ethnically pure, the nation-state is not an ethnic state, Arendt insists, but rather is possible only where "the great principle upon which national organizations of peoples are built, the principle of equality and solidarity of all peoples guaranteed by the idea of mankind," is accepted. In short, racism was kept in check in the Europe of emerging nation-states because racism "tends to destroy the body politic of the nation" (*OT*, 161). Racism is a vital part of totalitarianism precisely because totalitarianism aims at just that destruction of the body politic. In its own hostility to the political, imperialism is of a piece with the general bourgeois hostility to politics.

Marginalized "race-thinking" becomes "racism" and thus becomes more respectable during the late-nineteenth-century imperialistic rush for Africa. (Note not only that Arendt's argument is Eurocentric and thus does not consider racism in the United States, but also that she has nothing to say about Spanish history or about the much earlier imperialism of Spain, France, and England in the Americas.) Racial justification for rule does not risk civil war when the rule is to be held over alien, non-European peoples. "What imperialists actually wanted was expansion of political power without the foundation of a body politic" (*OT*, 135), and racism provided them with exactly the shortcut they desired.

In place of the plural nation-state at home—a political space in which various groups stood in various competitive and cooperative relationships to one another and all such groups had legal access to the institutions of government—imperialism instituted a racially justified imposition of power from above, an imposition that could be accomplished only by violence and whose only aim was: "the unlimited accumulation of power" and its corollary, "the unlimited accumulation of capital": "The state-employed administrators of violence [the imperialist functionaries] soon formed a new class within nations and, although their field of activity was far away from the mother country, wielded an important influence on the body politic at home." The establishment of the "aimless accumulation of power" as the "never-ending, self-feeding motor of all political action" makes the "foundation of new political bodies . . . well-nigh impossible" (*OT*, 137). Imperialism, then, gives its practitioners a taste for the kind of power they can accumulate in the absence of a body politic; the effort to destroy the body politic at home is totalitarianism, for Arendt. But, as we shall see, totalitarianism, unlike the tyrannies of the past (of which imperialism is a new, but still recognizable, variant), does not aim just at the accumulation of power. It aims to remake reality itself.

In analyzing the destruction of the body politic by totalitarianism, Arendt already suggests (by negation) the understanding of the political that she will explicitly formulate in her "middle" works. The political is a space in which powers must be multiplied (by the delegation and decentralization of power and by the active participation of large numbers of citizens), diversity and plurality produced and respected, and distinctive or creative action cherished. In such a polity, in which our interactions before and with others are the focus, something besides power can be the goal of political activity—and that something is the achievement of meaningful identity. Arendt will later call this goal "freedom" and connect it to the distinction, glory, and identity that can be achieved by action itself. As "freedom," it is everything that totalitarianism attempts to obliterate.

Imperialism cannot localize its effects: "its logical consequence is the destruction of all living communities, those of the conquered peoples as well as of the people at home" (*OT*, 137). We have already seen one consequence of this destruction, the characteristic isolation of the individual in twentieth-century Europe. (Arendt thought such isolation was still true of "modern" societies even after the defeat of Hitler; of course, Soviet totalitarianism persisted throughout her lifetime, even though it did move away from the absolute horrors of the Stalin years. Analysis of Mao's years as China's ruler, especially the years of the Cultural Revolution, might not only somewhat shift Arendt's account of totalitarianism but also shake her view that it was a peculiarly Western phenomenon.)

Another consequence of imperialism is the growth of bureaucracy.

As localized relationships wither, the individual is placed more and more in a direct relationship to the state, a relationship that takes the form of contact with state functionaries. The state is led to administer more and more areas of life that once were the province of the "living communities" it has effaced. The bureaucracies first developed for colonial administration are brought back home.

This return home of imperialist administration is inevitable, because imperialism itself must be understood as a response to the crises precipitated in "the European nations" by capitalism: "How fragile their institutions had become, how outdated their social system proved in the face of man's growing capacity to produce" (*OT*, 154).[6] Imperialist expansion is not needed just to establish new markets but, more crucially in Arendt's view, to counter the fact that the bourgeoisie's focus on accumulation has left "no other unifying bond available between individuals" (157) than exploitation of the outsider: "In a society of clashing interests, where the common good was identified with the sum total of individual interests, expansion as such appeared to be a possible common interest of the nation as a whole" (153–54). The chosen "means for preservation were desperate . . . , and in the end the remedy proved worse than the evil" (155). In this analysis, we see once again Arendt moving toward positions made much more explicit in later works: her insistence that economic concerns cannot provide the commonality that the political requires, and her belief that contestation, not unanimity, is the sign of a vital political sphere. The bourgeoisie is apolitical insofar as it wants to focus all its energies on economic activities, and it is antipolitical, a positive danger to the political, insofar as it desires a conflict-free public realm. The end of conflict can be achieved only by tyranny, by a totalitarianism whose method is terror and whose aim is the destruction of plurality.

It follows that the use of racism to achieve unity (like the similar use of nationalism) is deeply antipolitical: "[A]nti-semitism was . . . an instrument for the liquidation not only of the Jews but of the body politic of the nation-state as well" (*OT*, 39). Arendt's reasoning here is partly historical, partly a consequence of her understanding of the political. Historically, she argues that the European nation-state arises with the collapse of monarchy and in the struggle between the residual aristocracy and the emergent bourgeoisie. Neither side is able to gain the upper hand, a situation that leads "to the full development of the nation-state and its claim to be above all the classes, completely independent of society and its particular interests." The result in Europe was "a deepening of the split between state and society upon which the body politic of the nation rested. Without it, there would have been no need—or even the possibility—of introducing the Jew into European history on equal terms." No social group is willing to identify itself with the state, and thus these groups concentrate their energies on advancing their interests in society, primarily in the economic sphere. Because European Jews were at a disadvantage in social transactions, "the Jews were the only part of the population willing to finance the state's beginnings and to tie their destinies to its further development" (17). In return for this support, wealthy Jews were granted "great privileges," the greatest of which was "equality" (18). But such privileges were not extended to all Jews, which meant that the Jews as a group were anomalous in nineteenth-century Europe: "In contrast to all other groups, the Jews were defined and their position determined by the body politic." Other groups were defined primarily by class position in the economic sphere, but Jews, whether privileged or not, acquired their status through their relation to the state, not through their social relations: "[T]hey were, socially speaking, in the void" (14).

The Jews were safe so long as the contending non-Jewish classes were mostly indifferent to the state, passively accepting the services it rendered in enterprises too unprofitable for the bourgeoisie to undertake. But with imperialism, bourgeois indifference comes to an end. The imperial state is an active partner in, and a necessary ingredient for, a new kind of business opportunity. The bourgeoisie now has a reason to try to capture the state for itself. Thus, imperialism brings a new push for a unified state that represents the interests of the "whole" nation. This push borrows the racist ideology that has justified imperialism and turns it against those internal groups that can be seen as frustrating the effort to get the state to act from a single motive; hence the rise of anti-Semitism in the 1890s, with the Dreyfus case in France and the formation of the Pan-Germanic and Pan-Slavic parties in Central and Eastern Europe. Having defined the nation-state as encompassing a variety of peoples unified only by sharing a place, Arendt characterizes these new groups as advocating a "tribal nationalism" that is hostile to the nation-state and to "the body politic of their own nation" (*OT*, 41). The Jews, because they are associated with the nation-state, are an obvious target of such hostility. That the Jews can also be designated as racially different seals the tragedy. Attacks on the Jews, both as racial others and as the hidden powers behind a recalcitrant state, prove the perfect vehicle for bringing imperialism back home.

Domestic imperialism is not quite yet totalitarianism. For that transition to occur, totalitarian parties not only must exploit desires for unity and economic advantage along with the pathologies of isolation and superfluity, but also must actively employ terror to destroy any lived relations outside the totalitarian web. It is this destruction of a lived world and its replacement with a fabricated one that marks the totalitarian assault on reality and leads to the ontological questions of my second theme. But first let me indicate how Arendt's analysis of the prehistory of totalitarianism suggests how she develops in her later works the theme of politics as identity disclosure.

At stake is where identity is located. Although her position is not fully articulated in *The Origins of Totalitarianism*, Arendt already indicates that she sees identity as a marker of distinctiveness (such that the full diversity of identities constitutes the world's plurality) and that such distinctiveness is achieved through relationships with others. Hence, identity is not something one possesses inherently, internally, or essentially as an individual entity. In fact, it is probably wrong to think of identity as the kind of thing that can be possessed. One doesn't so much *have* an identity as *discover* an identity when it manifests itself in various interactions with others. It is easy to see that such an understanding of identity is totally incompatible with racism. For racism to make any sense at all, racial traits must function in the same way in each person of a particular race, irrespective of context and of the others with whom the self interacts. (Of course, racism also assumes that race "trumps" whatever other traits a person might possess.) Arendt is wary of any appeal to traits as inherent or possessed; for her, the self's distinctiveness manifests itself in drastically different ways depending on the circumstances that call that self (and its characteristics) into play. Take the example of fear. It is difficult to label a person a "coward" once and for all, because different circumstances may call forth different responses (this time fearful, that time brave) in the same person. In answer to the question where identity is located, then, we might say it exists between the self and others, a product of the relations that pertain between the self and those others and of the actual circumstances that call me to act or speak with, against, or toward those others.

Arendt is interested in specifying those different possible kinds of relations. Already, in *The Origins of Totalitarianism*, she characterizes the bourgeoisie as focused on social relations as opposed to political relations, an insight she will expand into the full-scale distinction between the social and the political in *The Human Condition*. Different kinds of identities, different possible human activities, are called into being by involvement in different sorts of relationships. Plurality, then, means not only that individuals exhibit unique identities in their relations to others, but also that the full diversity of those identities is displayed only by the involvement of the individuals in a variety of relationships. Work relationships, family relationships, the internal dialogue with oneself that is called thinking, the spectatorial relationship to books and movies, and citizenship all call forth different manifestations of identity. (We will see in the next chapter, however, that all these facets of identity are not equal for Arendt; she believes that humans are most free, most fully creative, in their political activities.) The world is diminished when this full plurality of relationships is truncated. Arendt means this quite literally; reality shrinks where plurality is scaled back. Totalitarianism offers the most extreme case of such diminishment, because it destroys all relationships except one: the relation of the individual to the totalitarian power that dominates him through terror. But totalitarianism is only one example of working against plurality. The Jews, because their spheres of possible activity were strictly circumscribed, led diminished lives throughout the European history Arendt describes. But so did the bourgeoisie, albeit out of choice rather than compulsion, in focusing so exclusively on the economic. Much of Arendt's lifework can be seen as an effort to recall for us the joys of political action (the *vita activa*) and the joys of thinking, of philosophy (the *vita contemplativa*). Both joys have been lost in the bourgeois emphasis on economic achievement and on the pleasures and satisfactions of domestic (family) life. Arendt has nothing against economic activity and family life per se, but she is distressed by what she sees as their dominance of our attention in the modern world. She wants to brings us to the possible richness of a world that embraces a full range of activities and sites in which to discover, experience, and display our identities. Totalitarianism marks our times not just because it dominated Europe during the middle years of the twentieth century, but also because it is in tune with the modern indifference to a fully pluralistic existence.

The plea for plurality might be called the "existentialist" component of Arendt's views on identity, her concern for the conditions under which a fully activated identity could exist. But her thoughts on identity also have a specifically "political" component, one especially relevant to the experience of totalitarianism. I will discuss in the next chapter the potential elements of the self that Arendt associates with "citizenship." What concerns us here is what the self loses when it loses citizenship, when it becomes "stateless." Because Arendt in her later work will place such stress on "action," on what the self can possibly do in the realm of freedom that is the "political," the crucial importance of "rights" in her political philosophy might be overlooked. There is the additional problem that rights in Arendt are not at all the same as rights in the liberal tradition of Locke and John Stuart Mill. In liberal political philosophy, rights almost always define the limits of state power and thus function to secure areas of individual activity separate from the state. Hence, liberalism's bias is toward a statist definition of the political that also sees most individuals as not wanting to get involved in the political, as just wanting to be left alone. (It is easy to see that this binary—government involvement understood as either beneficial or perniciously interfering—dominates political debate in the United States today. One thing Arendt has to offer us is a way to think of the political that abandons this increasingly fruitless configuration of the issues involved.) In liberalism, the state is viewed as potentially (perhaps even inevitably) encroaching on individual prerogatives, so rights (which define those prerogatives) must be firmly established in a founding document (a constitution) or on the basis of natural law to secure them from the political process itself. A power must be set up over and against the power of the state to curb the state's inbuilt tendency to increase its sway over individual citizens. Liberalism, then, is premised on the belief that the most significant part of human life is lived in an apolitical realm and that the state is a necessary evil that should be kept strictly bounded. Thoreau summed up this position succinctly when he wrote that the best government is the one that governs least. Rights in liberalism protect the individual from interference; the good that the liberal political order tries to promote is freedom, where freedom is understood as "negative liberty," the absence of external constraints on the self's choices and actions.

Arendt does not totally scorn the liberal tradition. As we shall see in the next chapter, she strongly believes in the efficacy of constitutions, which follows from her general adherence to the liberal doctrine of the separation of powers. And she is also a strong supporter of rights. But for her, rights are defined primarily as enabling equal and full participation in the political. Rights, we might say, are, for her, the minimal conditions of citizenship but hardly the major benefit of citizenship. Her nonstatist conception of the political, with its stress on the interaction of citizens in a public sphere, means that rights are not so much a protection against the state as the terms of equal membership in the polity. Rights are not the bedrock for achieving the good of negative liberty, but the enabling condition for achieving the goods one gains through action with others in the public sphere. In other words, Arendt stresses the positive goods that political action can secure, rather than the negative good of protection from tyranny. As first steps toward positive goods, rights are absolutely crucial, but they are the beginning, not the end, of the story.

Because rights in Arendt are tied to specifically political goods and action, she vehemently insists that rights could never be natural. The political is a specifically human creation and rights are human-made, like everything political. Less vehemently (she is not utterly consistent on this point), her understanding of rights entails that they cannot be universal. We do not have rights simply by virtue of being human. Rather, we have rights by virtue of membership in a particular polity— a polity that creates those rights through its coming into existence and its including certain people, and a polity that preserves those rights so long as it continues to afford equal participation to all its members. Rights and equality are, in short, thoroughly political in Arendt. They are created and maintained politically. Hence, the "stateless" person has no rights—a point that the Nazis understood perfectly and that makes Eichmann's situation after his kidnapping appear utterly fitting to Arendt: "[I]t was Eichmann's de facto statelessness, and nothing else, that enabled the Jerusalem court to sit in judgment on him. Eichmann, though no legal expert, should have been able to appreciate that, for he knew from his own career that one could do as one pleased only with stateless people; the Jews had had to lose their nationality before they could be exterminated" (*EJ*, 240).

To those who would protest that human-made polities are too contingent, too potentially corrupt a foundation on which to stake so much, Arendt's only reply is that we have nothing else. Look at the history of the twentieth century. Its whole lesson is that rights are easily overwhelmed and never guaranteed. There is no safeguard against human mistreatment of other humans except human action that protests and works against that mistreatment. Rights are worth striving for precisely because they can be lost. We are utterly in the realm of human powers ranged against one another here. No nonhuman power, no institutional arrangement, can save us from human evil.

The conclusion to be drawn, however, is not that we should hate or abandon the political. Rather, citizenship and the political are recognized as even more precious, albeit more fragile, than we might have supposed. Totalitarianism shows us that the political can be utterly obliterated—and with horrible results. The political is the only source of rights, even if the political cannot successfully protect rights in every case. The power that constitutes the political (which, as we will see in the next chapter, Arendt calls "acting in concert") is what constitutes and protects rights. Thus, the freedoms (of movement, of speech, etc.) and possibilities for action that rights create for individuals are products of citizenship, not of some innate humanness. In this respect, Arendt can be seen as an advocate of "positive liberty." As distinct from negative liberty, the position articulated by positive liberty insists that the very possibility of selfhood, of meaningful individual activity, is based upon membership in a human community, membership that entails certain constraints and conditions on a (fantasized) absolute freedom. The distinctiveness of identity that Arendt values can be realized only within the political, within the realm in which rights and equality make freedom possible. Thus, the "existential" components of identity are dependent upon, and can be activated only within, specifically political conditions of possibility.

We can begin a consideration of the ontological dimension of totalitarianism by thinking about its assault on rights. (Ontology refers here to the reality that totalitarianism is willing to acknowledge, the [anti]world that it strives to create.) The "body politic" for Arendt exists as a space of interaction among equal participants. If the participation is not equal, plurality (a full diversity of selves, actions, and opinions) cannot result. Rights exist to protect that equality, just as the political exists to foster that plurality. For Arendt, finally, it is that plurality which constitutes our world as the rich and fascinating place it can potentially be. Freedom in Arendt is enjoyable—and the political realm is where we get to be free. Humans freely acting in the political realm create a satisfyingly complex and textured reality (the "world," in her parlance) along with satisfyingly complex and textured identities. Totalitarianism, in this view, is hatred of plurality.

The "totalitarian contempt for reality and factuality" (*OT*, 458) manifests itself in the effort to "establish the fictitious world of the movement as a tangible working reality of everyday life" (391). Totalitarianism replaces "the recognition of my fellow-men or our fellow-nations as subjects, as builders of worlds or co-builders of a common world" (458), with the attempt "to organize the infinite plurality and differentiation of human beings as if all of humanity were just one individual" (438). What totalitarianism cannot "bear" is "the unpredictability which springs from the fact that men are creative, that they can bring forward something so new that nobody ever foresaw it" (458). Because reality is the product of such creative activity and because it is an intersubjective product, the path of history cannot be controlled by any human power. The outcomes of human action always exceed intention, because no agent (whether an individual or a collective agent) can calculate in advance all the other factors with which one action will interact, and, most importantly, no calculus can determine in advance the responding actions of other human agents in the world.

Totalitarianism tries to deny this fact—and Arendt insists that it is a fact. She steadfastly poises the totalitarian "fiction" against the "reality" of a common world forged through intersubjective interaction. The "totalitarian contempt for reality and factuality" goes hand in glove with its conviction "that everything is possible" (*OT*, 459), that a totalizing power can create the world completely according to its own will. And because Arendt's ontology rests on the assertion that the world we inhabit comes into existence as the result of our creative actions in front of and with others, it follows that "[w]hat totalitarian ideologies therefore aim at is not the transformation of the outside world or the revolutionizing transformation of society, but the transformation of human nature itself" (458). What is terrifying is how close totalitarianism comes to succeeding, how it can rescript the world and the humans who inhabit it so that we get figures like Eichmann who take murder as the normal business of everyday life.

Much of *The Origins of Totalitarianism* considers the means by which this transformation is attempted (and, to a certain extent, accomplished) not just through ideology but also through terror. One paradox Arendt highlights is that only the constant instability and uncertainty that terror imposes can incapacitate the potential for spontaneous, creative, distinctive action, yet that very need to perpetuate instability robs totalitarianism's "fictitious world" of any solidity. Arendt links the specific forms terror took in the activities of Hitler's and Stalin's secret police forces and in the concentration camps to this overall totalitarian strategy to offer a powerful account of the experience of living under totalitarian rule. Her brilliant reconstruction of that lived reality is gripping reading as well as a first coming to terms with this new configuration, and by itself justifies her book's reputation. Passing over the details of her account here, I will just note that terror utterly dismantles all relations between the individual and anyone else apart from the totalitarian power that holds each person mesmerized by the very enormity of the threat held over the individual and the fickleness with which that threat is enacted. That such terror views all individuals as superfluous is demonstrated not just by the arbitrariness with which victims are selected, but also in the fate those victims suffer. That fate is not death but total oblivion; the victim is not just killed, but any trace of her ever having lived is obliterated.

The success of such tactics of total obliteration points to a profound ambiguity in Arendt's ontology. She insists that the totalitarian world is "fictitious," yet that world manages to exist, manages to displace the "real" world for a time. (And that time need not be short. Stalin's Russia was still intact when Arendt wrote her book, and she had no way of knowing how long it could or would last.) In fact, Arendt wants to be clear that we cannot expect reality, some resilient nature of things, to do the work of destroying totalitarianism for us. Just as there is nothing beyond human activity that can remedy human violations of rights, so Arendt does not want us to rely on suprahuman factors to resist or overcome totalitarianism. "The tragic fallacy" of "all these prophecies" that totalitarianism must collapse of its own accord, she writes, "was to suppose that there was such a thing as one human nature established for all time, to identify this human nature with history, and thus to declare that the idea of total domination was not only inhuman but also unrealistic. Meanwhile we have learned that the power of man is so great that he really can be what he wishes to be" (*OT*, 456). Because our common world is humanly created (although never humanly controlled) through pluralistic action, there is no ontological *fact* that can stand over and against human action. If some human power manages totally to dominate human interactions by destroying the very possibility of those interactions in all their multiplicity, then the world can be utterly transformed. In other words, totalitarianism has profound ontological implications. There is no guarantee against the totalitarian fashioning of the night-marish reality of the concentration camps. Reality, it seems, can be remade by humans.

But hasn't Arendt herself claimed that we can call one reality a fact and the other a fiction? Yes—and she is not utterly consistent here. Basically, Arendt's ontology is grounded on the insistence that plurality is a fact—that is, on "the human condition of plurality, . . . the fact that men, not Man, live on the earth and inhabit the world" (*HC*, 7). Totalitarianism tries to negate this fact of plurality—and is frighteningly successful in that attempt. The concentration camp is a world in which plurality has been utterly destroyed. Arendt's argument (it seems) is that totalitarianism can destroy the "world" but cannot create a new world: "The totalitarian belief that everything is possible seems to have proved only that everything can be destroyed" (*OT*, 459). Thus, the reality that is fact can be destroyed, but the fictional reality that totalitarianism would put in that fact's place cannot be sustained. But we should be wary of accepting this way of account-ing for the apparent inconsistency in Arendt's thought, because Arendt herself is dissatisfied with traditional views (notably Augustine's) that dismiss the reality of evil precisely by claiming that it exists only as the negation of the good and thus has no existence in its own right. Evil is real—nothing is realer—for Arendt.

Given these confusions, it makes more sense to say that totalitari-anism is the antithesis of the political for Arendt, a kind of "evil twin" to the political, because it does create a world (albeit the unstable world of terror) for humans to inhabit. The political is the realm of "acting in concert" and, as such, the realm in which a public, shared world, is created. Totalitarianism is antipolitical because it destroys acting in concert, replacing such action with the total domination of one partner in interaction over all the other participants. Such total domination is unstable, because all it can do is perpetually try to maintain its sway over any and all threats from the subjected; this per-petual vigilance, we might say, means that totalitarianism is endlessly destructive but never creative. It never engages in the creation of a common world, because such a world would threaten its dominance. Instead, all of its energies are directed to continually undoing that commonality, to fostering the atomization on which it rests.

We reach here my third theme, the problematic of understanding. To describe totalitarianism as the antipolitical is, as I have suggested, to recall Augustine's musings on evil. And it makes sense to say that if traditional theodicy undertakes to comprehend, to account for, the goodness of God's creation in spite of "apparent" suffering and evil, then Arendt's self-appointed task is to "understand" the utter depravity of human behavior in the terrible century it was her fate to inhabit. What motivates her work, she says in an interview, is not an interest "in how my work might affect people. . . . What is important to me is to understand. For me, writing is a matter of seeking this understanding, part of the process of understanding" (*EU*, 3). And the greatest puzzle posed to understanding is the "radical evil" exhibited by totalitarianism.

The term "radical evil" comes from Kant, but neither he nor Augustine helps us understand it, Arendt tells us: "[O]ur entire philosophical tradition . . . cannot conceive of a 'radical evil.' . . . Therefore, we actually have nothing to fall back on in order to understand a phenomenon that nevertheless confronts us with its overpowering reality and breaks down all standards we know." The irrelevance of known standards leaves Arendt with very little to say about radical evil in *The Origins of Totalitarianism*: "[W]e may say that radical evil has emerged in connection with a system in which all men have become equally superfluous" (*OT*, 459). She repeats this notion, while confessing her lack of comprehension, in a letter to Randall Jarrell written in the month (March 1951) her book was published: "What radical evil really is, I don't know, but it has something to do with [this] phenomenon: the superfluity of men *as men*" (qtd. in Y-B, 255). Plurality holds that no human being is superfluous, because each brings something utterly distinctive to the intersubjective creation of the world. That world is lessened, is impoverished, by the loss of even one individual. Guided by this ontological conviction, Arendt accepts the notion of "crimes against humanity" as a category separate from violation of rights (or other crimes, such as theft). Although rights are generally political and nonuniversal for Arendt, the right to a distinctive existence does emerge as universal in her work—and it is the violation of that right, the hostility to and destruction of individual life in its individuality, that she designates "radical evil." Such acts are a crime against humanity—not just against the individual destroyed—because they diminish the very world, the very reality, that humans get to inhabit.

As we will explore in chapter 3, Arendt returns to the problem of evil in the wake of the Eichmann case, devoting much of her final work, *The Life of the Mind*, to this issue. She consistently refuses throughout her career, however, to speculate on the possible motives for a hostility to plurality. We could postulate a desire for control or a fear of the contingent, the unknowable, and/or the different (all ways of thinking about how the possibility of freedom might be terrifying), but Arendt generally avoids offering a psychology of evil. (She will later stress "courage" as a crucial political virtue, but she never specifically links the absence of courage to the attack on plurality.) The origins of totalitarianism, insofar as her book traces them, lie in a conjunction of historical forces and ideas, not in the psychology of "mass man," of fascists, or of any other historical agents. Her refusal of such psychological explanations undoubtedly stems in part from her profound indifference to Freud and, more generally, to any conception of the unconscious. This, of course, does not mean (to take one example) that the nineteenth-century bourgeoisie consciously intended to destroy the body politic and bring about totalitarianism. Arendt does not believe that any agent gets to create history that directly. What it does mean is that the bourgeoisie—and all agents, for Arendt—act from conscious motives (a preference for economic rather than political distinction, in the bourgeoisie's case) that, in conjunction with numerous other historical factors, result in the world humans create. So, for her, radical evil cannot be explained as the manifestation of some unconscious malignancy. Instead, such evil is a radical hostility to, a rage against, the very conditions of human existence—and it is this will to destruction of the very bases of human life that confounds us whenever we encounter it.

It is this being confounded that, for starters, Arendt wants to keep in front of our eyes. She is adamant that no articulable motive and no philosophical theory is even remotely adequate to these evil deeds. She wants to prevent us from sliding away from the enormity of these deeds to an explanation that reincorporates them within a framework of the comprehended, the mastered, the assimilated—worst of all, the accepted. "This should not have happened" is her response to learning of the Holocaust—and she wants to preserve that incredulity. Hence her use of the bald word "evil." It is the deed itself to which she wants to draw our attention, not to the words that would try to comprehend it. If to understand all is to forgive all, then Arendt wants to prevent any comfortable belief that we understand the Holocaust. And she is equally sure that here we confront deeds that cannot be forgiven:

> [I]n their effort to prove that everything is possible, totalitarian regimes have discovered without knowing it that there are crimes which men can neither punish nor forgive. When the impossible was made possible it became the unpunishable, unforgivable absolute evil which could no longer be understood and explained by the evil motives of self-interest, greed, covetousness, resentment, lust for power, and cowardice; and which therefore anger could not revenge, love could not endure, friendship could not forgive. Just as the victims in the death factories or the holes of oblivion are no longer "human" in the eyes of their executioners, so this newest species of criminals is beyond the pale even of solidarity in human sinfulness. (*OT*, 459)

Totalitarianism has bequeathed us a crisis in understanding. And although Arendt insists that the "horrible originality" of totalitarianism "exploded our categories of political thought and our standards for moral judgment" (*EU*, 309–10), she also insists that we must make the effort to understand. Nothing less than our ability to go on is at stake. Understanding, she tells us in the essay "Understanding and Politics," is an "unending activity by which, in constant change and variation, we come to terms with and reconcile ourselves to reality, that is, try to be at home in the world. . . . The result of understanding is meaning, which we originate in the very process of living insofar as we try to reconcile ourselves to what we do and what we suffer" (308–9). The monstrosity of the death camps makes reconciliation impossible; without some kind of reconciliation, we cannot go on. That is the impasse Arendt has reached in the early 1950s at the end of her first attempt to come to terms with the horrible reality of totalitarianism. She responds to that impasse, I believe, in two ways, The first is to develop an ideal, even utopian, theory of the political as an expression of how it could and should be for humans living and acting in concert in the world. Chapter 2 describes and discusses this work. The second response is to conduct a lifelong inquiry into the means of un-

derstanding, of theorizing, of giving meaning, an inquiry that leads
Arendt to return again and again to the problem of evil and to her investigations of thinking, judging, and storytelling. Chapter 3 is devoted to exploring this work. For the moment, I will close this chapter
with words Arendt wrote in 1967 (in a preface to a new edition of *The
Origins of Totalitarianism*) about comprehension and its active (non-
passive) relation to a reality we cannot simply accept but are called to
question, to "face up to," even (sometimes) to "resist":

> This book is an attempt at understanding what at first and even sec-
> ond glance appeared simply outrageous.
>
> Comprehension, however, does not mean denying the outra-
> geous, deducing the unprecedented from precedents, or explaining
> phenomena by such analogies and generalities that the impact and
> the shock of experience are no longer felt. It means, rather, examin-
> ing and bearing consciously the burden that events have placed on
> us—neither denying their existence nor submitting meekly to their
> weight as though everything that in fact happened could not have
> happened otherwise. Comprehension, in short, means the unpre-
> meditated, attentive facing up to, and resisting of, reality—whatever
> it may be or might have been. (*OT*, xiv)

2
Politics as Identity-Disclosing Action

To a large extent, Arendt's mature political philosophy stems from a set of definitions the elaboration of which generates a whole world in which there is a place for everything and everything is in its place. "Utopia," of course, means "no place," but Arendt's political vision is utopian exactly in its rootedness, in its insistence on location. A man needs a place to stand up, asserts the novelist Ford Madox Ford, and the political—the public realm—is that place for Arendt, "the proper place for human excellence" (*HC*, 49). The polis is where each human being can be distinctive and can display that individuality, that identity, which makes him or her indispensable to the unfolding of a fully particularized and plural world. The goal of Arendt's political philosophy is to articulate how the full possibilities of individual action are enabled when an ideal polis is in place.

Works that proceed by definition, as well as works that outline utopian visions, are almost inevitably contrastive. To define things is to draw boundaries around them, to separate them from what they are not. To describe a utopia is to criticize the way things are currently arranged and done. Arendt strongly condemns the modern world, especially what she sees as its devaluation of the political in favor of the "social." To get out from under modern presuppositions and prejudices, Arendt turns to the Greeks—and, to a lesser extent, to the Romans of the republican era and the American founding fathers. This move is problematic for a number of reasons that I can only note without examining here. The most obvious danger is nostalgia, with its attendant danger of idealizing a past both unexperienced and irrecoverable. Arendt is hardly free of nostalgic idealization, but she is equally adamant that no return to the glories of Greece and Rome is possible. If we bear in mind that her historical examples are primarily philosophical tools, important only insofar as they can alienate us from the assumption that our current arrangements are the inevitable way things must be and not meant to serve as models by which we should attempt to reconstruct antiquity, we can avoid (as Arendt herself usually does) the more grotesque errors of nostalgia.

It is not quite as easy to defend Arendt from the charge that her notion of modernity is a gross oversimplification. When she generalizes about the Greeks, we can say that these generalizations are educative, meant to function as examples of a different way of conceiving things and not presented as an accurate historical account of how life in fifth-century Athens was actually lived. But in describing modern arrangements and modern sensibilities, Arendt is making more substantial historical claims. She is guided here by her belief that totalitarianism in Germany and Russia is not "exceptional" but is an outgrowth of tendencies found throughout the modern world. Arendt aspires to nothing less than a diagnosis of modernity itself—and much of the grandeur and force of her work derives from this sweeping ambition. But we should register the cost of her way of proceeding. Not only does her definition of modernity fit just Europe and North America, thus excluding from her vision the rest of the world and how humans live and engage in political activity there, but she is also increasingly blind (after her recognition, in *The Origins of Totalitarianism*, of the different positions occupied by Jews, capitalists, workers, and nationalists in the Europe leading up to the totalitarian regimes of the 1930s) to the internal differentiations within the populations that live within modernity. If there is something called "modernity," with an accompanying sensibility, cluster of desires, and characteristic institutional forms, then members of modern societies participate to a lesser or a fuller degree in that modernity. Hence, Arendt's constant use of the generic "man" is problematic not just (or even primarily) because it is sexist but also because it marks her failure to see that "modern man," if he exists, is not everyone living in a modern country in modern times.

I should hasten to add that, when writing analyses of particular incidents (for instance, of the civil disobedience of students in the 1960s), Arendt was often very shrewd about the relations of different social groups to the polity of which they were citizens. My point is that her political theory takes insufficient notice of these differences. This fact does not lessen the theory's usefulness as a heuristic device, by which I mean that the theory serves as a way to interrogate the world we inhabit by highlighting what we might ask the political to accomplish. For me, the great value and crucial importance of Arendt's work lies precisely in what it teaches us to demand of democracy and in its meditation on the conditions that might allow those demands to be met. This value is, to a large extent, independent of the fact that her insufficient attention to differentiation lessens the validity of the descriptive moments in her theoretical works. As we shall see in chapter 3, Arendt is hardly unaware that she is no ordinary historian, and she explicitly formulates an account of the kind of historical "story-telling" that she practices in her work.

Arendt's understanding of modernity is not exactly the same as, but shares many similarities with, critiques of the modern West that have come to be associated with "postmodern theory."[1] To be schematic about it, modernity replaces premodern or "traditional" society through a series of events between 1400 and 1800: the invention of the printing press; the Protestant Reformation; the decline of feudalism and the emergence of the nation-state; the discovery by Europeans of non-European cultures they had not known existed; the explosion in productive capacity generated by technological advances and by the capitalist organization of economies, with the resultant population explosion and the growth of large cities. These various events hardly hold a single significance or determine an inevitable line of historical advance. But they do tend (or so, at least, Arendt argues in the essay "What Is Authority?" [*BPF*, 91–141]) to produce "the general doubt of the modern age," which "undermine[s] . . . religion and tradition" (93). The Enlightenment philosophers sought to replace lost authority with the rational, self-directed, autonomous individual—either the self-legislating, "mature" moral agent championed by Kant or the rational pursuer of self-interest found in Adam Smith. Reason would do the job authority, religion, and tradition had once done. The very word "modern" captured this sense of a break from the past, of a new order of things unbound to former beliefs and pieties.

The postmodern critique of Western modernity has been quite varied, but two themes are especially relevant to Arendt, although she could be assimilated to a postmodern view of either theme only by ignoring certain aspects of her thought. The first is the insistence that autonomous individuality is a myth. Postmodern theory stresses that all individuals are socially embedded from the moment of birth and that their choices, beliefs, emotions, and thoughts are (in the current jargon) "socially constituted." We have already seen how Arendt insists that identity can occur only in company with others and can be meaningful only when lived out amid others. She, like many postmodern theorists, stresses the interrelatedness of humans. But her equally crucial emphasis on freedom and on "natality" (the introduction of something new into the world in the birth of each human being and in the novelties introduced by action) means that she is very distant from the social determinism that haunts much postmodern thought.

The second postmodern theme might be called the "insufficiency of reason," at least of the kinds of reason that the Enlightenment philosophers thought would insure that the modern world would be a far better place for humans than the premodern world had been. It is not just that technological advances have caused as many problems as they have solved while also increasing the capacity of humans to harm one another, but also that the very definitions of reason that the philosophers advanced could be used to distinguish between the rational (the "fully human") and the nonrational (the immature, the mad, the criminal, the uncivilized, who are "subhuman"). Reason, in other words, tends to be used to establish a single, unitary standard for what counts as "human," and thus it can serve as a justification for the treatment, confinement, punishment, and/or exclusion of those who do not meet the standard. Postmodernism has been obsessed with crimes against humanity that have been committed in the name of reason, from the West's violence against non-Westerners to its treatment of women and children to the murders of millions of people deemed unfit to live in Nazi Germany and Stalin's Russia. As with the theme of social embeddedness, Arendt stands in a complex relation to this postmodern critique. On the one hand, she, like the postmodern theorists, condemns modernity for not valuing what she calls "plurality" (which seems very similar to what postmodernists call "difference"). And she is highly critical of the modern supposition of progress: that the present is better than the past and that the future will be even better than the present. But, on the other hand, she is not as completely skeptical of reason as are the postmodernists; she still looks to philosophy as a valuable resource for showing us how to live and (in the moral writings that follow the Eichmann book) tries to establish that "thinking" is crucial to doing good and avoiding evil.

In what follows, I emphasize that Arendt's major complaint against modernity is that it does not provide the proper place—the political realm—where the full plurality of identities could be generated through action undertaken with and in front of others. Her use of the Greeks, then, is an attempt to confront modern sensibilities, modern assumptions about the good life, with an alternative orientation to what it means to live amid others. In this context we might say that modernity, for Arendt, is the breeding ground of totalitarianism because it introduces the crucial shifts in attitudes—away from identity-disclosing action toward economically rewarding work, away from intense involvement in the political toward a concern with the "social," and away from a focus on "freedom" to a focus on "life"—that render the individual superfluous and attenuate the political realm to the point where its obliteration appears both feasible and desirable. The core of Arendt's political theory is the attempt to make us moderns see what the political distinctively is, what it and only it can accomplish, and why we should desire what it offers.

The Political and the Public

Arendt's emphasis on place and extensive reliance on definition come together in her reminder that "the word *polis* originally connoted something like a 'ring-wall'. . . . We find the same connotation in our word 'town,' which originally, like the German *Zaum*, meant a surrounding fence" (*HC*, 64 n. 64). Arendt is determined to specify the distinctive content of the political—and the distinctive human activities that only the political enables. The specific place of the political is the "public" realm; the identification of "the political" with "the public sphere" is so intense for her that the two sometimes seem coterminous. But, as the following definition of the "public" shows, it is perhaps more accurate to think of the "public" as the place in which the activities that Arendt would recognize as "political" can be enacted:

> The term "public" signifies two closely interrelated but not altogether identical phenomena.
>
> It means, first, that everything that appears in public can be seen and heard by everybody and has the widest possible publicity. For

us, appearance—something that is being seen and heard by others as by ourselves—constitutes reality. Compared with the reality which comes from being seen and heard, even the greatest forces of intimate life—the passions of the heart, the thoughts of the mind, the delights of the senses—lead an uncertain, shadowy kind of existence unless and until they are transformed, deprivatized, and deindividualized, as it were, into a shape to fit them for public appearance. . . .

Second, the term "public" signifies the world itself, in so far as it is common to all of us and distinguished from our privately owned place in it. . . . To live together in the world means essentially that a world of things is between those who have it in common, as a table is located between those who sit around it; the world, like every in-between, relates and separates men at the same time.

The public realm, as the common world, gathers us together and yet prevents our falling over each other, so to speak. What makes mass society so difficult to bear is not the number of people involved, or at least not primarily, but the fact that the world between them has lost its power to gather them together, to relate and separate them. (50–53)

Modernity has witnessed the gradual destruction of the public realm in both its senses—a destruction that also dismantles a private realm of intimacy that can exist only in contradistinction to the public space of appearances. Public and private are codependent, but their symbiotic relationship rests on their absolute separation from one another. Mass society—and what Arendt generally calls "the rise of the social" (38)—overwhelms that separation and thus threatens the activities specific to each realm. Arendt's theory relates public to private and separates them, just as she calls upon the public realm to relate individuals, to gather them together, *and* to separate them, to distinguish them from one another.

The quoted passage highlights that what the public realm most crucially enables is the achievement of identity. It is not just the reality of a common world that is constituted by the public, it is also the reality of our own individuality. Public and political become practically synonymous in Arendt, because even if we call the public "the space of appearances" and the political the activities through which we create and display our distinctive identities, there is an unanswerable chicken-or-egg question about which comes first. Our political activities constitute a common world in which the relationships established with others also provide us with a distinctive identity, while the existence of some commonality already in place gives us a location for our political actions. The best analogy here is probably to language, which also poses an irresolvable problem of origins. We use a preexisting language to express ourselves, and thus the language constantly changes by virtue of the creative uses to which it is put. But how could self-expression occur outside language, which supplies the very resources for imagining ourselves? And how could language have started, since to creatively express oneself requires the very resources of language? In other words, transformation of language or of a public world held in common is easily conceivable, just as we can conceive how a language (or a public world) might die out; but there is no way to imagine the human activity that could have instituted a language or a common world where there was not one before. What Arendt addresses, then, is not the origin of the public but its attenuation in the modern world. (Arendt is interested, especially in *On Revolution*, in the founding of a polity, but such a founding, although it is a new beginning, is never a creation ex nihilo.)

One source of that diminishment of the public in modernity is the liberal sensibility that locates one's "real" self in intimate relationships, in the private home (that haven from a heartless world). Arendt's insistence that the ability to experience our identities as "real" depends on "publicity," along with her conviction that "reality for us" consists of "appearances" that "can be seen and heard by everybody," flies in the face of both the modern epistemologies that locate the real in the depths that lie out of sight, beneath deceptive appearances, and the modern privileging of "private" satisfactions, from family life to the accumulation of private property.[2] Modernity has turned its back on the public and so has lost its sense of reality, of worldliness. Modern people have no common sense, Arendt tells us, by which she means that we no longer share a world in common. We live shut off from each other, isolated in private spaces. And she insists that the result of such isolation (even in the company of intimates) is not a heightened experience of individual identity, but just the opposite. Just as public and private are codependent, so a sense of one's individual uniqueness is dependent on occupying a shared world with others. Only in such a shared world can the difference that I make as an individual be registered, be noticed. Only by taking up my position amid others and among the things of a shared world can my identity be recognized by others and realized by me. Later, in *The Life of the Mind*, Arendt will turn to animal psychology to posit a fundamental urge to display, to make an appearance in the world before others. In *The Human Condition*, this fundamental urge is the striving for distinction, with the double meaning of that word very much intended. Distinction entails being recognized as distinct, as an individual, and the very means toward such recognition is to be distinguished in some activity that garners attention, respect, admiration, or acclaim. The path to distinction is "excellence": "Every activity performed in public can attain an excellence never matched in privacy; for excellence, by definition, the presence of others is always required, and this presence needs the formality of the public, constituted by one's peers, it cannot be the casual, familiar presence of one's equals or inferiors" (*HC*, 49). A fully flourishing public realm, then, is a world held in common that generates plurality, the fullest possible multiplicity of distinctive identities.

Plurality and freedom are the two fundamental goods that Arendt's version of the political strives to produce and to protect. Plurality is presented on the first page of chapter 1 laconically as "the human condition of plurality, . . . the fact that men, not Man, live on earth and inhabit the world. While all aspects of the human condition are somehow related to politics, this plurality is specifically *the* condition—not only the *conditio sine qua non*, but the *conditio per quam*—of all political life" (7). It is this "fact" that totalitarianism tries to deny, so that totalitarianism might be called the antipolitics that attempts to construct a world dominated by "Man" to evade the contingencies introduced by the presence of "men"—and by their differences from one another: "Plurality is the condition of human action because we are all the same, that is, human, in such a way that nobody is ever the same as anyone else who ever lived, lives, or will live" (8). The very existence of the public realm—and hence of reality as a common world—depends on this combination of sameness and difference in plurality. There are two conditions under which reality can be lost, Arendt tells us: when "nobody can any longer agree with anybody else," so that "the sameness of the object [under consideration] can no longer be discerned," or when agreement is so complete, so total, that a whole society becomes "imprisoned in the subjectivity of their own singular experience. . . . The end of the common world has come when it is seen only under one aspect and is permitted to present itself in only one perspective" (58). Reality is dialogic for Arendt; it depends on more than one angle of vision: "The reality of the public realm relies on the simultaneous presence of innumerable perspectives" (57).

Labor and Work

The key terms for a correct view of the political are freedom and action, where freedom is contrasted with necessity and action is one of three contrasting terms: labor, work, and action.[3] As freedom in Arendt is always the freedom to act, the cluster of terms are all interrelated. Labor is the effort required to secure the necessities of life: "Labor is the activity which corresponds to the biological process of the human body, whose spontaneous growth, metabolism, and eventual decay are bound to the vital necessities produced and fed into the life process by labor" (*HC*, 7). Arendt follows a traditional (both Platonic and Christian) denigration of the body here, although she recognizes that "the modern age . . . discovered how rich and manifold the realm of the hidden can be under the conditions of intimacy; but it is striking that from the beginning of history to our own time it has always been the bodily part of human existence that needed to be hidden in privacy, all things connected with the necessity of the life process itself" (72). Although she comments that the "bodily" at times has been associated with specific categories of people (the slaves who did the labor necessary to sustain life and the women who did the labor necessary to reproduce life [see 72]), Arendt consistently associates labor and necessity with sameness, with the absence of plurality and distinction. Labor is beneath public notice because when laboring, when driven by the necessities of biological existence, we are all the same. In fact, when laboring we are not even distinctively human; we are just "*animal laborans*," the "victory" of whom in modern times Arendt deplores (320). In labor we are moved by necessity as an animal is—and being moved by necessity is the opposite of acting freely, where freedom is the distinctive characteristic of the human.

Work, as distinct from labor, "is the activity which corresponds to the unnaturalness of human existence, which is not embedded in, and whose mortality is not compensated by, the species' ever-recurring life cycle. Work provides an 'artificial' world of things, distinctly different from all natural surroundings. Within its borders each individual is housed, while this world itself is meant to outlast and transcend them all. The human condition of work is worldliness" (*HC*, 7). Work occupies a strange position in Arendt's theory because it is utterly necessary for the creation and maintenance of the political but itself is not political, itself not free action. (On a more structural level, we can say that Arendt almost always proceeds by contrastive pairings—public/private, ancient/modern, freedom/necessity, French Revolution/ American Revolution—and even where these pairs are codependent, she almost never introduces intermediate or mediating terms. Work is an exception to this pattern.) To complicate matters even further, work is definitely not political in *The Human Condition*, whereas it appears to be political in *On Revolution*, with its stress on the "founding" activities of the framers of the American Constitution.

Arendt is trying here to distance herself from the Marxist and Hegelian (at least, in Hegel's master/slave dialectic) position that productive activity is both the ultimate human activity—the basic site for the manifestation of human creativity and freedom—and the site of a potentially disastrous alienation. The slave in Hegel is saved through work, but, Marx would add, only where the product of that work is recognized as the slave's own, with all the attendant fruits of recognition and ownership. Arendt very much wants to resist this association of production with the be-all and end-all of human activity. She wants to reserve her highest terms—freedom and action—for activities that do not aim at production, that are not completed by ownership, enjoyment, or (most crucially) mastery. (*The Human Condition* [105–13] contains a complex argument about property that I cannot outline here. Suffice it to say that Arendt connects the obsession with private property to modernity's destruction of the public. Marx's notion of collective property is no solution for her, because he remains fixated on ownership.)

Yet Arendt does see work as producing the stage upon which political activity takes place. And she sees in work the same basic drive that she finds in action: to produce something that outlasts one's life. Work attempts to create a thing that will have a permanence the worker herself does not have. Action attempts to insure a "remembrance" that survives both the action itself and, ideally, the actor herself. The transience of individual lives threatens humans with a sense of futility and a sense of irreality. The solidity and relative permanence of made things creates a world between humans on which they can rely, more than they can rely on the evanescence of their own private sensations and their own fleeting lives. In a parallel fashion, the polis "is a kind of organized remembrance. It assures the mortal actor that his passing existence and fleeting greatness will never lack the reality that comes from being seen, being heard, and, generally, appearing before an audience of fellow men" (*HC*, 198).

How, then, does work fall short of action? The answer is not utterly clear, but the crucial factor appears to be that work involves the individual with material things, whereas action places the individual in intersubjective relations to others. Work involves instrumental relationships in which the human worker uses material stuff as a means toward creation of an artificial, nonnatural world. ("Nonnatural" is in no way a negative term for Arendt.) There is, then, a kind of dominance, a will to power, present in work: an "element of violation and violence is present in all fabrication, and *homo faber*, the creator of the human artifice, has always been a destroyer of nature. . . . [*H*]*omo faber* conducts himself as lord and master of the whole earth" (*HC*, 139). Arendt concedes that "the experience of this violence is the most elemental experience of human strength" and, as such, is a source of "joy" and "elation" (140). But she refuses to equate dominance—the control over material things or over others—with freedom. Successfully doing what one wants to do in spite of the potential resistance of things and/or others is not freedom for Arendt, it is "strength." Control through strength is the result of the application of "force," and both "strength" and "force" are to be sharply distinguished from "power." The full import of this particular set of distinctions will be clarified as we pursue the freedom/necessity and work/action distinctions. For the moment, it will suffice to say that strength and force, like work, are individualistic; they are unilateral interventions in the world that attempt to make it bend to one individual's purposes. For Arendt, only the fully intersubjective, an "acting in concert with [equal] others," qualifies as political and free. Yes, work can be expressive of identity, and it creates the artificial world that people require to become present to one another in public, but the solitary interaction of the artisan with the materials she fashions is too isolated, too private, and too predictable in its results to render it "political." The element of dominance in work calls for its careful separation from the political lest it introduce relations of instrumentality and force into that realm. Arendt, like Kant, wants a "kingdom of ends," that is, a separate human realm in which the primary recognition that each and every human is always an end and never to be treated as a means stands as the guiding principle of all action. The "specifically human achievement" of political action "lies altogether outside the category of means and ends" (207).

Behavior and the Social

What would action guided by a principle outside all instrumental means-ends calculations look like? We reach here one crux of *The Human Condition*—and its greatest puzzle. Much of Arendt's discussion of action proceeds by negation. She is at great pains to tell us what action is not. So I am following her path in continually delaying a positive description of action by describing those things it is not. To further complicate matters, Arendt introduces a binary opposition between "behavior" and "action"—an opposition that stands in an unspecified and unclear relation to the threefold distinction between labor, work, and action. My account of Arendt's views here will hardly strike all readers of Arendt as adequate. But I daresay that all her readers can agree that only action counts as freedom and that the political exists—and is justified—only to the extent that action and freedom are possible in the world. Where action and freedom are, there is a polis—and vice versa. The reason politics is important is that we value freedom. Freedom is a good valued for its own sake, not for anything it allows us to produce, gain, or achieve. And freedom is exercised only in action. Thus, Arendt's effort to call the people of modernity to politics is an effort to awaken their (presumably latent) desire for freedom.

The moderns have lost that desire, Arendt believes, by focusing too exclusively on "life." We might say (although Arendt does not put it this way) that each of the three activities—labor, work, and action—is connected to a specific fundamental good. Labor is tied to the good of life: it is better to be alive than dead; it is better to be healthy than sick; it is better to be comfortable (well fed, warm, sheltered) than to be miserable (starving, homeless). Arendt hardly denies these goods when she groups them under the term "life." She explicitly acknowledges their primacy and the fact that they are inescapable; that is why she deems their satisfaction "necessary." The activities (labor) that satisfy these *needs* are not free; they are activities performed under the compulsion of need.

The good connected to work is (a never complete) control over the contingencies of existence. All human activity would be utterly futile if we were never able to move successfully from our present conception of the future into a future we managed to shape in accord with that conception. Purposive behavior is possible because humans experience their ability—through work—to shape the world they inhabit. Only such successes allow us to have purposes, allow us not just to live from moment to moment, but also to take up projects that entail development over time. Continuity—reaching toward permanence (at least a permanence that outlasts a single life)—is the great good achieved by work and its forceful mastery of this world we find ourselves in.

But labor and work are examples of behavior only, not of action, because they are calculable. It is easy to see why labor is not free, as it is driven by necessity. The case for work's unfreedom is harder to make out. Arendt implies that work is so bound to the laws of matter that the routes it takes are mapped out in advance. What she seems to have in mind is a notion of rationality that reduces reason to a means/ends calculus. Rational behavior in such a schema is evidenced when a person chooses the means best suited to achieving the end she has in view. This understanding of rationality is characteristic of classical political economy (Adam Smith) and utilitarianism (Jeremy Bentham) and is still alive and well in what today is called "rational choice" theory. Versions of rational choice theory, connected with a liberalism and a notion of academic disinterestedness that talked of "an end of ideology," were much more dominant in the social sciences during the 1950s than they are today. Of course, rational choice theory still has many adherents, but its hegemony is much more widely challenged today, with a much more diverse range of approaches, methods, and theories contending for the allegiance of social scientists. Insofar as she thinks of work as behavior, then (earlier I suggested ways in which work lies between labor and action), Arendt appears to accept the notion that efforts at control, efforts to achieve one's purposes, require bending to the necessities of the circumstances in which one finds oneself and forging a strategy that suits those circumstances. Work is behavior because it is the predictable outcome of a calculation about how to proceed.

Although it cedes work to the instrumental rationalists, Arendt's concept of action is meant to insist that there is more under heaven and earth than can be explained in their philosophy. The dominance of rational choice theories is one symptom of the general modern loss of a taste for, a focus on, freedom. How is it that "life" and "instrumental control" have come to be our central concerns? Arendt introduces yet another distinction as she tries to address this point—the distinction between the "social" and the "political." This is a distinction that makes even Arendt's most ardent admirers queasy, and it will be easy to see why in what follows. But we must recognize that Arendt would expect that her thought would be most resisted at exactly this point, because for her it is precisely the valuing of the "social" more than the "political" that characterizes modernity. In other words, her attempt to downgrade the "social" in favor of a revalued "political" is as aggressive an assault on modern sensibilities as anything essayed by Nietzsche in his proclamation of a "transvaluation of values." To reject Arendt's social/political distinction out of hand, to refuse to think through its challenge to our received ideas and heartfelt convictions, is to evade precisely what she wants us to confront about modernity. Perhaps, after going all the way with Arendt, we shall finally conclude that our modern understanding of these issues is the best we can do, but at least (even in this case of sticking with our beliefs) we will no longer think that our modern understanding is the only possible one and we will better understand the choice we are making. Our beliefs are the product of a certain history yet are not completely determined by that history, and they could be different.

Arendt defines the "social" as the undifferentiated result when the separate goods of "life," "instrumental control," and "freedom" are collapsed together. As we have already seen, Arendt thinks the polis is possible only where there is a strict division of spheres. Labor (hence the concern for "life") is a matter for the household; in the original Greek, "economics" refers to the household. Work (the concern for the production of permanence) is a matter of the public realm; it creates the common world. Action (the concern for freedom) is a matter of the political; it is the creation of plurality, of individual identity, before and with others in the space of appearances. What modernity has lost is the sense of these distinctions—and of their absolute importance. The crucial problem is that concerns of "life" have come to dominate: "The distinctive trait of the household sphere was that in it men lived together because they were driven by their wants and needs" (*HC*, 30). That humans live together as a means toward better addressing those wants and needs makes sense. But those wants and needs should not stand as the *sole* reason for human sociality. However, that is just what has happened in modernity, under cover of the "rise of the social" (38):

> The distinction between a private and a public sphere of life corresponds to the household and the political realms, which have existed as distinct, separate entities at least since the rise of the ancient city-state; but the emergence of the social realm, which is neither private nor public, strictly speaking, is a relatively new phenomenon whose origin coincided with the emergence of the modern age and which found its political form in the nation-state.
>
> What concerns us in this context is the extraordinary difficulty with which we, because of this development, understand the decisive division between public and private realms, between the sphere of the *polis* and the sphere of the household and family, and finally, between activities related to a common world and those related to the maintenance of life, a division upon which ancient political thought rested as self-evident and axiomatic. In our understanding, the dividing line is entirely blurred, because we see the body of peoples and political communities in the image of a family whose everyday affairs have to be taken care of by a gigantic, nation-wide administration of housekeeping. . . . [T]he collective of families economically organized into the facsimile of one super-human family is what we call "society," and its political form of organization is called "nation." (28–29)

The "social" confuses realms that Arendt wants to keep separate because it is neither fully private nor fully public. Think of our phrase "private enterprise." In what way is it private? Certainly not in the sense that intimate, familial relationships are. The social, Arendt claims, is the quasi-public realm that arises when matters of life (of economy) are (halfheartedly, we might say, in the liberal democracies) recognized as issues of the public good and thus as matters that the state cannot ignore (even though the extent to which state action in such matters is justified will be continually contested). The very confusions to which the proper relation of the state to the market (the "private sector") is prone suggest this unwise mixture of the political with concerns that Arendt insists are not appropriate for or amenable to its intervention.

The rise of the social at the expense of the political is the replacement of freedom as the good (end, or telos) of politics with the "general welfare" as the good of politics: "[G]overnment, which since the beginning of the modern age has been identified with the entire domain of the political, was now considered the appointed protector not so much of freedom as of the life process, the interests of society and its individuals" (*BPF*, 150). At her most extreme (and, on this point, she is more often extreme than not), Arendt insists not only that politics should have nothing to do with welfare or economic justice, but also that any attention paid to such concerns will jeopardize the ability of politics to deliver the one good—freedom—that is actually in its power to provide. To saddle politics with welfare issues is utterly futile, because politics and political institutions cannot successfully address such issues. *On Revolution* can be read as a morality tale meant to impart just this lesson. The French Revolution failed because its leaders were carried away by a well-meaning, even admirable, but fundamentally misguided "compassion" for *les misérables*, and hence they diverted politics from its true ends. Unfortunately, the French Revolution has been the model for all subsequent modern developments, most notably the modern nation-state (whose internal tensions and contradictions lead to its collapse into totalitarianism), the Russian Revolution (which had no motive but "compassion"), and, generally, the growth of the "social" (with its production of modern mass society to replace the differentiated plurality of a political realm strictly separated from the private household).[4] Compassion leads only to terror: "No revolution has ever solved the 'social question' and . . . the whole record of past revolutions demonstrates beyond doubt that every attempt to solve the social question with political means leads into terror, and that it is terror that sends revolutions to their doom" (*OR*, 112). Compassion leads to terror, Arendt argues, for two reasons: First, because we humans are all alike in our needs, a focus on needs makes us lose our sense of plurality, of each individual's precious uniqueness. Once individuals are not unique, they become "superfluous." One more or one less makes no difference—and the door to mass society and mass killing is opened. Second, acting on compassion inevitably leads to frustration, because leaders soon discover that they cannot alleviate material suffering. In their frustration, someone is inevitably blamed for their failure. The elimination of these blocking figures will bring the utopia of plenty, the leaders argue, and the killing begins.

Such pessimism about the modern political project of insuring general prosperity (not just in Marxist countries but in the liberal welfare state as well) is just one reason Arendt's views about the "social" have proved so offensive to many readers. Her pessimism seems fatalistic when she goes on to say that the French revolutionaries could not have avoided their mistake of turning their attention to the "social question" of poverty:

> [I]t can hardly be denied that to avoid this fatal mistake is almost impossible when a revolution breaks out under conditions of mass poverty. What has always made it so terribly tempting to follow the French Revolution on its foredoomed path is not only the fact that liberation from necessity, because of its urgency, will always take precedence over the building of freedom, but the even more important and dangerous fact that the uprising of the poor against the rich carries with it an altogether and much greater momentum of force than the rebellion of the oppressed against their oppressors. (*OR*, 112)

The American Revolution may be an exception, then, because of the highly unusual prosperity of the colonists as they entered into rebellion. If "liberation from necessity . . . will always take precedence over the building of freedom," then how could the political act of building freedom ever get started, as poverty is all too obviously all around us?

Arendt offers only two answers, one not very palatable, the other not very plausible. The first answer is that freedom and politics can be enjoyed only by the few who are prosperous and that their prosperity is gained at the expense of the many who devote their entire lives slaving to produce life's necessities. The Greeks faced this fact squarely in openly making the division between free citizens as one category and slaves and women as another. We moderns live the same fact to a certain extent: the prosperity of the West is unequally shared by all the people living in the West and is built upon the overwhelming "mass poverty" in the non-West. However, Arendt's work seems to imply, our modern sensibility does not allow us simply to state this fact of unequal access to prosperity (and hence to freedom) and thus to live by that fact. Instead, because we want to believe in equal access for all, we have simultaneously turned the political toward the effort to make all prosperous and have placed all humans in the same boat of establishing liberation from necessity as the sole goal of our activities. We lose the political as freedom because we sentimentally say that freedom is not worth having if not everyone can have it—yet we have no means to make freedom available to all. The means we do try to use toward that end create something worse than the poverty and inequality they try to alleviate: terror. Arendt recognizes the Marxian point that some "poverty . . . is a political, not a natural phenomenon, the result of violence and violation rather than of scarcity" (*OR*, 63). It is important to identify such instances of "artificial" poverty; but she also insists that there are natural necessities and scarcities, ones that simply are part of the human condition and that stand opposed to freedom: "[N]ecessity, which we invariably carry with us in the very existence of our bodies and their needs, can never be simply reduced to and completely absorbed by violence and violation" (65). Marx and Hegel are wrong "to believe . . . in a dialectical process in which freedom would rise directly out of necessity" (63). The effort to gain the necessities of life is separate from the political striving for distinction and freedom.

Arendt's second take on poverty—her implausible answer—turns away from the view that poverty is natural but takes its solution to be a merely "administrative" matter, where "administrative" is strictly distinguished from "political." Modern technology, she says, gives us the means to achieve prosperity for all, so that the modern world, in sharp contrast to the ancient world, does offer the possibility of political participation and action to all. But it is not a political matter to see to it that modern technology actually delivers on this promise of prosperity to all (see *OR*, 65-66 and 114, for the fullest statements of this argument). The logic of Arendt's position here, it seems, is that administrative matters are simply questions of means and ends: "Public debate can only deal with things which—if we want to put it negatively—we cannot figure out with certainty. . . . On the other hand, everything which can be figured out, in the sphere Engels called the administration of things—these are social things in general. That they should be subject to debate seems to me phony and a plague" (Hill, 317). Arendt's example is the building of a bridge: we can debate whether or not to build the bridge, but once having decided to build it, the matter is turned over to the engineers. But this distinction becomes implausible once we are dealing with an issue as complex as the alleviation of poverty. Not only is there no certainty about what means will do the trick (various experts will disagree with each other), but we also cannot do everything necessary at once. There will be trade-offs, risks, and benefits going to some groups before others, not to mention the benefits accruing to the experts who are given the task. All these uncertainties pull the issue back into the public forum of debate—and thus, in Arendt's view, contaminate that public forum with matters that will have material consequences for participants in the debate. There just does not seem to be, in practice, any way of keeping the social and the political, the administrative and the political, separate.

Explaining the Rise of the Social

The difficulties posed to modern sensibilities by Arendt's notion of the "social" only increase when we consider her explanations for its triumph in our era. Arendt recognizes that the polis in Greece was founded on the violent exclusion of women and slaves:

> [A]ll Greek philosophers . . . took for granted . . . that freedom is exclusively located in the political realm, that necessity is primarily a prepolitical phenomenon, characteristic of private household organization, and that force and violence are justified in this sphere, because they are the only means to master necessity—for instance, by ruling over slaves—and to become free. Because all human beings are subject to necessity, they are entitled to violence toward others; violence is the prepolitical act of liberating oneself from the necessity of life for the freedom of the world. (*HC*, 31)

In this Greek view, the violence Arendt associates with the compassionate modern nation-state is not avoided; it is merely displaced to a "prepolitical" moment in the private sphere, although talk of "entitlement" to such violence is chilling. If the Arendtian polis cannot be achieved through better means than the exclusionary violence of the Greeks, we might very well prefer to take our chances with the liberal welfare state, even when accepting Arendt's and other critics' complaints that liberal universalism breeds a violence distinctive to the modern West. At issue here is whether some form of violence is inevitable and whether the violence characteristic of liberal humanism is so likely to lead to totalitarianism as to be much more dangerous than other violences.

Whether Arendt believes (à la Nietzsche) that violence is an inevitable part of human affairs, so that all that is left to us (to paraphrase Marlow in Conrad's *Heart of Darkness*) is a "choice of violences," is not clear.[5] On the one hand, certain passages in *On Revolution* suggest that she thinks modern technology gives us the means to overcome scarcity and, thus, a nonviolent means to make politics accessible to many more people (if not everyone) than was true in ancient Greece.

Amidst plenty, the violence of the struggle for life (there is something Darwinian as well as Hobbesian and Nietzschean in Arendt's view of necessity) is mitigated, perhaps even eliminated. On the other hand, there is an incipient elitism in Arendt that leads to the pessimistic fear that the many will never abandon the quest for necessities in favor of the charms of freedom and action.

Arendt's ambivalence on this point manifests itself in the differ- ent—and contradictory—points of view she evidences on the ques- tions of what people do and can be expected to desire and of why it is that moderns have the desires they have. In some moods, her com- plaints against modernity can seem very like traditional reactionary and aristocratic denunciations of the leveling, mediocrity, and vulgar- ity characteristic of egalitarian societies. In this view, the courage, cre- ativity, and attachment to "higher" pleasures that are required to adopt the exercise of freedom as one's primary good are simply out- side the ken of the many. In this explanation, desires seem to be self- chosen, not resulting from historical or cultural factors. Given more time, freed from the need to devote all time and energy to securing ne- cessities, the many do not know how to do anything but more of the same. They use their newfound extra time and energy to produce and consume more goods; they create a consumer society, a world in which effort, identity, self-worth, and meaning are exclusively attached to what one owns and consumes. Such commodities are not things held in common in a public world, but things held away from the world for private use. In our present-day "consumer's society," we have not used our escape from necessity to pursue other ends, but "we have al- most succeeded in leveling all human activities to the common denom- inator of securing the necessities of life and providing for their abun- dance." Giving these former laborers "admi[ssion] and . . . equal rights in the public realm" (*HC*, 126) didn't raise them to the "free- men's" level but pulled the "freemen" down to the laborers' level.

In other moods, Arendt hardly blames the modern masses them- selves, taking those masses instead to be the product of the historical shift from ancient to modern that she is delineating. It is not that the masses—out of perversity, ignorance, or some other inherent failing— refuse to devote their newfound leisure to the political, but that the political has already become so attenuated—both as a motive and as a realm—that the masses (almost literally) have no place to enact what- ever political desires they might latently possess. A taste for freedom and politics can be activated only through an experience of political action—and it is just that experience that is denied to almost everyone under modern conditions. The "lost treasure" of the revolutionary tradition is exactly this joy and exaltation of political action itself, a joy that Arendt says is rediscovered in the spontaneous revolutionary action of certain people in moments of crisis. That this rediscovery is made in "the absence of continuity, tradition, and organized influence" (*OR*, 262) testifies to modernity's repression of everything that might foster a love of freedom. Each revolutionary group (those who formed the soviets in 1905 Russia, or the workers' councils in 1956 Hungary, or the various protest groups of the 1960s) forges the participatory and egalitarian protoinstitutions of a renewed polis in almost total ignorance of their predecessors' similar efforts.

In this scenario, played out most optimistically in Arendt's two essays on the student protests of the 1960s, "On Violence" and "Civil Disobedience" (both collected in *Crises of the Republic*), not only is modernity (not the masses) to blame for our collective failure to value the political, but also violence itself is understood as the product of the continual frustration of the political capacities of each and every citizen. In these two essays, Arendt is deeply impressed by the nonviolence of many of the political activities within the Civil Rights and antiwar movements; she ascribes the violence of the times not to extremists within the movements or even to the movements' revolutionary goals, but to the absence of an adequate public space for fully political activity. Violence, she contends, stems from the baffled sense that something is amiss, something is lacking in a bureaucratized modern society that leaves nothing for citizens to do, no way from them to participate, to act. This sense of something missing is baffled (and thus becomes all the more frustrated and prone to violence) because modernity has deprived us of even a memory or a tradition of the political.

If democracy and creeping egalitarianism are not to blame for the attenuation of the political and the rise of the social, then how do we account for modernity's turn away from action and freedom? At one point in *The Human Condition*, Arendt periodizes this movement, associating the move from action to work with early capitalism, and the triumph of labor over both work and action with late capitalism:

> Historically, the last public realm, the last meeting place which is at least connected with the activity of *homo faber*, is the exchange market on which his products are displayed. The commercial society,

characteristic of the earlier stages of the modern age or the beginnings of manufacturing capitalism, sprang from this "conspicuous
production" with its concomitant hunger for universal possibilities
of truck and barter, and its end came with the rise of labor and the
labor society which replaced conspicuous production with "conspicuous consumption" and its concomitant vanity. (162)

Is there any way to explain these shifts in loci of ultimate concern, in
the basic structure of people's desires?

Arendt, in fact, is neither very good at nor very interested in offering underlying causes for the shifts in sensibility that she describes.
Her resistance to explanation stems in part from her rejection of ne-
cessitarian views of history, which she associates primarily with Hegel
and Marx. Deterministic narratives reduce all human activity to behavior and thus neglect what Arendt (borrowing and transforming a
term from Augustine) calls "natality": "[T]he new beginning inherent
in birth can make itself felt in the world only because the newcomer
possesses the capacity of beginning something anew, that is, of acting.
In this sense of initiative, an element of action, and therefore of natality, is inherent in all human activities" (*HC*, 9). We preserve our sense
of natality only when we retain our wonder at the "miracle" of action
and at its introduction of the unexpected:

> Every act, seen from the perspective not of the agent but of the
> process in whose framework it occurs, is a "miracle"—that is, some-
> thing which could not be expected. . . . It is in the very nature of
> every new beginning that it breaks into the world as an "infinite im-
> probability," and yet it is precisely this infinitely improbable which
> actually constitutes the very texture of everything we call real. . . . It
> is because of this element of the "miraculous" present in all reality
> that events, no matter how well anticipated in fear or hope, strike us
> with a shock of surprise once they have come to pass. The very im-
> pact of an event is never wholly explicable; its factuality transcends
> in principle all anticipation. (*BPF*, 169–70)

Natality not only limits our ability to foresee the future but also renders causal accounts of the past reductionist and limited:

> Causality . . . is an altogether alien and falsifying category in the his-
> torical sciences. Not only does the actual meaning of every event al-
> ways transcend any number of past "causes" which we may assign to
> it (one has only to think of the grotesque disparity between "cause"
> and "effect" in an event like the First World War), but this past
> comes into being only with the event itself. Only when something

irrevocable has happened can we even try to trace its history back-
ward. The event illuminates its own past; it can never be deduced
from it. (*EU*, 319)

This emphasis on "natality," on what we might call the "plurality" produced by the infinite novelties of action, obviously exists in
tension with Arendt's willingness to make sweeping generalizations
about the behavior of modern consumers. Similarly, her resistance to
reductive explanatory narratives confronts her attempt—halfhearted
and not fully worked out though it is—to explain the transition from
the ancient to the modern world. Arendt, of course, was fully aware of
other accounts of this transition, most notably Marx's. A Marxist-
inspired class analysis, focusing on the bourgeoisie, provides the basic
narrative of *The Origins of Totalitarianism*, even though that narrative is crucially supplemented by attention to racism and nationalism.
Similarly, *The Human Condition* follows Marx in taking the economic as the dominant factor in modern society. For Arendt, however,
Marx is a major part of the problem, not a resource for a cure, because Marx is quintessentially a part of his age, not a critic of it, when
he locates the most fundamental human satisfactions in work. Marx's
explanatory history, then, reveals the very obsession with productive
activity that needs to be explained—and, furthermore, takes production as the cause itself. Arendt's whole effort is directed against the
modern reduction of all activity to work (or, even worse, to labor), so
she must reject the Marxist location of causes and explanation in production. Of course, we could just say that capitalism, which names a
social organization geared toward "conspicuous production," man-
dates the modern obsession with the productive—and Arendt seems
to say just that in places. But this idea doesn't answer the question,
why does capitalism arise and gain dominance between 1500 and 1800
in the West?

Arendt looks to modern forms of knowledge, particularly the
modern science ushered in by Galileo, Newton, and their brethren, for
an answer. Modern science deprives us of the world of common sense,
Arendt argues; then she implies (I do not know that she makes this
point explicitly anywhere) that work—the production of human-
made things—compensates for the anxiety generated by loss of access
to nature. In other words, nature has always been problematic because it is changeable and not particularly tuned to human needs, but

in ancient times it was a stable point of reference held in common, just as the artificial "world" of objects made in work was a stable point of reference. But nature becomes unknowable in any direct, common-sense way with the advent of modern science, and so we frantically up the pace of the production of artificial objects to combat an attenuated sense of reality. At the same time, the doubt that now assails the possibility of holding things in common afflicts human-made objects as well; there is a new impulse to accumulate things in private, because what we hold in common with others seems threatened. Private accumulation, meant to confront the threat of losing a common world, only serves to make that possibility a reality. When the public world is fully furnished (so to speak), there is no need to construct a lavish private space. But the more people who retreat from the public world into a privately owned one, the less full that public world becomes and the more reason there is to retreat from it.

Science empties out the public world because it deprives us of common sense—a term that Arendt uses in its double meaning, first, to describe an experience of sensual impression (rendered by sight, touch, hearing, taste, and smell) that is commensurate with the experiences of other humans and is thus held in common with them. The existence of common sense, according to this meaning, makes appeals to sensual impression serve as confirmations of reality in cases where questions arise. What settles such matters is showing the questioner something, letting her see and hear for herself. But modern science deprives us of such appeals. The most obvious example is the claim that the earth moves around the sun, not vice versa. The evidence for the truth of Copernicus's claim is utterly removed from the evidence of common sense. The senses, in fact, are not to be trusted. Cartesian doubt, Arendt tells us, "resides ultimately in the loss of self-evidence" and "spreads from the testimony of the senses to the testimony of reason to the testimony of faith." An abyss is opened up between how things appear and their truth, an abyss that is fatal to the sharing of a world in common: "If Being and Appearance part company forever, and this . . . is indeed the basic assumption of all modern science, then there is nothing left to be taken upon faith; everything must be doubted" (*HC*, 275). (As I will discuss in chapter 3, Arendt's ontology rests on establishing the reality of appearances, as contrasted to the modern tendency to locate the real in hidden depths.)

In its second meaning, common sense refers to the unquestioned, habitual assumptions by which we organize our daily rounds of activities and experiences. This meaning comes close to what political theorists today are more likely to call "ideology" or what Pierre Bourdieu (1984) calls the "habitus." It is hard not to read Arendt here through the lens of the intense and intricate discourse on ideology that has taken place in the twenty-five years since her death. The issues here are complex—and I will return to them in chapter 3 when considering Arendt's use of Kant's *sensus communis,* the version of common sense that plays a key role in Kant's *The Critique of Judgment.* For the moment, I will venture to say (fully admitting that this is an interpretation of Arendt more shaky and more tendentious than most of what I have to say in this book) that common sense in Arendt functions positively as a bond that holds groups of people together and that its unquestioned, even unconscious, quality does not particularly disturb her. That said, it is crucial to recognize that Arendt is under no illusions that such common sense—or its cousin, the unquestioned and unquestionable authority of religion and/or tradition—can be restored under modern conditions. The premodern world (as described by Arendt in the essay "What Is Authority?" in *Between Past and Future*) was organized around shared values, beliefs, and truths in a way that is simply no longer possible. Nostalgia is fruitless. Authority cannot be restored; the unquestioned sway of some monolithic religion and some canonical tradition is gone from human society forever. "I do not believe that we can stabilize the situation in which we have been since the seventeenth century in any final way," she declares (Hill, 314). We must reconcile ourselves to the modern situation, which requires "thinking without a bannister" (336): "The tradition is broken and the Ariadne thread is lost. . . . [O]ne has got to start thinking as though nobody had thought before, and then start learning from everybody else" (337).

From a contemporary leftist viewpoint, however, Arendt falls into an error rather different from nostalgia. The loss of common sense generates, in her view, modern subjectivism, the isolation of each individual in "the prison of his own mind, into the limitations of patterns he himself created" (*HC*, 288). In her prologue to *The Human Condition,* Arendt tells us that "the purpose of the historical analysis" presented in the book "is to trace back modern alienation, its twofold flight from the earth into the universe and from the world into the self, in order to arrive at an understanding of the nature of society" (6).

Modern society, in Arendt's view, appears to suffer from what the French sociologist Émile Durkheim called "anomie," which can be defined as the chaotic condition of modern societies in which the centrifugal forces of constant innovation (technological, cultural, and commercial), increased mobility (both in status and from place to place), and an individualistic ethos overwhelm any residual centripetal focus that could promote social cohesion. Durkheim's legacy to modern sociology was the "problem of order." Anomie focuses on the worry that there will be no "social glue" capable of holding society together in the face of the dissolving effects of economic competition, the decay of commonly held belief systems (notably religion), and modern individualism.

Such an outlook misses entirely the power of ideology. To see us today as living in an utterly chaotic, fragmented society is to miss the extent to which beliefs about (to name a few examples) the desirability of growth and change (both economic and personal), the unique ability of capitalism to provide prosperity, the appropriate and acceptable relation of "developed" to "underdeveloped" nations, and the appropriate and acceptable relation of men to women and among the different "races" are, in fact, held in common—and reinforce a "globalization" of capitalism that is anything but chaotic and anarchist. There is plenty of evidence that individuals are no more "subjective," no more autonomous, no more separated from unquestioned assumptions and beliefs today than at any time in the past. It is just that some of the traditional sources of authority have given way to new ones. (And we shouldn't be too hasty in making even this limited claim. Religion has shown itself far stronger in the past thirty years—think of Islamic and Christian fundamentalisms—than most commentators on "modern" society have ever been willing to acknowledge.) Anomie goes hand in hand with what has increasingly come to seem the myth, not the fact, of modern subjectivism. In any case, the pendulum has swung almost entirely the other direction in postmodern thought. Much postmodern theory posits a subject so utterly constituted by social forms and powers that the puzzle has become how to explain individual agency at all.

Arendt, of course, clings to action and "natality" precisely to combat the social determinisms already evident in various social, historical, and political theories of her own day. And she is hardly a simple-minded adherent of the view that modern society is anomistically (atomistically) subjective. After all, in her historical account modern subjectivism calls forth its opposites: mass society and totalitarianism. The modern, isolated subject is vulnerable to the siren calls of an ersatz communality, one that results in obliterating individuality. That mass society and totalitarianism do not have to rely on brute force to gain adherents means that Arendt must address the issue of ideology, which explicitly enters her thought when she is considering totalitarianism's appeal. Here is a centripetal force that works via persuasion—and the basis of its appeal seems to be that modern subjectivism has been experienced more as a burden than a blessing, a situation that provides considerable leverage to ideologies purporting to bind people together again.

Here, as elsewhere, mass society and totalitarianism can seem remarkably like "evil twins" in Arendt's conception of the political. They address the same anxieties and deficiencies of modernity, but they propose solutions that are worse than the disease. Yet it is hard to see how Arendt's own prescriptions do not qualify as an "ideology" in the way she uses that term to describe totalitarianism. The only differences appear to be that her view has fewer adherents and that it offers a more explicit analysis of the disease it sets out to cure and, hence, of the basis on which it solicits our adoption. Perhaps such explicitness is all we need when we are talking about ideology, especially if we focus on the unquestioned or unconscious element of an ideology, but we also know that no theory can be totally lucid about its assumptions and commitments. In any case, Arendt's historical explanation of how the ancient world cedes to the modern one, and her political theory as an exhortation to revive certain desires lost under modern conditions cannot completely disentangle themselves from the very epistemological problems that she thinks have been bequeathed to us by modern science and that she locates as a primary cause for the crisis of the political in modernity. Such an entanglement is hardly surprising; Arendt herself is, of course, a modern, even if only a "reluctant" one, as Seyla Benhabib (1996) puts it, and it invalidates neither her thought nor her critique of her own society if she, at times, partakes of modernity's perplexities.

Action, Freedom, and Identity in the Space of Appearances

Enough about all the pretenders to the throne. It is time to turn to action and freedom, to see why action is free but other activities are not, and how action can generate both a common world and a full plurality of distinctive identities. The first point to stress is that, for Arendt, action is its own good, is for its own sake. Nothing justifies action; nothing is gained or accomplished through action. Action is simply the embodiment, the realization, of freedom—and requires nothing further to be experienced as a good. Arendt recognizes the paradoxes involved in declaring anything a good in, of, and for itself. Not only do we habitually justify activities as means toward ends, but we also habitually justify ends by reference to other goods that they foster or enable. Thus, if we were to ask what makes freedom a suitable goal (end) of human efforts, the answer would probably involve either explaining the benefits of freedom (what it produces as direct products or as by-products) or offering a series of synonyms for freedom. Arendt wants to bypass these complexities altogether by removing action—and the realm in which action occurs, politics—from a means/ends vocabulary. She wants to resist "the substitution of making for action and the concomitant degradation of politics into a means to obtain an allegedly 'higher' end" (*HC*, 229). She wants a "pure" politics in the way that aesthetes, the advocates of "art for art's sake," want a "pure" poetry separated from any instrumental calculus—and especially from the economic rationale of commodities. The desire is for poetry or politics as a state of being, sufficient unto itself and desired for what it is, not for what it can do. In fact, readers of Kant's *Critique of Judgment*—the great founding text of modern aestheticism—will recognize that Arendt's notion of action is strikingly similar to Kant's notion of the beautiful, in its emphasis of form over content, its insistence on the purposeless and disinterested, and its stress on the particular and distinctive over the general.

I need to emphasize Arendt's desire to imagine action and the space of politics as existing outside any means/ends calculus precisely because I am not going to honor that desire in what follows. Arendt wants to set herself against what she sees as the dominance of instrumentalism in the modern age, and I don't know whether she fails to disentangle herself from that instrumentalism or whether I am the one who can't escape instrumentalist thinking. In any case, one way to read the modernism/postmodernism divide is to say that the modernists, following Kant, desperately tried to erect realms—usually aesthetic ones—free from the contaminating touch of instrumentalism (utilitarianism) and the market. In other words, modernism in the arts attempts to oppose the dominance of the market in modernity. (Inspired by Arendt, J. M. Bernstein has called the aesthetic realm of the modernists "the cipher for an absent politics" [1992, 13].) Arendt's attempt to repudiate modernity by imagining a pure politics resides firmly within modernity as another example of the oppositional tradition that begins with romanticism and carries through to modernism. Postmodernists deconstruct the dream of purity, revealing (in Pierre Bourdieu [1984], for example) that such pretensions to purity have their own payoff in "cultural capital" or (in Terry Eagleton [1991], for example) that illusions about the possibility of escaping the market's relentless domination of every phase of life merely serve to reconcile the modern age to capitalism, not to establish an escape from it. Postmodernists proclaim that there is no outside to modern instrumentalism—and then are left with the problem of imagining what kind of challenge to the dominant order can be mounted from within that order. I am enough of a postmodernist to find it impossible to credit the claims to purity, autonomy, and disinterestedness that Arendt makes for action. But this may be my blind spot, not Arendt's. In attempting to circumvent the notion that everything is interested, that everything is undertaken as a means to achieve something else, she is pushing at the very limits of modern thought, striving mightily to indicate that there should be and perhaps even already are other vocabularies, other ways to think. A postmodern denial of these possibilities should hardly be allowed to set itself up as true. Many critics of postmodernism have seen it as simply caving in to modernity, whereas at least the modernists waged a valiant, if failed, battle against it—keeping alive the dream, if not the reality, of something "other."

It seems to me that, despite her insistence to the contrary, Arendt in fact identifies a whole series of goods that action produces, and that she somewhat relies on these produced goods to justify action. The most crucial products of action are the political realm itself, and plurality (distinctive individual identity) and freedom. The achievement of individual identity is synonymous with freedom—and only the free person is fully human: "Speech and action reveal this unique distinctness. Through them, men distinguish themselves instead of being merely distinct; they are the modes in which human beings appear to each other, not indeed as physical objects, but *qua* men. This appearance, as distinguished from mere bodily existence, rests on initiative, but it is an initiative from which no human can refrain and still be human" (*HC*, 176). The stakes, then, are quite high. To act is to be human—in other words, only those who are free, who initiate something in the world, and who "distinguish themselves" as "unique" count as human. We have here a significant movement through a set of interrelated goods (freedom, humanness, plurality, initiative) as well as a number of things (identity, uniqueness, humanness) produced by means of action. Within this interpretive framework, what is important is not so much that action is not a means, but that action is the means to a different set of goods—a set of goods that modernity, with its emphasis on labor and work, seems to have lost sight of. The complaint, then, is not against means/ends relations per se but against the reductionist modern understanding of the range of ends that humans might pursue. Modern instrumentalism recognizes only economic interests and thus misses the full range of what might motivate humans.

Action in Arendt can be best defined as an activity staged in front of others that reveals the agent's identity. Arendt can make no more pointed differentiation between the "social" and the "political" than to write "that the best 'social conditions' are those under which it is possible to lose one's identity. This unitedness of many into one is basically antipolitical" (*HC*, 214). In political action one achieves one's identity, one doesn't lose it. Only that which creates identity counts as action in Arendt—a condition with the somewhat confusing consequence that speech, in certain ways, is the most readily identifiable action, given Arendt's definition of the term: "[For the ancient Greeks,] [t]hought was secondary to speech, but speech and action were considered to be coeval and coequal . . . ; and this originally meant not only that most political action . . . is indeed transacted in words, but more fundamentally that finding the right words at the right moment, quite apart from the information or communication they may convey, is action" (25–26). The polis is "the most talkative of all bodies politic" (26).

Arendt offers an intricate account of how action produces identity. Recall, first, that identity is utterly intersubjective for Arendt: "[W]e become one whole individual, in the richness as well as the limitation of definite characteristics, through and only through the company of others. For our individuality, insofar as it is one—unchangeable and unmistakable—we depend entirely on other people" (*EU*, 358). By the time we get to *The Human Condition*, however, Arendt is no longer committed to the "unchangeable" part of this formulation. Identity is "revealed" through speech and action, but that revelation comes as a discovery to the agent as much as to the audience. Identity does not preexist action as its cause but is produced by action as its result. And, given Arendt's emphasis on action as initiative, the identity produced by one's past actions is always susceptible to transformation via the action I am performing now. The examples of writing or of a conversation with others can illustrate Arendt's insight here. The thrill of writing or of a good conversation is that it leads me to discover what I believe through the process of articulating my thoughts in a way that makes them presentable to others. In some inchoate way, perhaps, those beliefs and ideas were "in" me, so that when I articulate them now, I can acknowledge them as "mine"; but, in another way, what I write or say under the pressure of others as the audience for those words surprises me as much as it does them. If I believed or thought those things, I didn't quite know I did. It is just this sense of excitement and discovery at the birth of something novel yet familiar (recognizably mine) that Arendt tries to express as the relation between action and identity. Circumstances reveal my capacities; thus, I can discover new things about myself by encountering new situations. But that discovery, for Arendt, is not complete until it is articulated. That is why the presence of other humans—and of the speech they elicit—is crucial:

> Action and speech are so closely related because the primordial and specifically human act must at the same time contain the answer to the question asked of every newcomer: "Who are you?" This disclosure of who somebody is, is implicit in both his words and deeds; yet obviously the affinity between speech and revelation is much closer than that between action and revelation, just as the affinity between action and beginning is closer than that between speech and beginning, although many, and even most acts, are performed in the manner of speech. Without the accompaniment of speech, at any rate, action would not only lose its revelatory character, but, and by the same token, it would lose its subject, as it were. . . . Speechless action would no longer be action, because there would no longer be an actor, and the actor, the doer of deeds, is possible only if he is at the same time the speaker of words. The action he begins is humanly disclosed by the word. (*HC*, 178-79)

Words, then, insure that actions disclose the agent to human others: "Without this disclosure of the agent in the act, action loses its specific character and becomes one form of achievement among others."

Because the agent does not know in advance what her actions will reveal, action requires courage: "Although nobody knows who he reveals when he discloses himself in deed or word, he must be willing to risk the disclosure" (*HC*, 180). This risk is heightened in the public sphere, where I reveal myself not to intimates but to strangers. I might make an utter fool of myself—with everybody watching. Arendt's model of action is performative, even theatrical, through and through. Striving to distinguish oneself is akin to the stage performance of the virtuoso. Arendt acknowledges that this Greek understanding of action is competitive and individualistic, founded on the contest among participants to be recognized as excellent:

> No doubt this concept of action is highly individualistic, as we would say today. It stresses the urge toward self-disclosure at the expense of all other factors. . . . As such it became the prototype of action for Greek antiquity and influenced, in the form of the so-called agonal spirit, the passionate drive to show one's self in measuring up against others that underlies the concept of politics prevalent in the city-states. (194)

In the essay "What Is Freedom?" (in *Between Past and Future*), Arendt connects virtuosity with Machiavellian *virtu* while also making clear that politics is justified (as least for a republican tradition she traces from the Greek city-states and the Roman republic to Machiavelli) insofar as it enables "freedom as virtuosity" to appear. Because her discussion in this essay makes clear the connection between freedom, action, and politics, while highlighting her performative, agonistic model of action as well as the reason she insists action should produce no tangible, material thing, it is worth quoting at length (note Arendt's explicit identification of an "end or *raison d'être*" of politics):

> Men *are* free—as distinguished from their possessing the gift of freedom—as long as they act, neither before nor after; for to *be* free and to act are the same.
> Freedom as inherent in action is perhaps best illustrated by Machiavelli's concept of *virtu*, the excellence with which man answers the opportunities the world opens up before him in the guise of *fortuna*. Its meaning is best rendered as "virtuosity," that is, an excellence we attribute to the performing arts (as distinguished from the creative arts of making), where the accomplishment lies in the performance itself and not in an end product which outlasts the activity that brought it into existence and becomes independent of it. . . .

> The performing arts . . . have a strong affinity with politics. Per-
> forming artists—dancers, play-actors, musicians, and the like—need
> an audience to show their virtuosity, just as acting men need the
> presence of others before whom they can appear; both need a pub-
> licly organized space for their "work" and both depend upon others
> for the performance itself. Such a space of appearances is not to be
> taken for granted wherever men live together in a community. . . .
>   If, then, we understand the political in the sense of the *polis*, its
> end or *raison d'être* would be to establish and keep in existence a
> space where freedom as virtuosity can appear. This is the realm
> where freedom is a worldly reality, tangible in words which can be
> heard, in deeds which can be seen, and in events which are talked
> about, remembered and turned into stories. (*BPF*, 153–55)

Action is individualistic because it gains one the freedom to be
oneself. But I cannot be an individual unless there are others who witness, acknowledge, applaud, and remember my words and deeds. I
must accompany my deeds with words so that they may have a human
significance. But those deeds take up a presence in the world when
they are recounted and remembered in the words of others. Actions
breed stories. And those stories are communal; they are, in certain
ways, the social fabric itself, the binding together of humans who
share the memory of certain great deeds, who form the audience in
this specific space of appearances. Action is not complete until it has
been witnessed, taken up, recounted, and (we might say) judged by
the audience. Applause and memory must be won; the agent must act
in ways worthy of acclaim (hence virtuosity). Individual identity, although it arises out of what the agent does, can be conferred only by
others.

In some ways, Arendt has far too little to say about the process by
which the agent secures the attention and acclaim of others. Is such attention granted as part of a reciprocal pact—I'll watch you during your
turn on the stage, if you'll watch me? Or is there a fundamental competition in which there are losers as well as winners, some persons who
will not be talked about or remembered, who could be said never really
to achieve distinction or even individuality? Even worse, are there
some who never even get their moment onstage? Does the polis develop
an asymmetrical split between those who mostly act and those who
mostly serve as the spectators of such action? To a certain extent, Hegel's
notion of "recognition" as expressed in the master/slave dialectic lurks
behind Arendt's understanding of identity. For Hegel, individual iden-

tity depends on the individual being "recognized" as such by others. Only the response of others to my presence in the world as making a unique difference grants me the reality of selfhood. (The connection to "natality," "plurality," and Arendt's ontology is, I trust, obvious.) But Hegel tries to think through the repercussions of this radical dependence on others; he suspects that where there is dependence, there is the potential for extortion and other kinds of exploitative power imbalances. The master extracts recognition from the slave without returning a reciprocal recognition. (In another parallel with Arendt, the master gains this power over the slave because the master has managed to transcend a concern with "life" in a way that the slave has not.) Hegel believes such nonreciprocal recognition is, in the long run, self-defeating, because the recognition granted me by someone I do not recognize as unique cannot confer a reality on my individuality. The non-recognized slave has been deprived of the power needed to recognize another, including the master himself. But even if nonequality eventually frustrates the very desire that generates it, Hegel shrewdly understands that humans often find radical dependence on others intolerable and adopt various means—from psychological denial to the establishment of relations of force—to circumvent such dependence and the vulnerabilities that accompany it.

Of course, in one way I have already suggested that Arendt's analysis of totalitarianism focuses on its fear of plurality, its fear of an inability to control destiny. And although I do believe that her subsequent work devotes too little attention to the possibility of unequal and nonreciprocal relations among humans in public spaces, that deficiency is remedied to some extent by the great attention paid to the agent's lack of control over her actions. Three distinct factors contribute to the agent's lack of control. First, as I have already discussed, there is no preexisting intention or identity that governs action from the agent's side. "Action 'produces' stories," Arendt tells us, yet "the stories, the results of action and speech, reveal an agent, but this agent is not an author or producer. Somebody began it and is its subject in the twofold sense of the word, namely, its actor and sufferer, but nobody is its author." We are not the "authors" of our stories not only because we do not know ahead of time what we are going to do or who we are going to turn out to be, but also because we are unable to predict or control the consequences of our actions. We are "sufferers" as well as "actors" because of factors two and three: the external world and other people. "Action almost never achieves its purpose" (*HC*, 184), Arendt writes, because she does not think the will has the force, the ability, to impose unilaterally its patterns on the world and on others. Instead, in the meeting of the various vectors that make up the lines of force in any situation, my action is diverted and transformed. A story records the interaction of my deed not just with the responses of others but also with their deeds; with the movement of objects in response not just to my action upon them but also to the pressures that circumstances exert on me. Action, for Arendt, "always establishes relationships" (190), and both the extent of those relationships and their consequences are impossible to know (and hence to control) in advance:

> Because the actor always moves among and in relation to other acting beings, he is never merely a "doer" but always and at the same time a sufferer. To do and to suffer are like opposite sides of the same coin, and the story that an act starts is composed of its consequent deeds and sufferings. These consequences are boundless, because action, though it may proceed from nowhere so to speak, acts into a medium where every reaction becomes a chain reaction and where every process is the cause of a new process. (190)

Our radical dependency on others is paired with the radical contingency that accompanies all our deeds. We cannot know in advance where we are headed. There are no ways to guarantee the satisfaction of the desires that underwrite action.[6]

Here, once again, we meet the "existentialist" Arendt, portraying humans as acting out a fundamental freedom that is rendered mostly ineffective because of the radical contingency of the universe they inhabit. Humans must act, the existentialist would argue, but those actions are futile because we can never gain what we desire. And the ultimate sign of that futility is the fact that we will die. For the existentialist, the world is absurd, meaningless. Only human action imposes meaning and order on the utterly random chaos of the nonhuman. The crucial difference between this existentialist stance (most fully expressed in Sartre's early work) and Arendt's views is that she believes that the political realm is humanly created precisely to mitigate this radical contingency. Perhaps the universe is absurd; but humans "acting in concert" can create a realm—which Arendt calls the "world" and distinguishes from the "universe"—in which acting out our freedom is neither meaningless nor utterly futile. Our desire for immortality is granted in the only achievable fashion, if the polis acts as an "organized remembrance." Far from believing that "hell is other people" (as in Sartre's famous aphorism), Arendt believes that only a resourceful, intersubjective human coping with what, after all, is the *human* condition can make life worth living. We cannot expect help from nature or from the gods. It is the world that humans create, the space of appearances they clear for themselves, that allows for action and freedom. As the experience of totalitarianism demonstrated, this political realm is itself contingent; it offers no guarantees against the disaster of its own disappearance. But where it does exist, Arendt firmly believes, it offers the best possible lives that humans can ever hope to live—and its collapse in mid-twentieth-century Europe created her sense of its unique preciousness. There can be no substitute for the political and the distinctive freedom it enables. From the perspective of this emphasis on the political, existentialism looks like a despairing philosophy that explores what freedom could possibly be in a world where the political has been irrecoverably lost.

The utter reliance on others both for my identity and for the intersubjective creation of the space of appearances moves us from the agonistic, individualistic component of Arendtian action toward its cooperative component. Both are equally crucial; they must coexist for action to be possible. The idea that cooperative action is underwritten by the contingency that surrounds all human action and the realm in which that action can be staged is most obvious in Arendt's discussion of two particular actions that she identifies as peculiarly necessary for the creation and survival of the political: promising and forgiving. Promising tries to lessen the terror of an unknown future by assuring that you can at least rely on me to do this in the future; forgiving mitigates the terror of action by extending a human acceptance that what was revealed in your action—and the consequences that it engendered—was not under your control: "The possible redemption from the predicament of irreversibility—of being unable to undo what one has done though one did not, and could not, have known what he was doing—is the faculty of forgiving. The remedy for unpredictability, for the chaotic uncertainty of the future, is contained in the faculty to make and keep promises." These two faculties establish "islands of security without which not even continuity, let alone durability of any kind, would be possible in the relationships between men" (*HC*, 237). What must be stressed is that promising and forgiving are completely human and totally excessive. Both are foolhardy gestures in a universe marked by change, unpredictability, and all the other potential sources of harm toward human aspirations. But they are absolutely necessary foolhardy actions if humans are to create a world that attempts to stand against the "twofold darkness of human affairs" (the unreliability of our own characters and the inability to know the consequences of our actions in advance) without resorting "to a mastery which relies on domination of one's self and rule over others." Arendt admits that promises are "dangerous" because they "leave the unpredictability of human affairs and the unreliability of men as they are"; but this is the "price [humans] pay for plurality and reality, for the joy of inhabiting together with others a world whose reality is guaranteed for each by the presence of others" (244). That is, if we eschew forceful mastery in order to preserve the freedom that allows for the miracle of action as initiative, we are left with only nonenforceable promises (the voluntary binding of ourselves to others) and the free bestowing of forgiveness from others to maintain the political community over time. If Arendt is an existentialist, it is because she believes that humans facing the potential meaninglessness of utter contingency create a political space of appearances that has "no more to support itself than the good will to counter the enormous risks of action by readiness to forgive and to be forgiven, to make promises and to keep them" (245). In *On Revolution*, Arendt tells us that "the making and keeping of promises, . . . in the realm of politics, may well be the highest human faculty" (175). Courageous promises and generous forgiveness, which leave us utterly vulnerable to the unpredictable others on whom we are dependent, are the only foundations of the political, which we produce in concert with others. No wonder that "mastery which relies on domination" is such a temptation.

A Pickup Basketball Game

In turning now to the cooperative component of Arendt's concept of action—especially to her distinctive understanding of power—I will rely on the example of a pickup basketball game. I like this example because it makes remarkably clear, almost obvious, various Arendtian positions that seem eccentric or paradoxical. Her way of thinking no longer seems so foreign when something as ordinary as a basketball game can be adequately explained only with the aid of her concept of action. We will take a pickup game as our model here: there is no money or other external reward for winning; there are no spectators, just the players themselves; and anyone who walks into the gym is able to join the game.

It is easy to see that the game exists only as it is being played. Action on the court produces nothing but the game itself. Action and the game coexist; when one stops, so does the other. The players—and this is a crucial element of the Arendtian political realm that I have not mentioned yet—are absolutely equal in the sense that nothing about their lives off the court (how much money they have, their sexual identity, their educational level, etc.) has any impact on their participation in the game. Joseph Heller's *Catch-22* offers a good example of how nonequality in the limited sphere of the game renders it unplayable. Major Major comes to join the bomber crews' pickup games. The other players treat him as their superior officer—they always pass him the ball, never foul him, and barely guard him. Frustrated, he decides to come to the next game disguised. The players pretend to be taken in by the disguise and now use this opportunity to abuse him, fouling him as hard and as often as they can. Needless to say, the major has to give up. He doesn't come back, and the game goes back to something that is recognizably basketball. Given the rigidities (and the resentment) built into military hierarchies, a major can't just go out and play a game with the "boys."

When equality has been successfully established within the limited sphere of the game, players are judged solely on their performance in the game. And that performance has no reality apart from its appearance. It's what you do on the court that matters; you don't get any extra points for a basket because you've had to overcome horrendous psychological or physical hardships to manage to play at all. Your motives for playing or your attitude toward this game are irrelevant except insofar as they manifest themselves in your performance. There is no deeper reality, beyond the appearance of that performance, that in any way influences the unfolding of the game. Equality, then, means that anyone in the gym is eligible to play, that all are expected to play by the same rules (there aren't exceptions for certain privileged participants), and that all will be judged solely by how well they play.

Starting from a position of equality, players strive for distinction. The pleasure here is the striving against competitors, and the goal is to be good (if not the best), to have one's abilities recognized by the other players. It is the action of playing that brings these abilities into existence. The game is endlessly fascinating to the players, because new situations and new competitors disclose new facets of my abilities. I cannot know ahead of time the "moves" I will make; they are called into existence by my action in playing. I reveal my ability, my identity as a basketball player, to myself as well as to the other players—as, of course, they reveal themselves to me. It is worth noting that the game can still be highly pleasurable if I am not the best player on the court. In fact, the game is often more pleasurable when I play with and against people better than I, rather than when I am the best. Arendt does not consider the possibility of "resentment" in collective human activities, a possibility that obsesses Nietzsche. But the fact that the losing players in a basketball game do not inevitably resent the winners suggests that processes of distinction need not breed resentment. (Of course, when the rewards garnered by winners stand in stark contrast to deprivations endured by losers, the possibilities for resentment are greatly increased. I will return to this point when I consider the "consequences" of action on the basketball court.)

A basketball game is a structured world. The rules of the game are what is held in common, and those rules both "relate and separate" players. The players are related, of course, by partaking in the same game; they are separated not just into two teams but also among differentiated "positions" on each team. Anyone who has ever watched schoolchildren attempt to play the game by converging on the ball knows that basketball is transformed into the very different game of "keep away" when the players are not sufficiently separated. Collective activities involve many actors, not all of whom are doing the same thing at any given moment. In fact, the product of that activity depends on the plurality of actions pursued by the actors within the overarching framework of the activity. These different actions are coordinated insofar as they produce the collective activity. What do the players' actions produce? Nothing but the game itself.

In similar fashion, Arendt believes that the political realm is produced by the actions of the individuals who strive for distinction in that realm. We reach here Arendt's distinctive definition of power: "Power is what keeps the public realm, the potential space of appearance between acting and speaking men, in existence" (*HC*, 200). Power names the creative, public side effects that attend acting. The space of appearances, like a language or a cultural practice, is "utter[ly] dependent upon further acts to keep it in existence" (*BPF*, 153): "[P]ower [is] generated when people gather together and 'act in concert,' [and it] disappears the moment they depart" (*HC*, 244). The basketball game exists only as a product of the intersubjective collaboration of the players who are competing against one another, so the game is both agonistic-individualistic *and* cooperative-intersubjective. If a dispute breaks out about the interpretation or applicability of the rules, or if one player is simply ignorant of the rules and must be informed of them, or if the agonistic play gets so heated that two or more players start to fight, the game dissolves. Whether this suspension of the game is permanent or not depends on whether the constitutive agreement among all the participants—an agreement that is not necessarily explicit—can be restored. No single participant has the power to make the game resume.[7] In exasperation at some suspension of the game, I may say, "Come on, let's play," but I have no way beyond that verbal call to make the players go back to playing. Each of the players—irrespective of his or her individual abilities—is equally necessary to the playing of the game and thus equally capable of making it impossible for the game to continue by refusing to participate. And since the only good involved here is the game itself, there is no leverage over a player who decides that this game is no longer good to play (because someone is violating the rules, for example).

Thus, power in Arendt—as distinct from almost all other theories of power—is tied to equality, not to the production and maintenance of inequalities. As we have seen, Arendt uses the terms "force" and "strength" to designate unilateral impositions of necessities by one party upon others. The political realm in Arendt is the realm of freedom and equality precisely because the realm dissolves when it is not the product of an intersubjective "acting in concert" in which every participant engages willingly. But she pays a seemingly high price for this insulation of the political from force and strength. The political is immune from force because there is no threat that could coerce participation. Just as the only thing the basketball players lose is the game itself, so participants in the political lose the space of appearances if the intersubjective agreement that constitutes that space (an intersubjective agreement enacted through the ongoing activities that keep that space alive—an enactment that Arendt designates "power") breaks down. This is not a trivial loss, of course, especially as Arendt posits such free activity as the space that makes possible a fundamental good.

But this loss is not life threatening. The political offers "public happiness" (see *OR*, 119 and 127); but nothing *necessary* to life is at stake in the political, so it is a realm of freedom in two senses: it is free because it is not connected to necessity, and it is free because there is no way to compel anyone to participate. In fact, Arendt calls "freedom from politics" one "of the most important negative liberties" (280), apparently believing that the freedom of the political is guaranteed only when people are free *not* to participate: "The joys of public happiness and the responsibilities for public business would then become the share of those few from all walks of life who have a taste for public freedom and cannot be 'happy' without it" (279).

To return to the basketball analogy: There is no stigma nor any material penalty incurred by those who don't like to play basketball. But most readers of Arendt have found it impossible to accept that the political is as "sealed off" from the rest of life as a basketball game is. There are two ways to phrase this objection to Arendt's concept of the political. The first is to insist that there are consequences to participation in the political that extend beyond just having an opportunity to act. Arendt's own account of action already suggests this fact. Recall that she remarks on the "boundless" consequences of action, on its establishment of relationships whose formations and the interactions they enable constitute an "event." Actions on a basketball court are not boundless but strictly bounded; whether I play today and how I play if I choose to play have just about no potential connection to other portions of my life. We can, of course, imagine scenarios—involving injuries, say, or playing with people with whom I also interact in the workplace or in political activities—where my playing would have such consequences. Any activity, I would argue, can "leak" into other activities in certain circumstances. But to say it *can* happen is not to say that it *must* happen in every case. Much of the charm and fascination of games stems precisely from their insular nature, from how completely they can be sealed off from the concerns that usually dominate our time and energy. At stake is whether politics can be similarly sealed off—and thus whether it can enjoy the peculiar freedom and happiness that games often, albeit not always, possess. Games seem to have "gone wrong" when their consequences expand beyond their boundaries, but political action has "boundless" consequences as part of its normal functioning.

The problem is that Arendt somehow wants politics to have no consequences with regard to "life" and yet to have "boundless" consequences with regard to my identity and my relations to others and to the world we share in common. It is very difficult to see how she can erect such an absolute barrier in one direction (between "freedom" and "life") while collapsing barriers in the other direction (between "my" activities and the "others" to whom those activities connect me). She clearly believes that the political should neither address nor influence any material issue; the political should have no material consequences. But because she recognizes that material prosperity is a necessary condition for participation in the political and that gaining the right to participate is a political matter (see *OR*, 127)), it is hard to see how the political could be purged of all material questions.

The second way to question Arendt's exclusion of all "social" questions from the political is to ask, just what do political actors do? Mostly they talk: "[P]olis-life . . . to an incredibly large extent consisted of citizens talking with one another" (*BPF*, 51). What did they talk about? As Hanna Pitkin (1981) and others have pointed out, Arendt rules out as nonpolitical almost everything we usually think of politics being "about." If political actors distinguish themselves in agonistic public debate, then we would imagine debates on issues with momentous consequences. But Arendt so much wants politics for its own sake, an action that is its own good, that she strives to separate political action from consequences. That the future of slavery and the fate of the Union were at stake in the Lincoln-Douglas debates somehow distracts us from simply admiring the virtuosity of the speakers' performances. Questions of right and wrong, of truth and falsity, are irrelevant to political action in its purity. (In the next chapter I will discuss Arendt's insistence that truth is outside politics.) Politics is threatened with becoming as trivial as a basketball game—full of intensity but signifying nothing—a situation that recalls Eugene McCarthy's observation that a good politician, like a good basketball coach, has to be smart enough to play the game well, but dumb enough to think it's important.

Arendt has been particularly faulted for excluding two considerations that currently are central to almost all definitions of the political: justice, and the ongoing negotiation or struggle concerning the line dividing the public and the private. Arendt's definition of power is useful to those arguing against her. Arendtian power calls our attention to what can be accomplished by people acting together. Thus, power is not just the force that makes some social actors do things they would not freely choose to do, but also the force that makes it possible to achieve some ends that cannot be reached individually. Justice is a classic example of such an end. Various theories of the origins and purposes of political bodies (including, but not limited to, social contract theories) focus on the collective establishment and enforcement of standards of justice. Such concepts of justice encompass more than issues of economic justice, but it is hard to see how all considerations of economic fair treatment (e.g., protection against fraud, for starters) could be excluded from considerations of justice. Arendt herself, insofar as she acknowledges that certain basic rights are indispensable and that the collective power of the political is the only creator and sustainer of such rights, locates some functions of justice in the political sphere. But she pays scant attention in her middle works to the ways in which debates about justice are the matter, the "about," of politics. (In some ways, however, her concern with "judgment" in her later work remedies this lack.)

On the negotiation or struggle concerning the dividing line between public and private, Arendt has less to offer. We owe much of our current focus on this element of politics to feminism and its famous slogan "The personal is political." What feminism has highlighted is the extent to which modern societies are organized around the designation of some spheres of activity and intersubjective relations as appropriate objects of concern for collective power, and other spheres and relations as "private" and thus, in theory at least, not subject to political intervention. The dividing line between public and private is not at all stable; in fact, it is crucial to recognize that much political effort, energy, and struggle center precisely on defining that line. Hence (to use two examples), to declare the family "private" is to say that how husbands exercise force (in Arendt's sense of the term) over their wives and how parents discipline their children are matters that brook no outside scrutiny or interference. Similarly, to propose political regulation of the practices of "private" business corporations is to extend the political into a sphere of activities that usually resists such extensions. *Pace* Arendt, the definition of the political is not and cannot be stable. The definition of what is "properly" political cannot be grounded on anything except human agreements and conventions—and such agreements and conventions will be continually contested and will change over time. It is a political matter of the greatest import to decide what activities should be the focus of our applied collective power and what activities should be untouched by that power. (It is no help to say that the political is defined as any activity that is created and sustained through collective power. If that were the case, our basketball game would be political, which is patently absurd. So what makes an exercise of collective power political must be something about the kinds of concerns it addresses, in particular concerns about guaranteeing citizens the opportunity to experience the freedom of acting within the framework of activities generated by collective power.) No solution to the riddle of the division between the public and the private—neither an extreme one nor some middle course—can ever solve it once and for all, in part because different groups within any society will benefit disproportionately depending on where the lines are drawn. Arendt clearly tries to draw the boundaries of the political in such a way that all disproportionate results—and hence all possible conflicts of interest about the definition of the political—are ruled out. But in creating a political realm so disinterested, so severed from all consequences for which groups of citizens might be expected to struggle with other citizens, she seems to have created a politics devoid of all content whatsoever.

But let us not be too hasty. One last appeal to our basketball analogy will help clarify Arendt's understanding of the political in ways that not only make it more plausible but also stand as potentially helpful correctives to the contemporary viewpoints that produce the critique I have just outlined. For starters, we should recognize the benefits of purity. Postmodernism consistently denigrates the quest for purity as a modernist obsession that has the pernicious effect of wholesale exclusion. We can achieve purity only by ruthlessly casting out all the elements that would threaten homogeneity. Arendt's exclusions of the body, the household, and the economic from the political seem an obvious case. But let's flip this critique around and think about what exclusion enables. What would a pickup basketball game look like if we had to take into account considerations of sexual preference, economic well-being, and educational achievement? What Arendt understands is that certain activities are possible only if the participants meet in an equality that does not apply to them vis-à-vis each other in *all* their relations but does apply within this sphere and for the goal of engaging in this activity. If we can keep our activities walled off from one another, we can create conditions that enable various activities to occur and develop.[8] That you play basketball better than I does not influence our respective relations to one another or our performances in a town meeting about a proposed landfill—and vice versa. Postmodernism persistently argues that leakages will always occur between spheres that we try to keep autonomous, just as it persistently argues that our motives are always mixed, that they never achieve the purity associated with "disinterestedness." And Arendt would surely agree that the vigilance against a falsely claimed autonomy suggested by the postmodern critique should always be maintained. She simply wants us to see that the effort to create and maintain autonomous spheres of activity is well worth the trouble, because that is the only way that the very possibility of engaging in some activities can be preserved. If matters of "life" are inevitably our strongest motives, then even a temporary focusing of attention and energy on activities that do not promote life requires a separate sphere. What does a basketball game turn into if the players are concerned with its consequences on their lives as a whole? Think of such a game played by business associates, some of whom are utterly dependent on the boss, who is also playing. As in the *Catch-22* example, this game would be altered significantly. Arendt's reasoning is that wherever matters of "life" intrude, they must dominate. Thus, if we abandon the effort to construct purified spheres, all our activities will be reduced to a single set of motives. There is no reason to believe she is wrong.

However, it would be foolish to claim that we often achieve the kind of purity Arendt advocates. Look at how hard I have had to strain, even in the simple example of a pickup basketball game, to make all things equal and to keep out extraneous motives and desires. Yes, purity is potentially productive of recognizable goods, but the achievement of purity is so difficult and (often) so costly that the game may not be worth the candle. I want only to argue that we could make such a judgment solely in particular cases; there is no general formula that proves all purity pernicious. To be more specific, we can say that there are two key issues: equality of opportunity to participate and equality of participation once involved. If the gym is closed to some members of the community, then the pickup games may be equal in themselves but not equally open to all. Even if all can play, the games might be structured in ways that place newcomers or women or older people at a consistent disadvantage (maybe no one passes the ball to these people, or the procedure for turning the court over after each game results in their playing fewer games). What I extrapolate from Arendt's argument is that eternal vigilance is necessary to avoid the many abuses that stand in the way of achieving equality. But she refuses the fatalistic position that equality can never be achieved—as well as, perhaps more crucially, the perfectionist position that only utter equality will do. This does not mean, I hasten to say, that we should comfortably settle for inequalities or for the mixing of economic motives or powers with activities of a different sort. What it does mean is that spheres of activity are worth defending from the hegemony of the economic and that we can still have some good basketball games in an imperfect world.

One last example might help show how this point applies to democratic politics. The role played by money in current politics—and in the running of our government—is clearly corrupting. It is not just that people with more money have greater access to the government, but also that money is used predominately as a way to further the economic well-being of those who wield it. Arendt's work calls us to protest and strive against this corruption of politics in every way possible, but it does not place us in the binary position of declaring American politics utterly corrupt. Money is a necessary but not a sufficient ingredient for winning elections; there are still other ways to influence politicians, and the candidate who spends the most money does not invariably win. Corruption, like anything else (including democracy itself), rarely comes in absolute form—and it is important to be able to judge degrees. Such judgments are not just a matter of assigning appropriate blame but, much more crucially, a way of understanding what we can positively do. Democracy, like a pure basketball game, is an ideal (an Arendtian "principle"?) that guides our actions and sometimes affords us memorable and satisfying interactions with others, even as it leads us at other times to bemoan the ways in which the ideal is violated. Democracy has not utterly vanished from the earth, but it is a sapling that must be nurtured in a fairly hostile environment. A disgust with its current manifestations because none of them is absolutely perfect does little to further such nurturance. What we need to do instead is to participate in the practices of democracy that seem to us to approach the ideal, while protesting vigorously against practices that violate that ideal.

Arendt's vision of the political, it can be argued, is demonstrably about something. It is about identity—and, by extension from an individual's identity to the identity of all individuals, it is about plurality. Here Arendt seems more postmodern than the postmodernists. Against a reductionist account in which economic motives or some form of the "will to power" reigns supreme, Arendt calls our attention to another set of fundamental motives, those centering on identity and distinction, which exist alongside concerns for "life." The emergence of "identity politics" during the past forty years only confirms her insight that humans as political animals do not live by bread alone and that they look to the political to enact identities that they wish to be recognized as distinct from others. Time and again, such strivings for identity (from nationalistic struggles to ethnic, racial, and/or subcultural movements) have precipitated sacrifices, demands, and political actions that are pointless or even harmful to the participants' economic interests. A striking case in point is the separatist movement in Quebec, which came within a very few votes of winning the most recent referendum on separation from Canada even though all parties in the dispute agreed that the result would have been economic hardship for the Quebecois. To economic self-interest as the primary motive of all action, political or otherwise, Arendt adds action and its orientation toward the public manifestation of identity. The difficulty of her portrayal of the political—our having a hard time figuring out what politics is "about" in her work—may reflect not so much any deficiencies in her thought as the real-world difficulty of establishing a public space in which the performance of identity can take place without being swamped by issues of economic well-being. It is not that her politics is not "about" anything, but that it is hard to create the conditions under which politics can be successfully about identity. Certainly most of the manifestations of "identity politics" in our own time register frustrated protests against political institutions that seem incapable of addressing the concerns that motivate the protesters. It's as if we haven't imagined the body politic in ways suitable to a new set of needs that have arisen—needs that have taken all the policy experts of the welfare state by surprise. Arendt may be of great use to us today precisely because she devoted so much attention to the deficiencies of the prevalent conception of the public—and struggled so mightily to forge an alternative model of the public realm.

It is crucial to note that Arendt's notion of identity is at odds with many of the kinds of group identifications that constitute much of contemporary "identity politics." (I take up this issue in chapter 4.)

The limitations of wondering what politics could be "about" may be what is misleading us here. Just as political agents do not aim directly at producing the public space of appearances (I play basketball for the pleasure of it, not to insure that basketball exists or that it does not disappear from the planet), so identity might be seen more accurately as a by-product of action. The political debates in which I engage need not be "about" identity. In fact, if they are not about identity, I am much more likely to uncover aspects of my identity that I never suspected. I will never disclose new capabilities if I engage only in activities that are designed to reaffirm the identity I already claim as mine. Because Arendt's notion of action is oriented to the novel, to the miraculous production of something new under the sun, she is interested in identity not as something that "fixes" the self but as the excessive, unpredictable surpassing of what I thought I was before I engaged with others in a particular interaction.

Participatory Democracy

All this theorizing about the political and the identity-disclosing activity it enables is fascinating enough, but the reader almost certainly finds it terribly abstract compared to Arendt's concrete analysis of the form taken by the political's opposite, totalitarianism. In *On Revolution*, Arendt goes a long way toward trying to imagine an institutional, even a constitutional, framework for the kind of politics she advocates. She takes her inspiration from the American founding fathers—John Adams, Thomas Jefferson, and James Monroe in particular—and from the soviets of the Russian Revolution, the workers' councils of the 1956 uprising in Hungary, and the work of Rosa Luxemburg (a strange set of influences to cite in a book published shortly after the Cuban missile crisis). A precise name for Arendt's political vision is tricky. As we have seen, her ideas dovetail with some ways of understanding liberalism, yet some commentators have tried to enlist her within the "republican virtue" tradition (a tradition that she explicitly invokes at times [see Hill, 330] and that her reliance on Machiavellian *virtu* calls to mind). My own preference is "participatory democracy." I want to emphasize Arendt's important contribution to the effort to critique and rethink radically the political institutions of the contemporary West.

Arendt has any number of objections to the way that democracy is currently understood and practiced, but one theme dominates her critique: the exclusion of most citizens from "participating, and having a share, in public power" (*OR*, 255). Modern liberal democracies evidence little awareness of the kind of power that Arendt associates with "acting in concert" but instead "identif[y] power with the monopoly of the means of violence" (256). The state acts as judge and enforcer, adjudicating disputes among citizens who are seen as having conflicting interests with one another, and monopolizing the means of violence so that no group of citizens can gain dominance over other groups. The state, in other words, acts mostly to insure the security of all citizens by depriving them all of the force to impose their separate wills. Of course, if we devise a state like this because we believe that the threat of domination is primary, we will also need to secure ourselves against the threat of domination by the state itself, especially because we have lodged the means of violence in that state. The most familiar guarantee in a liberal democracy is the list of rights in the constitution—in the United States, the Bill of Rights. The liberal assumption of a society comprising competing or conflicting interests breeds a state whose primary function is to prevent these conflicts from completely disturbing the peace and to develop a set of "negative liberties"—rights that define all the ways the state cannot use its force to dominate its citizens.

The result, as Arendt freely admits, has been the fairly successful defense of citizens against outside interference in their lives. Arendt hardly scorns the usefulness of rights and their effectiveness in ordinary times. Her own terrifying experience of losing all rights insures her respect for them. But she has three objections to what we might call this "minimalist" version of the political, a version that focuses on the state as the guarantor of security with its field of operations sharply delimited by rights.[9] Her first point, as we would expect, is that a minimalist politics ignores the very activities that she looks to the political to enable. To define freedom negatively as freedom from the interference of the state or of others makes sense only within a totally individualistic worldview—a view that denies that individuality itself is intersubjectively produced and that freedom, identity, and reality can be established only in public. From Arendt's point of view, a minimalist politics is a pathological denial of dependence on others, a pathology indicated by its being able to acknowledge others only as threats to the individual. Others exist in the minimalist vision only as what I need to be protected from.

Second, Arendt points to a contradiction within the minimalist vision when she insists that rights are politically created and sustained. Rights are obviously not "natural," not some kind of "universal" birthright, because they exist only under very specific political conditions—namely, where there is a constitution that delineates them and where there is the collective power to enforce them. Rights, in other words, are a perfect example of power in Arendt's sense. Rights exist only where the polity "acting in concert" sustains them by continually respecting them. And rights disappear in the very moment that the collective, as a collective, stops respecting them. As we have learned in trying to improve civil rights in the United States, in trying to end the violations of rights predicated on racism and sexism, there are very severe limits to what the state or isolated individuals or groups can achieve. I say this not to deny the crucial importance of governmental antidiscrimination laws and their enforcement, or the advocacy work of various "social movements," but only to emphasize that rights, like Arendt's version of the political itself, are a product of power in her sense, and hence are easily destroyed by force or strength but not readily created by force or strength. The very fragility of rights, like that of the political, marks their preciousness. Rights depend on that contingent "good will" (*HC*, 244) which is but a thin cloak against the nakedness of exposure to brute force. But we do ourselves no good, in Arendt's view, if we think that an appeal to "nature" or to the "universal," or the construction of a strong yet delimited state can solve this vulnerability for us outside our radical dependence on others. To look to nonhuman grounds or institutional mechanisms for security is to try to replace power, understood as "acting in concert," with force—a move that fails to see that force is unable to produce some of the things that only power can create.

This discussion leads to Arendt's third objection to a minimalist politics. Because it utterly fails to register power as "acting in concert," minimalist politics thinks of power as something to be "seized" and held against others, not as something to be multiplied through the actions of various groups working together toward "the constitution of a public sphere where freedom could appear" (*OR*, 255). Arendt insists that the people, in revolution after revolution, have reinvented a "council" model of politics that aims at a "direct regeneration of democracy" through the proliferation of local sites that allow for "the direct participation of every citizen in the public affairs of the country" (263). Councils are spontaneous local organizations that direct activities of the local participants in the revolution, usually depending on open meetings where plans are discussed and debated. An example is the kinds of meetings that were held to plan demonstrations on various college campuses during the 1960s. Although representatives from various national organizations might be present at such meetings, final decision-making power rested with the local participants, who reached their decisions through extensive discussion followed by a vote. Realists of every stripe, including professional revolutionaries, have always scoffed at councils as "some sort of fantastic utopia," failing to recognize that historically "the councils . . . were always organs of order as much as organs of action" (263). Councils simply represent a very different kind of order, one that sees what power can produce and what collective action can achieve, instead of viewing the proliferation of power, the empowerment of the many, as a formula for chaos. Councils, in short, affirm a positive view of liberty, one that looks toward the political realm as the stage of freedom, against the negative view of freedom found in the minimalist vision, where freedom is enjoyed in private, apart from others.

Councils confront not only modernity's predilection for negative liberty and centralized power but also the bias toward representational government in the modern polity. "What the councils challenged was the party system as such, in all its forms" (*OR*, 265), be it the one-party states of the postrevolutionary Marxist world, the two-party system in America, or the multiparty configurations in parliamentary democracies. Parties are built upon representation, not participation, and here Arendt's critique folds back to join her argument in *The Human Condition* that "social" rather than "political" concerns dominate modern politics. The only thing parties can represent, Arendt argues, is "interests," because interests (by which she means mostly economic considerations) come in aggregates. Interests are shared by particular groups; thus, a party can adequately present the case for those interests and can exert the pressure needed to achieve them. Arendt opposes "interests" to "opinions," with opinions understood as the distinctive, individual positions reached by political agents "in a process of open discussion and public debate" (268). One of the ways that democratic processes allow for the disclosure of individual identity is in the revelation of my opinions to myself and to others as I partake in the public encounter with others that is political debate. In a representative democracy, of course, only a very few are ever parties to such debates. The resulting dearth of "opinion" (most people never get to form opinions, because they can be formed only in intersubjective forums) contributes to the domination of modern politics by "social" issues (matters of interest) rather than "political" ones.

Arendt concedes that the "two-party system has proved its viability and . . . its capacity to guarantee constitutional liberties, . . . [yet] the best it has achieved is a certain control of the rulers by those who are ruled[;] . . . it has by no means enabled the citizen to become a 'participator' in public affairs" (*OR*, 268). She is scathing in her portrait of the modern voter and the increasingly restricted circle of his concerns: "[T]he voter acts out of concern with his private life and well-being, and the residue of power he still holds in his hands resembles rather the reckless coercion with which a blackmailer forces his victim into obedience than the power that arises out of joint action and joint deliberation" (269).

Fundamentally, Arendt's critique of liberal democracies is exactly in line with her critique of Marx. Both twentieth-century liberalism (the welfare state, as contrasted to the minimalist nation-state) and Marxism associate politics with a centralized administrative power whose major concern (aside from the security issues—domestic and foreign—that occupied the nation-state) is the general welfare of the people. In criticizing this kind of paternalistic concentration of power (no matter how benign), Arendt appears close to radical critiques of modern bureaucracies (such as that of the French philosopher-historian Michel Foucault) and to the conservative (neoliberal) critique of "big government." In fact, she is rather distant from both Foucault and the foes of big government. Today's conservatives want government out of their hair for classical liberal reasons: they locate all their hopes and aspirations in economic activity and simply think such activity proceeds better without government regulation. They are proponents of the creed of laissez-faire. Arendt is indifferent at best, contemptuous at worst, to a focus on the economic. She deplores big government because it displaces numerous local sites of deliberation, discussion, and political action. What irks her is the failure of liberalism and Marxism to recognize that what politics offers—freedom and action—is essentially noneconomic. Classical liberalism can understand politics only as a distraction, a painful necessity and burden that keeps us from the main business, which is business; hence liberalism's focus on negative liberties, on our rights to disentangle ourselves from the political. Marxism reveals a similar desire to escape politics when it imagines a conflict-free society in which all agonistic debate would cease. In short, Arendt's hostility to big government does not partake of the more general hostility to politics as such that characterizes the dominant modern political philosophies.[10] The whole system of centralized and representational government is founded on this modern failure to perceive the potential "public happiness" of political involvement: "The defenders of this system, which actually is the system of the welfare state, if they are liberal and of democratic convictions must deny the very existence of public happiness and public freedom; they must insist that politics is a burden and that its end is itself not political" (*OR*, 269).

Arendt's difference from Foucault points to a more troubling consequence of her position. In his influential *Discipline and Punish* (1979), Foucault traces what he sees as the historical rise of intervention in people's daily lives by various functionaries of power. One way to read Foucault is to see him as focusing on the threat to freedom posed by the growing power of "experts" whose dominion is institutionalized through the large organizations—schools, hospitals, corporations, the military, various governmental bureaucracies—that increasingly process, even produce, individuals who must wend their way through the appointed procedures. Foucault is interested in processes of routinization and examination, in the ways that individuals must submit to being codified and categorized according to standardized processes administered by credentialed "professionals." Various other writers (Christopher Lasch, in *The Culture of Narcissism* [1979], is one example) have explicitly understood the rule of experts as a threat to democracy, as a way in which power is siphoned away from the many toward the few. It is worth noting that this critique of experts and of the large institutions that house them can take rightist or leftist forms. The conservative version usually champions self-reliance, some version of rugged individualism accompanied by the "devolution" of the offending institutions. The leftist version is more likely to propose increased citizen input and control along with various strategies for decentralization, for the movement of decision making back to a local level with increased participation in debates and votes about policy formation by those who would actually be subject to those policies.

Although Arendt's work offers more support for the leftist than for the rightist take on this issue, her desire to distinguish very sharply between matters of "administration" and political matters makes her theory incapable of addressing the dangers experts pose. Arendt believes that "administration" is outside politics, because it entails answering the simple question of what is the most efficient and most effective way to do something. Where there is a correct answer, a truth of the matter, there is no point to political deliberation and debate. It is pointless and inappropriate, for example, to have a public debate about whether a doctor should prescribe an antibiotic for a patient with pneumonia. Arendt seems to endorse the rule of experts within their fields of expertise, reserving for public debate only those matters in which every person's "opinion" can be of equal weight.

As we have seen, the distinction between "administration" and "politics" seems impossible to maintain. It is not just that there are certain circumstances under which administrative issues can become political ones—when there are not enough antibiotics to go around, or when the use of antibiotics is not clear-cut because they contribute to the development of new, more resistant strains of the disease. Arendt's distinction not only could survive such cases, but actually could prove useful to deciding whether a particular case were of one type or the other. What her distinction cannot survive is any acknowledgment that "strength" accrues to the experts who "administer" things and that their ways of using that strength in their administrative functions alter the political freedoms, capacities, and access of nonexperts. Writers such as Foucault and Lasch convincingly demonstrate that there cannot be a neutral realm of administration. Rather, administration, like the representative party system, involves a displacement of action from the many to the few and, thus, has profound political consequences.

Arendt fleshes out her vision of participatory democracy with an extended discussion of three necessary components that she derives from the American founding fathers: a constitution, the multiplication of powers, and federalism. I will close this section with a discussion of each in turn.

A constitution, as Arendt understands it, is the formal equivalent of promising. It provides the only nonviolent alternative to the unilateral usurpation of power by one group in the founding of a polity. In the modern age, the authority that commands allegiance and fealty to a political entity cannot be derived from God, and even tradition is a very shaky reed. The founders of the American republic had to create something out of nothing, yet they also had to acquire somehow the right to create that something for others, the right to say, "We, the people of the United States . . ." Arendt sees the founding fathers as, in some sense, having taken the gamble of throwing themselves on the mercy of the people. They understood power precisely as Arendt does, not as something that could be seized but as something arising out of collective action. The written Constitution was their action, but it could become a source of power only when it was collectively ratified as a document uttered by the body politic as a whole. The success of this founding act was utterly dependent on the people's adoption of the document as their own; only when they agreed to live by it and came to live by it in their ongoing lives would the polity as a polity and the people as a people be created. Thus, the Constitution is an action in all the ways Arendt describes. It is the distinctive action of the individuals we know as the founding fathers, whose greatness we remember; but it is also an action that produces something only by virtue of its collective character. And what it produces—a polity and a people—is a network of relations among people that entails promises, obligations, capacities, and interactions that did not exist before and all of which could hardly be foreseen at the moment of founding. A constitution is a "mutual contract by which people bind themselves together in order to form a community . . . based on reciprocity and presuppos[ing] equality." It is this establishment of relations of interaction that is the key. The constitution's "actual content is a promise and its result is indeed a 'society' or 'cosociation' in the old Roman sense of *societas*, which means alliance. Such an alliance gathers together the isolated strength of the allied partners and binds them into a new power structure by virtue of 'free and sincere promises'" (*OR*, 170).

Because a constitution is utterly human-made, Arendt views it completely pragmatically. The law of a land, as embodied in a constitution, is not untouchable, not sacred. It simply outlines the "rules of the game" by which interaction is possible and proceeds. There is no reason, beyond the fact that it works, that it keeps us allied to one another, to remain faithful to a constitution, and there is no power beyond the continued allegiance of the citizens that can keep a constitution an honored and enforceable document. A constitution's guarantee of minority rights is not worth the paper it is printed on, if the ongoing power of the people, as manifested in their actions at this moment, does not protect and preserve those rights. Jürgen Habermas (1983) is one critic whom Arendt makes uneasy with her insistence that nothing external to the social contract itself, the agreement of a people to be a people within these rules of the game, secures the ongoing effectiveness of that people's constitution. But it is unclear (to say the least) just where such an external power would come from. The history of civil rights in this country suggests that Arendt is right. Constitutional guarantees of equal protection under the law have no force until public action, a public appeal to the neglected terms of the founding agreement, is undertaken. There is no substitute for public action—and no guarantee that such action will be successful. There is a continuum here, from a constitution fully honored and enacted by all; through the more usual situation of a community in which various parts of the agreement are honored, other parts (what they mean and how they should be enacted) are disputed, and still other parts are deliberately flouted by some, to the outrage and protest of others; to the extreme of having the agreement collapse altogether in situations of revolution and civil war. Where any given society with a constitution is located on this continuum depends entirely on the civic interactions among its citizens as they function within the framework established by the constitution, and on the institutions and relations the constitution fosters.

The citizen, then, is one who exists in relation to others—in relations that are political insofar as they are public—and, by virtue of those relations, gains certain capacities. She also gains certain protections, in that only as a member of a polity can she hope that its collective power will be brought to bear upon any who violate the rights stipulated as hers in the constitutional agreement. Arendt values citizenship, just as she values political community, for what it makes possible. She sums up her entirely "positive" or "productive" understanding of the law in the "Appendices" to the book *On Violence*. Note that Arendt believes that law is utterly necessary (some underlying set of agreements, of limits and constraints, is necessary to human intercourse) *and* utterly contingent (the precise form that such agreements take is completely open). She is as impatient with the idea that one could live outside the law altogether as she is with the idea that the law has a sacred validity and could take only one form:

> I think [the] comparison of the law with the "valid rules of the
> game" can be driven further. For the point of those rules is not that I
> submit to them voluntarily or recognize theoretically their validity,
> but that in practice I cannot enter the game unless I conform; my
> motive for acceptance is my wish to play, and since men exist in the
> plural, my wish to play is identical to my wish to live. Every man is
> born into a community with pre-existing laws which he "obeys" first
> of all because there is no other way for him to enter the great game
> of the world. I may wish to change the rules of the game, as the rev-
> olutionary does, or to make an exception of myself, as the criminal
> does; but to deny them on principle means no mere "disobedience,"
> but the refusal to enter the human community. The common
> dilemma—either the law is absolutely valid and therefore needs for
> its legitimacy an immortal, divine legislator, or the law is simply a
> command with nothing behind it but the state's monopoly of vio-
> lence—is a delusion. All laws are "directives" rather than "impera-
> tives." They direct human intercourse as rules direct the game. And
> the ultimate guarantee of their validity is contained in the old Roman
> maxim *Pacta sunt servanda*. (157)

Some readers will think that this understanding of the law gives
far too much leverage over the individual, who must play the game by
the rules to have any identity at all. (What choice does the would-be
basketball player have except to play by the rules or not to be a basketball player at all? Only after playing for quite a while would the
player have the standing required to suggest a revision of the rules,
and such a revision would go into effect only after some kind of collective discussion of its desirability and some kind of collective decision-making procedure.) Arendt is aware of the individual's vulnerability in the face of the others on whom he is so radically dependent,
and she thinks that the American founding fathers, inspired by the
French political philosopher Montesquieu, understood that the best
protection against the abuse of collective power lies not in hemming in
that power with various restrictions, but in multiplying the sites of
such power:

> Montesquieu's discovery actually concerned the nature of power,
> and this discovery stands in so flagrant contradiction to all conven-
> tional notions on this matter that it has almost been forgotten, de-
> spite the fact that the foundation of the republic in America was
> largely inspired by it. The discovery . . . spells out the forgotten prin-
> ciple underlying the whole structure of separated powers: that only
> "power arrests power," that is, we must add, without destroying it,
> without putting impotence in the place of power. (*OR*, 151)

Instead of disabling the potential power of this or that association of freedom, we should multiply associations, create as many public spaces as possible where people might act together and might appear to one another. Power gains the upper hand over individuals when it is the only game in town, when it is a question of associating with these people under these rules of the game or not associating with anyone at all. But there is no reason, Arendt believes, that there should not be various games going on, various places and ways in which one can participate in public associations that afford one the experience of collectively producing an ongoing activity. Against the centralizing tendencies of the nation-state—its propensity to draw all power to itself—must be poised the relative independence of more local sites. Not only do such sites offer smaller—and therefore more practical— venues for direct participation by citizens, but they also place a number of mediating associations, each with its own collective production of power, between the individual and the nation-state. Thus, in Arendt's view, a complete checks-and-balances arrangement not only separates functions at the nation-state level but also includes public spaces apart from and only semianswerable to the nation-state. The terrible loneliness of the modern individual, which is exploited by totalitarian movements, does not exist in a polity where multiple public spaces thrive.

The institutional form such decentralization takes within a large community is federalism. If the councils formed in revolutions are Arendt's model of political freedom in action, it is to Jefferson's "wards" that she turns for an institutionalized model of that freedom. Wards, for Jefferson, were "the only possible non-violent alternative to his earlier notions about the desirability of recurring revolutions," because only the wards could provide a place where " 'the voice of the people would be fairly, fully, and peaceably expressed, discussed, and decided' " (*OR*, 250) in such a way as to secure participation and "public happiness" for each citizen while counteracting the endemic "corruption" of representative governments. That corruption stems not so much from the representatives turning against the people as from the people looking to the government to fulfill their private desires. The ward system fights corruption, then, by maintaining the public desires of the people, desires which they experienced and acted upon during the revolution but which they are likely to abandon in more normal times: "What [Jefferson] perceived to be the mortal danger to the republic was that the Constitution had given all power to citizens, without giving them the opportunity of *being* republicans and of *acting* as citizens" (253).

What Jefferson had in mind was the institutionalization of something like the local meetings that accompanied ratification of the Constitution—meetings in which public debate precedes casting one's vote. The closest things we have to such meetings in present-day America are New England town meetings (on which Arendt commented favorably; see Hill, 317) and the Iowa caucuses in the presidential primaries. Unlike, say, an open town council meeting, the ward gives all who attend (not just the town council members) the right to vote, and a strict majority decides. There seems to be no reason—in either principle or practice—not to extend this idea of local public sites to include associations we normally do not think of as political—from Rotary clubs to food co-ops to sports clubs. The key element here is a public grouping in which members deliberate and then decide on a collective course of action. Such an extension brings Arendt's views even closer to Tocqueville's, which they already resemble. Tocqueville was explicitly alarmed by the tremendous power concentrated in the modern nation-state and believed that only allegiance to and participation in local associations protected citizens from a naked vulnerability to that state. Certainly, both Tocqueville and Arendt allow us to see that the destruction of local associations and their replacement by relations to the ruling party and/or the state are primary tactics of totalitarianism; hence Arendt's insistence that multiplying sites of power is actually the best safeguard against the abuse of power—or, more correctly, against the destruction of power by force.

Arendt admits that Jefferson is vague about the distribution of jurisdiction between the wards and the federal government. The point does not greatly trouble her, though, partly (as we have already seen) because she is not very interested in what governments can accomplish, but also partly because she does not consider the encouragement that federalism can offer to balkanization (the breakdown of polities into warring factions). Her failure here is epitomized by an essay on Little Rock (RLR), in which she sides with Arkansas segregationists (who included the state's governor at the time [1957]) against President Eisenhower's decision to send federal troops to enforce an integration order handed down by the federal courts. Arendt's argument is complicated, and I am not doing full justice to it here. I only want to highlight that she does not recognize this incident as typical and does not recognize that the principle of local jurisdiction often encourages splinter groups (whether ethnic, racial, religious, or ideological) to think that they can claim a territory to themselves, "purify" it of any who disagree with them, and live entirely according to their own precepts. Plurality—the fact that we live amid many different others—does not justify this unreal solution of isolation, of living only among one's own "kind." Such a denial of dependence on radically different others is destructive of the polity and of the world as Arendt understands them. Thus, she should be more aware that federalist decentralization can threaten the acknowledgment of plurality and that the question of what overriding principles all local wards will honor will be a continual source of friction, conflict, and negotiation in any federal system. All of this is to say that despite the Little Rock essay and despite Arendt's championing of federalism, just about everything in her writing suggests that she would be highly suspicious of the belief that we could solve the ongoing problems in the former Yugoslavia or in the Middle East by granting autonomy and a separate polity and/or territory to each "nationality" that declares a wish to separate itself from every other nationality.

Arendt also admits that Jefferson is vague about the purposes of the wards, about what they might be expected to accomplish. And here she addresses, as directly as anywhere in her work, her critics' charge that her own view of politics is too vague and lacks content. Such vagueness, she tells us, is a merit, at least to the extent that it makes us focus on what keeps sliding out of the picture: participation, action, and freedom. It is in our identity as citizens, and only as citizens, that we get to be free—and that should be more than enough to make the political precious to us. Yet somehow we continually slide away from a focus on freedom to ponder the "what" of politics— what it can do for us, or what we are to do when we engage in it:

> This vagueness of purpose, far from being due to a lack of clarity, indicates perhaps more tellingly than any other single aspect of Jefferson's proposal that . . . [he envisioned] a new form of government rather than a mere reform of it or a mere supplement to the existing institutions. If the ultimate end of revolution was freedom and the constitution of a public space where freedom could appear, . . . then the elementary republics of the wards, the only tangible place where everyone could be free, actually were the end of the great republic

whose chief purpose in domestic affairs should have been to provide the people with such places of freedom and to protect them. The basic assumption of the ward system, whether Jefferson knew it or not, was that no one could be called happy without his share in public happiness, that no one could be called free without his experience in public freedom, and that no one could be called either happy or free without participating, and having a share, in public power. (*OR*, 255)

Conclusion: Recovering Citizenship

Almost all the themes in Arendt's political theory that this chapter discusses can be gathered under the umbrella of the distinction between *le citoyen* (the citizen) and *le bourgeois* (middle-class man), established in her interchange with C. B. Macpherson (in Hill, 327–31). She accepts Macpherson's description of *le bourgeois* "as a calculating individual seeking to maximize his own interest." And she also accepts that the liberalism of Hobbes, Locke, and J. S. Mill follows from the "additional assumption . . . that every man's interest naturally conflicts with everybody else's" (330). Her argument, as I have presented it, is that *le bourgeois*, understood as exclusively pursuing his own interests, has become the dominant personality type of modernity. But there is another, "older tradition," the "tradition of Montesquieu," which "really go[es] back to Machiavelli and Montaigne" and, from there, "to Greek and Roman antiquity" (330). This is the tradition of *le citoyen*, with its focus on noneconomic motives and achievements, and its insistence on what can be accomplished *only* in public, only when and where we are citizens.

Arendt's fundamental position is that only as citizens do we get to have distinctive identities and that, having lost our knowledge of this vital connection between politics and identity, we now inhabit a mass society that obliterates individuality. The characteristic political forms of modernity—the nation-state, the welfare state, and totalitarian regimes—all fail to provide any public space for the achievement of identity. These forms all testify to the modern severance of the political from issues of identity, the modern loss of a basic understanding of the freedom and action that citizenship makes possible. Only participatory democracy—a dimly remembered possibility that makes brief appearances now and then in our era—rekindles a sense of what politics and those who participate in it can do.

Arendt's political vision is motivated by the attempt to rearticulate this "older tradition" of the potential of politics. Her vision has its negative and its positive side. Negatively, Arendt works to clear a space for action and freedom, as she understands them, by purging the "social"—matters of life and necessity—from the public realm of appearances. Positively, she sets out to delineate the various elements—action, freedom, equality, acting in concert, and participation in local associations—that make up a political realm in which full citizenship can be enjoyed.

That this vision of full citizenship is utopian follows from the fact that Arendt finds it only fleetingly present in all of modern history. The articulation of her vision serves as the standard by which she judges the deficiencies of modernity. And, because she insists on the reality-producing character of political action, her standard leads her to accuse modernity of a certain irreality, a peculiar insubstantiality. It is to these issues of ontology and judgment—to questions of how we are to understand our world and to conduct our lives within it—that the next chapter turns.

3
Understanding and Judging the Reality of Evil

It is always tempting to create a narrative of development when surveying a writer's lifework. Sometimes the writer herself identifies a turning point, a moment of transformation or conversion. Arendt's attendance at the trial of Nazi war criminal Adolf Eichmann in Jerusalem in 1961 seemed such a turning point to Arendt. Confronted with Eichmann, Arendt "spoke of 'the banality of evil.' Behind that phrase, I held no thesis or doctrine, although I was dimly aware of the fact that it went counter to our tradition of thought—literary, theological, or philosophic—about the phenomenon of evil" (*T*, 3). Both the attempt to understand Eichmann and the vituperative response to Arendt's book on the trial made Arendt return to the questions of "radical evil" and "understanding" that had played little part in her "middle" works. The Western philosophical tradition either psychologizes evil or denies its reality. The psychologists explain evil by attributing its cause to envy, resentment, weakness, or "the powerful hatred wickedness feels for sheer goodness" (4). The deniers of evil either subscribe to some holistic vision in which good always comes from (apparent) evil in the long run, or get lost in the swamp of trying to account for the fact that the will (the faculty that prompts action) can fail to do what reason knows is good (I know I shouldn't smoke, but I do anyway). Confronted by the Holocaust—by "the real evil [that] causes speechless horror, when all we can say is: This should never have happened" (SQ, 763)—the modern observer gets no help from tradition. There has been a consistent "evasion, . . . sidestepping, or . . . explaining away of human wickedness. If the tradition of moral philosophy . . . is agreed on one point from Socrates to Kant and . . . to the present, then that is that it is impossible for men to do wicked things deliberately, to want evil for evil's sake" (761). Arendt finds herself compelled, partly by the experience of the Eichmann trial and partly by the fierce reaction to her "report" (the word she always insisted on using) on the trial, to confront the problem of evil.

But, as we have already seen, Arendt had to tackle the problem of evil in *The Origins of Totalitarianism*, whereas the political vision of what I have called her "middle" works can be seen as describing the "good" that we are called to prefer to evil. So I think we would be unwise to split Arendt's career into two strongly contrasting halves. The continuities in her thought are much stronger than the differences. I will find much occasion in this chapter to quote from works written before Arendt went to Jerusalem. If, from 1963 on, she attacks the problem of evil in rather different ways, she is still often developing notions first articulated, if not fully pursued, in earlier works. In addition, I will argue that the crucial mental faculties of thinking and judging, as described in *The Life of the Mind*, closely resemble action, so that the Arendtian ideal remains recognizably the same even when the scene of activity shifts. And the third major mental faculty described in *The Life of the Mind*, willing, is nothing less than the mental faculty that guarantees free and spontaneous action, hence installing the key concept of Arendt's political theory directly into the more philosophical, less overtly political work of her later years.

Although Arendt, at the very beginning of the first volume of *The Life of the Mind*, identifies the problem of evil as a major motivation in undertaking this work, her speculations actually wander fairly far from that focus. None of *The Life of the Mind* was published during Arendt's lifetime. The first two volumes, *Thinking* and *Willing*, existed in complete versions at the time of her death in 1975, but there is no way to know how extensively she would have revised either volume before allowing it to be published. The projected third volume, "Judging," was not even started. Mary McCarthy, who edited and saw to publication the two existing volumes, tells us that "[a]fter [Arendt's] death, a sheet of paper was found in her typewriter, blank except for the heading 'Judging' and two epigraphs. Some time between the

Saturday of finishing 'Willing' and the Thursday of her death, she must have sat down to confront the final section" (*LOM*, "Editor's Postface," 242). In 1982, under the editorship of Ronald Beiner, Arendt's lecture notes for a 1970 course on Kant at the New School for Social Research in New York City were published under the title *Lectures on Kant's Political Philosophy*. These lectures, along with various discussions in essays that Arendt did publish, provide a pretty good indication of how Arendt viewed "judging," even if they do not flesh out her thoughts as fully as a completed volume would have done.

Several preliminary remarks about *The Life of the Mind* are in order. The completed volumes have, oddly enough, elicited much less comment from subsequent writers than has the work on judgment, a fact not solely attributable to the pleasures of speculating on what a writer might have said had she lived to write some more. *Thinking*, as we shall see, presents three different portraits of that activity, and the three are made compatible with one another only with great difficulty. The book is a treasure trove of insights, but (in my opinion, at least) it does not, in the final analysis, hang together very well. The result, I think, is that commentators on Arendt have really not quite known what to do with it. *Willing* has received even less attention, mostly (it seems to me) because it offers a philosophical justification for Arendt's claims about the freedom and novelty of action, but it adds nothing substantially new to her thought. I have taken the liberty of almost entirely ignoring *Willing* here. Judging, Arendt tells us, is "the most political of man's mental abilities" (*T*, 192), which provides another reason for its having attracted the most attention from commentators on her work. Arendt has become a "classic" of political theory, but she has not been much studied or regarded by philosophers, so it is no surprise that the most overtly political parts of her last work have attracted the most attention. *The Life of the Mind*, to a large extent, is Arendt's attempt to turn from political philosophy to what she would have thought of as philosophy proper—a discipline to which the question What is thinking? (a question put exactly that way by Heidegger) is central. If Heidegger (to a certain extent) introduced Arendt to the questions that she thinks philosophy should address (see *T*, 6–10), it is to Kant that she turns for a thread through the labyrinth. *The Life of the Mind* follows the Kantian division of pure reason (thinking), practical reason (willing), and judgment (the subjects, in turn, of Kant's three critiques), including the Kantian insistence on the autonomy of each of these mental faculties. But problems with this apparent acceptance of the Kantian triad surface just about immediately, because Arendt wants thinking (and here she invokes the problematic Kantian distinction between *Vernunft* [reason] and *Verstand* [intellect; see *T*, 13–16]) to be a matter of understanding and meaning, not of truth or knowledge. In addition, willing in Arendt, unlike Kant's "practical reason," is not moral but almost beyond good and evil, insofar as action, in its freedom, can be either good or evil and insofar as the will that moves us to act is pretty much indifferent to moral considerations. Instead, Arendt moves such moral considerations to judging, which in Kant is concerned only with aesthetic questions (Is this thing beautiful or not?), not with moral questions (Is this action right or wrong?). Thus, Arendt's apparent adherence to a Kantian framework can obscure how radically she realigns the Kantian account of these matters.

Finally, *The Life of the Mind* has proved difficult to assimilate because it is unclear just what its relation to Arendt's political thought is. Should we treat these final works as an attempt to provide a philosophical underpinning to her political theories? There are some indications that she had ambitions to do just that, but certainly any such task was far from completed at the time of her death. Alternatively, is this move to philosophy a retreat, an attempt to locate sureties in thought after stressing so adamantly the contingencies of action? I am somewhat sympathetic to the view that the last, philosophical works blunt that strong Arendtian insistence on what is at stake in and what can be accomplished only through politics by suggesting that similar results can be achieved through thinking, which is not fully intersubjective and public in the way Arendtian politics is.[1] Yet my own way of approaching the later works follows a somewhat different tack in this chapter. I want to work from the problem of evil, reading *Eichmann in Jerusalem, The Life of the Mind*, and other relevant works (both early and late) for Arendt's efforts to come to terms with the reality of evil, a reality that she feels the tradition denies. This focus on evil leads me to see the continuity between Arendt's political theory (which, in my view, is developed as an envisioned alternative to the evils of totalitarianism) and her philosophical meditation (which might be seen as exploring how the philosophical tradition must be revised to take adequate account of the fact of evil). Arendt's extended philosophical meditation on evil has four major foci: an insistence on evil's reality, an effort to understand evil, the link between evil and thoughtlessness, and the exploration of how we can judge right from wrong. The first three sections of this chapter address each of these foci in turn (with the second and third foci included in the chapter section "Thinking"). In the final section, I discuss how certain Arendtian comments on "storytelling" suggest a methodology (although that is too strong a term) appropriate to the work she asks thinking and judging to perform in the confrontation with evil.

The Reality of Evil

In insisting on the reality of evil against a whole philosophic tradition that denies that reality, Arendt develops the ontology of appearance that she suggested in her earlier works into a full-blown "reversal of the metaphysical hierarchy" (*T*, 26). I deliberately use the word "ontology," which my dictionary defines as "a particular theory about being or reality." Against almost the whole philosophic tradition, Arendt insists that *"Being and Appearance coincide."* She has no sophisticated or complicated metaphysical or epistemological argument for this insistence. Her appeal, as always, is to common sense, to the world given to us by our senses and confirmed by our interactions with things and (crucially) with others whose actions indicate that they recognize the existence of the same world of perceived, common objects: "The world men are born into contains many things, natural and artificial, living and dead, transient and sempiternal, all of which have in common that they *appear* and hence are meant to be seen, heard, touched, tasted, and smelled, to be perceived by sentient creatures endowed with the appropriate sense organs" (19). No matter how much we might protest against the way this given world of appearance is organized, its primacy cannot be gainsaid: "The primacy of appearances is a fact of everyday life which neither the scientist nor the philosopher can ever escape, to which they must always return from their laboratories and studies, and which shows its strength by never being in the least changed or deflected by whatever they may have discovered when they withdrew from it" (24). It is a protest against this reality that has led philosophers to claim that appearances are only fleeting and that the true reality lies behind them, or to extol withdrawal from appearances into the quiet of meditation or stoic indifference. But the success of all such attempts must be limited, in Arendt's view. Evil, especially, will not disappear just because I claim it is only "apparent" and not truly real; such maneuvers cannot make me immune to the real harm evil can inflict on me or on the world.

What philosophers really object to in appearances is their contingency, which means that things appear at some times but not at others, that the things that appear do not appear necessarily, and that things appear differently to different people (i.e., they can be viewed from different perspectives). Things (hence Being) might have been otherwise. In the whole tradition before Bergson, only the medieval philosopher Duns Scotus, Arendt tells us, was a "defender of the primacy . . . of the factor of contingency in everything that is." Contingency is "the ultimate of meaninglessness" for "classical philosophy" (W, 31), but for Arendt contingency is the necessary correlate of freedom. Only if circumstances and results could have been otherwise, only if action makes a difference in the realm of how things are (the realm of worldly appearance, for her), does it make sense to claim that humans are free. Thus, Arendt reasons, the possibility and reality of evil are the price paid for human freedom (see 31–34). The reality of evil and contingency (the possibility that it all might be otherwise) come together with the inefficacy of philosophical escapes from that reality in a comment by Duns Scotus that Arendt quotes twice: "Those who deny that some being is contingent should be exposed to torments until they concede that it is possible for them not to be tormented" (31, 134). Arendt's epistemology may be seen as pragmatic: whatever they might say, all humans act as if what appears to them is real. They pick up the fork and eat the food in front of them on the table; they flee the fire that approaches them.

But this ontology (like all positions on the nature of reality) is not quite so simple as the preceding paragraph might suggest. Arendt also recognizes that any ontology of appearance runs into the question of the difference between reality-for-us and reality-in-itself. Her response (typical of her human-centered work throughout) is simply to eschew any interest in reality-in-itself. What she talks about is what is real for humans—and that means that the real is a product of the meeting of humans with material objects that are perceived. (Such material objects, of course, include my own and others' bodies.) Things—and people—have reality only insofar as they appear and are perceived: "Reality in a world of appearances is first of all characterized by 'standing still and remaining' the same long enough to become an *object* for acknowledgment and recognition by a *subject*" (T, 45–46).

The dependence of the object on the subject (and vice versa) leads to the characteristic Arendtian position that reality is intersubjective, that it is established through the coincident perceptions of a number of subjects:

> That appearance always demands spectators and thus implies an at least potential recognition and acknowledgment has far-reaching consequences for what we, appearing beings in a world of appearances, understand by reality, our own as well as that of the world. In both cases, our "perceptual faith," as Merleau-Ponty has called it, our certainty that what we perceive has an existence independent of the act of perceiving, depends entirely on the object's also appearing as such to others and being acknowledged by them. Without this tacit acknowledgment by others we would not even be able to put faith in the way we appear to ourselves. (46)

Reality is given to us, then, only insofar as others live and act in ways that acknowledge that they confront and respond to the same objects that stand in front of me. The cure for solipsism is the perception that others react to the same realities with which I must deal.

Arendt moves from this epistemological-ontological argument to its ramifications for human psychology. Following the work of a Swiss biologist, Adolf Portmann, Arendt posits a fundamental "urge to self-display":

> [W]hatever can see wants to be seen, whatever can hear calls out to be heard, whatever can touch presents itself to be touched. It is indeed as though everything that is alive—in addition to the fact that its surface is made for appearance, fit to be seen and meant to appear to others—has an *urge to appear*, to fit itself into the world of appearances by displaying and showing, not its "inner self" but itself as an individual. (*T*, 29)

We are real only insofar as we appear to others; the reality of that appearance is insured only by our recognition by others; and it is only through this dynamic of appearance and acknowledgment that individuality is achieved, that is, takes on a worldly reality.

Moral considerations enter when Arendt tells us that "in addition to the urge toward self-display . . . , men also *present* themselves in word and deed, and thus indicate how they *wish* to appear, what in their opinion is fit to be seen and what is not" (*T*, 34). That appearance is a matter of publicness follows from the fact that the appearance's reality is not secured until it is witnessed. With the addition of the complicating fact that humans can choose what to display and what to conceal, morality also becomes a matter of public, intersubjective appearance. Hence, in the Kant lectures, Arendt is quite taken with (even though she does not fully endorse) Kant's notion that "publicity" can serve as a criterion for judging right and wrong. Whatever I am willing to display fully and openly to others is what I deem morally upright; what I wish and try to hide is what I am ashamed of, what I think is morally dubious: "To be evil, therefore, is characterized by withdrawal from the public realm. Morality means being fit to be *seen*" (*LK*, 49).

One problem with equating publicness with morality is that we lose any way to protest a corrupt society. The Nazis committed their crimes openly and publicly. Thus, totalitarian evil presents us with a crisis not only in "the standards of our moral judgment" (*EU*, 405) but also in the reliability of appearances. If evil appears as the legal and the upright, then don't we need the kind of maneuvers that philosophy has traditionally employed to identify the "true" nature of deceitful appearances? It is just this kind of logic, of course, that led premodern philosophers to deny the reality of evil. The wicked prosper only *apparently*; in reality, even if we can't see it, the world is just and the good will be rewarded, the wicked punished. The incentives for the post–World War II philosopher to deny the reality of evil are rather different, but they still make resorting to the traditional strategies attractive. Since the Holocaust, the philosopher wants some standard by which to judge the moral wickedness of what appears completely acceptable, and some safeguard against people just following along with what a corrupt society declares is appropriate, even praiseworthy, behavior. The perplexity presented by the Eichmann case, in Arendt's view, is that according to almost every conventional way of determining morality, Eichmann acted morally. Within Nazi Germany, where the courts had declared that "'the Fuhrer's words had the force of law'" (*EJ*, 148), the conscientious Eichmann was not acting on "criminal" or "unlawful" orders when he furthered the murder of the Jews. Hence, there was no competing standard of morality that he might have pondered to determine whether his actions had been fit to be seen. Everything that accompanies actions approved by others in the public space of acknowledgment (acceptance, promotion, respect, even acclaim) followed from Eichmann's doing his job well. No dissenting voice withheld its approval or expressed its outrage at Eichmann's actions.

Under such conditions, "to fall back on an unequivocal voice of conscience—or, in the even vaguer language of the jurists, on a 'general sentiment of humanity' . . . —not only begs the question, it signifies a deliberate refusal to take notice of the central moral, legal, and political phenomenon of our century" (*EJ*, 148). The tradition's recurrent blind spot in regard to evil contributes to this "deliberate refusal," but there is also a failure to see that what is crucial is not the actions of the criminals and sadists who led the totalitarian movements, but the actions of millions of "ordinary" citizens who followed those leaders. Arendt makes this point utterly clear in a 1965 lecture:

> Among the many things which were still thought to be "permanent and vital" at the beginning of the century and yet have not lasted, I chose to turn our attention to the moral issues, those which concern individual conduct and behavior; the few rules and standards according to which men used to tell right from wrong, and which were invoked to judge or justify others and themselves, and whose validity were supposed to be self-evident to every sane person either as a part of divine or of natural law. Until, that is, without much notice, all this collapsed almost overnight, and then it was as though morality suddenly stood revealed in the original meaning of the word, as a set of *mores*, customs, and manners, which could be exchanged for another set with hardly more trouble than it would take to change the table manners of an individual or a people. (*SQ*, 740)

The "moral phenomenon" of our century, then, is the discovery that people take their moral bearings so completely and so docilely from the world that surrounds them that the unthinkable can be transformed into the taken-for-granted almost overnight. (To be less dramatic, I should note that Arendt is careful in *Eichmann in Jerusalem* to consider the stages by which the Nazis approached the Final Solution: they got the general populace first to see Jews as aliens in their midst, then to accept the removal of Jews from German cities [to confine ourselves just to Germany for the moment], and only then to go along with the murder of people who had been their neighbors four to eight years previously.) The banality of evil, its becoming for most Germans ordinary and unremarkable, is thus part of the preponderant reality of appearance in human lives. So long as we claim that appearance is the *only* reality, we have no way to condemn the actions of those who went along with the way their daily reality was organized and the actions and words that were honored within that reality. Contingency comes to cover not just the actions humans perform and the words they speak, but also the very standards by which those words and deeds are judged. There are no "'permanent' . . . rules and standards."

We can now phrase precisely the problem animating Arendt's meditation on evil and how it eventually leads her to thinking and judging. She is committed to an ontology of appearance and believes that the tradition's inability to confront truly the reality of evil is part of its continual effort to deny the reality of appearance in favor of deeper, less changeable realities. (Plato's ideal Forms, the Christians' eternal God, Kant's things-in-themselves, Hegel's *Geist*, Heidegger's Being, and even Freud's unconscious would all exemplify these unchanging undergirding entities.) But she is also troubled by the suspicion that moving morality as well as reality fully into the realm of appearances offers us no safeguard against the evils perpetrated by the Nazis and by "the ordinary citizens" who did the Nazis' work for them. (It was Arendt's determination, of course, that even the Nazis' victims, the Jews, were among those who did that heinous work for them—and, thus, to themselves—that caused such angry responses to the Eichmann book. But Arendt believed that showing how even some Jews "participated"—to use her carefully chosen word—in the Holocaust would reveal the stunning totality of the moral collapse she was trying to delineate.) Evil becomes "banal" when it is *the* reality of the world people occupy, a reality whose sheer facticity makes it incredibly difficult to imagine or believe that things could be otherwise. Far from being "negative," always a "lack" and always "destructive" (as in Augustine's and Aquinas's enormously influential characterizations of evil [see *W*, 86–96 and 117–25]), Arendt's banal evil can create and sustain a full, if horrible, world, one that gives people a place, a role, and a series of chores that carry them from day to day without any stirring that things might be wrong. Arendt's problem is how to introduce some stirrings, some doubt, into this plenitude, this rich world of appearances. The tricky part is that she wants to retain her insistence on the reality of appearances, but she also needs to introduce some "otherness," some element distinct from that reality, into the mix. The vehicle she chooses is "thinking." And, as I have already hinted, she will speculate that appearance, although it is the primary reality, is not the *only* reality, that thinking gives us access to a reality that is not of appearances.

Before moving on to thinking, however, it is worth outlining how sticking strictly to appearances accords with Arendt's view of politics. One way to introduce "otherness" into the way I might judge my own or others' actions is to provide a place where I attend to others' opinions. That place is the public realm, in Arendt's political philosophy; judging, as she describes it, establishes a kind of inner simulacrum of that public realm. In *On Revolution*, Arendt is adamant that the public realm can deal only with appearances, which means that it judges deeds, not motives. When the fear of "hypocrisy," and the accompanying quest to determine whether actors are really "sincere," becomes a matter of concern to citizens, the public realm is doomed to an endless and unavailing sidetracking into private matters that should not be its concern. As members of the public world, we can deal with only what others do, with the deeds that manifest their identity and that have manifest consequences in the maintenance and transformation of the world we share in common because we all perceive it. To place as a matter of public concern what is beyond perception is to focus not on what we hold in common, not on what lies "between us" as the world, but on what makes us impenetrable mysteries not only to others but also to ourselves. Almost quite literally, Arendt believes that that way madness lies. The Terror in France was one manifestation of that madness.

Similarly, in the Eichmann case, Arendt wishes that the court had rested its judgment solely on Eichmann's deeds. She ends her report with what she wishes the judges had said to the defendant as they sentenced him. In this imagined address, the judges tell Eichmann that "[w]e are concerned only with what you did, and not with the possible noncriminal nature of your inner life and of your motives or with the criminal potentialities of those around you." The judges reason that even if they were to grant that Eichmann was unlucky, that under different circumstances he would never have done what he did, "there still remains the fact that you have carried out, and therefore actively supported, a policy of mass murder" (*EJ*, 278). That fact alone, the reality of Eichmann's manifest deeds, is what the court judges him on, in Arendt's imagined address, and what justifies the sentence of hanging.

The same logic that leads Arendt to consider Eichmann's deeds the only relevant public facts in the case (so far as judgment of him is concerned) also leads her, in the Eichmann book, to wonder whether conscience itself might be politically or publicly understood not as some inner, private voice but as something activated when others question or disapprove of us. This need for others to assist in the uti-lization of a capacity usually considered completely private is made evident both in the case of the millions of non-Nazi Germans who "did not act of conviction" but nonetheless "coordinated" themselves (SQ, 744) with the regime's policies, and in the loss of conviction by committed Nazis when they "met with *open* native resistance" in Denmark "and the result seems to have been that those exposed to it changed their minds" (*EJ*, 175). In this view, morality, like reality, is intersubjective and located in the public world of appearances; how-ever, we become utterly hostage to the quality of that public realm. When "the law of Hitler's land demanded that the voice of conscience tell everybody: 'Thou shalt kill'" (150), murder became one's duty—and most people adopted that code of behavior easily: "Morality col-lapsed into a mere set of mores—manners, customs, conventions to be changed at will—not with criminals, but with ordinary people, who, as long as the moral standards were socially accepted, never dreamt of doubting what they had been taught to believe in" (SQ, 744).

Arendt's political philosophy offers no guarantees against this col-lapse. If all others get into lockstep, if there are not those contending voices that characterize plurality for her and that serve to activate my conscience by infiltrating my unquestioned easiness with my own as-sumptions and opinions, nothing in Arendtian politics can prevent such disastrous unanimity. For me, this lack of guarantees is one of the strengths of Arendt's work. She is facing up to the fact of evil in the way few writers do when she says that evil is fully possible, that nothing can prevent the worst from happening, and that only the quality of our human togetherness, of our ways of living with others in public, can give us a world worth living in at all. But this nakedness of humans and of the polity in the face of evil made her blink (or so it seems to me). Alongside her stalwart claim that politics is our best and only way of avoiding evil, that we live together in a public realm of appearances that we are responsible for making a good or an evil one, in *The Life of the Mind* she places another safeguard against evil: a private dialogue of myself with myself, which she calls "thinking" and which can distance me from the collective evil of others at times when all the world is becoming murderous. As we shall see, Arendt is not fully consistent in making thinking private; one of the ways she de-scribes thinking places it at the service of reality as appearance. But she seems unwilling, in the final analysis, to trust fully in appearances; she retains an ace in the hole to be played in "special emergencies" (*T*, 192).

Thinking

It is difficult to present Arendt's description of "thinking," because she includes three different functions for that capacity within her discussion, and it is unclear just how these three fit together or even whether they are compatible with one another. Thinking is what generates understanding; thinking is the soundless dialogue of myself with myself that provides me with some distance from the reality of appearances and hence (in some cases) a way to resist its pressures on my beliefs and actions; and thinking is linked to taking others' viewpoints into account. This last of the three functions is often called "political thinking" by Arendt and will eventually come to reside in "judging." But it is fair to say that "thinking" and "judging" do not remain as distinct as we might hope in Arendt's work, because Eichmann's "thoughtlessness" (the catalyst that moves her to try to describe thinking in the first place) combines elements two and three: Eichmann has no interior place in which to distance himself from the voice of society (he can speak only in clichés and pat phrases [see *EJ*, 47–51]), and he is unable "to ever look at anything from the other fellow's point of view" (48). In this section, I will deal only with the first two elements of thinking in Arendt: thinking as producing understanding, and thinking as private dialogue. Political thinking—taking others' viewpoints into account—will be discussed in the section on judging.

Arendt turns to a description of thinking after she describes Eichmann as "thoughtless" (see *EJ*, 287):

> The longer one listened to him, the more obvious it became that his inability to speak was closely connected with an inability to *think*, namely, to think from the standpoint of somebody else. No communication was possible with him, not because he lied but because he was surrounded by the most reliable safeguards against the words and the presence of others, and hence against reality as such. (48–49)

This formulation is a bit perplexing, because, as we shall see, Arendt relies on thinking to distance us from the reality that "the words and the presence of others" establish, so that both thinking and thought-lessness are withdrawals from the intersubjective reality of appearances. But the main thrust is clear: thoughtlessness (which Arendt tells us is quite distinct from "stupidity" [*T*, 4]) is monologic, as opposed to the dialogues of the self with itself or of the self with others, which are involved in the different versions of thinking. The question that Eichmann's thoughtlessness poses for Arendt is articulated at the beginning of *Thinking*: "Could the activity of thinking as such, the habit of examining whatever happens to come to pass or to attract attention, regardless of results and specific content, could this activity be among the conditions that make men abstain from evil-doing or even 'condition' them against it?" (5).

It is a bold question to ask, for two (related) reasons. First, it had become a standard response to the Holocaust and Hiroshima (especially through the influential work of Horkheimer and Adorno of the Frankfurt school of "critical theory") that the monstrosities committed by the "most civilized" nations during the twentieth century indicated that Western culture was fundamentally flawed. The image of the SS man who relaxed from his murderous chores by listening to Bach summed up the sense that the whole Western tradition was, at best, ineffectual and, at worst, complicit with the century's horrors. To turn to philosophy and "thinking" as a safeguard against evil seems quaint from such a viewpoint. Second—and perhaps even more provocatively—to focus on "thinking" was to call to mind the most egregious example of philosophy's failure to protect the thinker from evil: Heidegger. The question "What is thinking?" comes from Heidegger's essay with that title, and Arendt puts an epigraph from Heidegger at the front of the volume *Thinking*. (Although I won't discuss it here, she also examines Heidegger's work on thinking—although in the second volume, not the first—and finds it wanting in several crucial respects [see *W*, 172–94].) Arendt, it seems, is out to save what can be salvaged from the discredited tradition in general and the discredited Heidegger in particular.

Thinking is the philosophical activity per se. It begins by withdrawing us from others and from the intersubjectively constituted realm of appearances. Hence, if philosophy has consistently portrayed as the truly real a realm apart from appearances, that portrayal, although it flies in the face of common sense, is not utterly inexplicable. The belief in a nonapparent reality reflects both the experience of thinking itself and an understandable (albeit potentially dangerous) bias among philosophers to accord their own activity and its characteristics the highest status among all human activities. (Highest status in philosophy is conferred by declaring something the greatest good or by announcing that it possesses the most Being, the most reality.) Thinking requires "a deliberate *withdrawal* from appearances. It is withdrawal not so much from the world . . . as from the world's being *present* to the senses. *Every mental act rests on the mind's faculty of having present to itself what is absent from sense*" (*T*, 75–76). Thinking is dependent on imagination, the capacity to re-present in thought that which is now absent to the senses. Only this capacity, this withdrawal "from the present and the urgencies of everyday life," permits us to develop a sense of time (recollecting a past and projecting a future distinct from the present perceived by the senses) and to transcend "the partiality of immediate interests as they are given by my position in the world and the part I play in it" (76). In withdrawal, then, is a kind of freedom, the negative freedom of not being ruled entirely by the demands of this moment—a freedom from immediacy and partiality that, of course, philosophers have extolled.

Arendt goes even further, claiming that thinking requires nonpresence: "In order for us to think about somebody, he must be removed from our presence" (*T*, 78). She lays down this requirement because she wants to distinguish thinking from actively responding to a situation. To see a car coming toward me on the highway and to pull off the road in response is not an example of thinking for Arendt. Here, as in her description of action, Arendt wants to separate purposive or calculated behavior from the "purer" activity, be it "action" or "thinking." Both action and thinking, for her, are "disinterested" not in that they arise out of the needs of the immediate situation, but in that they are free, spontaneous activities tied to experience yet also distanced from it. Imagination provides the vehicle of such distance for thinking, whereas spontaneity, natality, and what we might call the expressive relation of action to identity are the crucial elements of action's transcendence of immediate circumstances.

Arendt expresses thinking's nonpurposive nature in *The Life of the Mind* by returning to issues of meaning and understanding that occupied her in the early 1950s as she thought about what form history should take in the wake of totalitarianism. Here we encounter Arendt's description of thinking as understanding, the first of her three versions of thinking. Arendt recognizes that Kantian pure reason produces knowledge about the world, knowledge that we can use in instrumental ways to manipulate and control our environment. Thinking, in her sense, is not cognitive in this way; it produces not knowledge but meaning or understanding. This pursuit puts thinking in tension with common sense; it can even make thinking appear "unnatural" (*T*, 78; see also 80). Thinking "interrupts any doing, any ordinary activities," and this interruption, this withdrawal, is the "genuine experience of the thinking ego" that underlies all "the fallacies and absurdities of the two-world theories" that posit a realm of sensual appearances and another, more real realm beyond, behind, or below appearances (78).

The connection of thinking with meaning or understanding is not easy to reconcile with the link between thinking and the avoidance of evil found in the soundless dialogue of self with self and in political thinking. It is as if Arendt's residual concern with understanding is allowed to sneak into *The Life of the Mind*, with its very different agenda. I will offer a tentative way to forge a connection between these two concerns, but Arendt herself appears unaware that thinking performs more than one function in *The Life of the Mind*, or that these multiple functions might not be very compatible.

In any case, Arendt describes the process by which thought creates meaning as follows: "All thought arises out of experience, but no experience yields any meaning or even coherence without undergoing the operations of imagination and thinking. Seen from the perspective of thinking, life in its sheer thereness is meaningless; seen from the perspective of the immediacy of life and the world given to the senses, thinking is . . . a living death" (*T*, 87). At this juncture in Arendt's work, a chasm opens between the actor and the spectator, the ignorant present and the understanding that comes only with hindsight. The experiencing actor is fully in the world and open to view; the thinker has withdrawn from appearances, gaining a vantage point unavailable to the actor: "[O]nly the spectator, never the actor, can know and understand whatever offers itself as a spectacle. . . . [A]s a spectator you may understand the 'truth' of what the spectacle is about; but the price you have to pay is withdrawal from participating in it" (92–93). Connecting thinking with the withdrawal of the spectator from participation comes awfully close to describing action itself as "thoughtless," a conclusion Arendt surely does not want to reach. But her determination to protect thinking from the pressures of circumstances and of the present pushes her in that direction.

The understanding that the thinker pursues outrages common sense, because it is not knowledge that furthers our practical dealings with the world or with our fellow human beings. Such knowledge belongs to the order of "truth," where Arendt understands "truth" as fact. Truth belongs to the realm of necessity and it has its place—but that place is not political. Opinion is political, truth is not: "All truths—not only the various kinds of rational truth but also factual truth—are opposed to opinion in their *mode of asserting validity*" (*BPF*, 239);

> Seen from the viewpoint of politics, truth has a despotic character. . . . Facts are beyond agreement and consent, and all talk about them—all exchanges of opinion based on correct information—will contribute nothing to their establishment. Unwelcome opinion can be argued with, rejected, or compromised upon, but unwelcome facts possess an infuriating stubbornness that nothing can move except plain lies. The trouble is that factual truth, like all other truth, peremptorily claims to be acknowledged and precludes debate, and debate constitutes the very essence of political life. The modes of thought and communication that deal with truth, if seen from the political perspective, are necessarily domineering; they don't take into account other people's opinions and taking these into account is the hallmark of all strictly political thinking. (241)

In distinguishing understanding from knowledge, opinion from truth, and (as we have seen in chapter 2) opinion from interest, Arendt is trying to open up a space for "political thinking." In her view, the epistemological doubt introduced by modern science has led most philosophers since Descartes (with the notable exception of Kant) to be obsessed with a certainty they can't ever quite attain (that's why they are obsessed with it), to the neglect of those areas of nontruth that delineate the political. From this viewpoint, we can say that *The Life of the Mind*, just like Arendt's middle works, is oriented toward opening up the space of the polis that modernity has eclipsed. But now, instead of extolling the capabilities of humans when they "act in concert" and the rewards of political action, Arendt explores the mental resources that might foster political attitudes or orientations, if not quite a full-blown polis. I think it hard to dispute that *The Life of the Mind*, like Frost's oven bird, ponders what to make of "a diminished thing." Against the vision of humans acting together to create the polis found in *The Human Condition* and *On Revolution*, *The Life of the Mind* presents the solitary thinker who, through the pursuit of understanding and the formation of opinions by way of judging, keeps political attributes alive in bleak times. Maybe this is the best we can expect to do in the pass to which modernity has now brought us.

Although Arendt is clear about what "understanding" is not, it is a little harder to see just what it is. Recall that she locates her own need to write in the need to understand: "What is important for me is to understand. For me, writing is a matter of seeking this understanding, part of the process of understanding" (*EU*, 3). Understanding is linked to meaning and, crucially, reconciliation: "The result of understanding is meaning, which we originate in the very process of living insofar as we try to reconcile ourselves to what we do and what we suffer" (309). Unlike the search for knowledge, which ends when one discovers the truth, "[u]nderstanding is unending and therefore cannot produce final results. It is a specifically human way of being alive; for every single person needs to be reconciled to a world into which he was born a stranger" (308). "It is an unending activity by which, in constant change and variation, we come to terms with and reconcile ourselves to reality, that is, try to be at home in the world" (307–8). At stake in understanding, then, is our very desire to be in the world. What is not clear is whether understanding and the "reconciliation" it provides are a necessary first step prior to action. Can action itself reconcile us to this world? And why do we need to be reconciled at all? What fundamental outrages to the self, what sufferings, must be accepted "to be at home in the world"? In our time, totalitarianism is clearly such a fundamental outrage: "To the extent that the rise of totalitarian government is the central event of our world, to understand totalitarianism is not to condone anything, but to reconcile ourselves to a world in which such things are possible at all" (308). If our response to the Holocaust is "*This ought not to have happened*" (14), then understanding is now faced with the monumental task of finding ways to make us at home again in the world in which what should not happen can happen and did.

In the 1954 essay "Understanding and Politics (The Difficulties of Understanding)," from which I have been quoting, Arendt is clear that understanding is the wisdom acquired by the spectator of history after the event and hence is unavailable and useless to the actor: "We cannot delay our fight against totalitarianism until we have 'understood' it, because we do not, and cannot expect to understand it definitively as long as it has not definitively been defeated." Totalitarianism is so novel that "the wisdom of the past . . . dies, so to speak, in our hands as soon as we try to apply it honestly to the central political experiences of our own time" (*EU*, 309). But if we remember that the "miracle" of action for Arendt is precisely that it introduces something new ("natality") into the world, it becomes clear that the wisdom of the past is repeatedly insufficient for the present. Understanding, then, is not pursued as a guide for present actions or present reactions; at best, it offers "'heuristic,' not 'ostensive' concepts; they are tentative—they do not demonstrate or show anything" (*T*, 64). Such results might easily be deemed purposeless. Arendt quotes Kant: "Pure reason is in fact occupied with nothing but itself. It can have no other vocation" (65). We meet here, once again, the Arendt who has a strong predilection for purity. Thinking, in its pursuit of understanding, is to withdraw from the world (and hence with the partialities of involvement) in a dialogue with itself that produces nothing of use.

This uselessness is carried over from the sections of *Thinking* that stress "understanding" to the sections in the second half of the volume that stress thinking as "the soundless dialogue of the I with itself" (*T*, 74–75). The model for such thinking is Socrates, both in his endless questioning of all received meanings and in his concern with his own integrity in contrast to his agreement with others. Arendt gives the crucial Socratic passage that articulates this priority of a harmony with oneself over harmony with others: "It would be better for me that my lyre or a chorus I directed should be out of tune and loud with discord, and that multitudes of men should disagree with me rather than that I, *being one*, should be out of harmony with myself and contradict me" (181). In thinking's soundless dialogue, I am not primarily for others, as I am in action and appearance, but in this withdrawal from appearance am "for myself" (193): "It is this *duality* of myself with myself that makes thinking a true activity, in which I am both the one who asks and the one who answers." In this process, "we constantly raise the basic Socratic question: *What do you mean when you say . . . ?* except that this *legein*, saying, is soundless and therefore so swift that its dialogical structure is somewhat difficult to detect" (185). "The only criterion of Socratic thinking is agreement, to be consistent with oneself . . . ; its opposite, to be in contradiction with oneself, . . . actually means becoming one's own adversary." Arendt quotes Aristotle at this point: "'[T]hough we can always raise objections to the outside world, to the *inward discourse* we cannot always object,' because here the partner is oneself, and I cannot possibly want to become my own adversary" (186).

Here is the first answer to how thinking guards us against evil: "It is characteristic of 'base people' to be 'at variance with themselves' . . . and of wicked men to avoid their own company; their soul is in rebellion against itself" (*T*, 189). If conscience means anything aside from the pressure that others' views place on us, it means this harmony with oneself. The thinker, by withdrawing into this duality of the soundless dialogue, which Kant describes as "talking with oneself . . . hence also inwardly listening" (qtd. on 186), risks a dissonance that the unthinking can avoid altogether:

> [When the thoughtless] Hippias goes home, he remains one, for, though he lives alone, he does not seek to keep himself company. . . . When Socrates goes home, he is not alone, he is by himself. Clearly, with this fellow who awaits him, Socrates has to come to some kind of agreement, because they live under the same roof. Better to be at odds with the whole world than be at odds with the only one you are forced to live together with when you have left company behind. (188)[2]

Arendt recognizes that this concern with integrity, with the internal agreement of the self with itself in the dialogue of thinking, is not political, because it turns away from others and from the world of appearances. Furthermore, the moral effects of thinking are not the thinker's aim; he pursues the activity of thinking for its own sake, because for him, as for Socrates, "to think and to be fully alive are the same" (*T*, 178). The unexamined life is not worth living. Thinking is a pure activity, like Arendtian action. But just as action produces benefits as by-products not directly intended, so thinking has a "moral side effect":

> For the thinker himself this moral side effect is a marginal affair. And thinking as such does society little good, much less than the thirst for knowledge, which uses thinking as an instrument for other purposes. It does not create values; it will not find out, once and for all, what the "good" is; it does not confirm but, rather, dissolves accepted rules of conduct. And it has no political relevance unless special emergencies arise. That while I am alive I must be able to live with myself is a consideration that does not come up politically except in "boundary situations." . . . When everybody is swept away

unthinkingly by what everybody else does and believes in, those who think are drawn out of hiding because their refusal to join in is conspicuous and thereby becomes a kind of action. In such emergencies, it turns out that the purging action of thinking . . . is political by implication. For this destruction has a liberating effect on another faculty, the faculty of judging, which one may call with some reason the most political of man's mental abilities. (192)

Before turning to the political faculty of judging, let me try to specify the various perplexities still left in Arendt's account of thinking. For starters, Eichmann's "thoughtlessness" was characterized by his mindless going along with the crowd and by his inability to see anything "from the standpoint of the other." Only the first of these two characteristics is addressed by the model of Socratic thinking. Thus, Socratic thinking is not "political thinking," which involves debate and dialogue with others, not with oneself. This second kind of thinking, in company with others as contrasted to in company with myself, Arendt will call "judging." The terminology is confusing here, because Eichmann's thoughtlessness involves his inability to practice two kinds of thinking: thinking proper and judging (or "political thinking"). (The terminology is even more confusing when we note in the long passage just quoted that there is also cognitive or purposive thinking.) Thinking proper is a safeguard against evil in extreme boundary situations in which society is utterly corrupt, and it can have a "liberating" (presumably this means an enabling) effect on judging. But since judging, as we shall see, involves taking into account the "possible" viewpoints of others, not necessarily involving oneself in an actual dialogue with those others, it is not clear what kind of social crisis could render "representative thinking" impossible. In other words, thinking as a dialogue with oneself and judging as a dialogue (in one's mind) with others are two different possible ways of thinking, and Arendt is very unclear about what would make one form of thinking or the other more appropriate in this or that situation. And she certainly never considers the possibility that I could reach two different conclusions as a result of following the two different ways of thinking. If that happened, how would I begin to choose between the alternatives? I can only suspect that lurking behind the thinking/judging distinction is Arendt's division between the private and the public. Thinking is mostly nonpolitical, because it deals with private matters; this fits with Arendt's intuition in *The Human Condi-*

tion that the *vita contemplativa* stands in sharp distinction from the *vita activa* that is the realm of politics. But Arendt never makes an argument to this effect, with the result that the boundaries between thinking and judging remain fuzzy.

Finally, there is the problematic relation of Socratic thinking to the "reconciliation" achieved in "understanding." Recall that "understanding" produces "'heuristic' concepts" (*T*, 64) and is linked to "meaning." (The dictionary, rather unhelpfully, tells us that "heuristic" means "helping to discover or learn" and notes that it comes from the Greek word *heuriskein*, "to invent or discover.") Heuristic concepts are those which provide models or frameworks for comprehension; such concepts do not designate what we confront as definitively this or that, but instead suggest ways to approach something that may prove fruitful. Take, for example, Wittgenstein's advice that we think of language as a toolbox. (My own proceeding here by offering an example is a heuristic way to illustrate the meaning of "heuristic.") His statement does not designate the rules that govern how language functions; rather, his suggestion opens up some possibilities for how we might interact with language. His advice might serve to make our encounters with and our uses of language more meaningful. His analogy suggests a new way to view language, a new appreciation of possibilities to which we might have been blind before. The analogy unfolds being or—to use the word Arendt would prefer—the world. Reality is enhanced, broadened, diversified, deepened, expanded, opened up by this new perspective on it, this new way of interacting with it. I take it that Arendtian understanding aims in the same direction as Wittgenstein's late works, to move us from a protest against the limitations and imperfections of the world to a reconciliation with that world via the fullest possible realization of its multiple possibilities. When those possibilities include the Holocaust, there is much to be said for a defiant and eternal refusal to be reconciled—the position, say, of Camus's rebel. But Arendt, like Wittgenstein, is searching for what will enable us to "go on" even after the Holocaust. And if she looks to understanding to provide resources for going on, it is because she sees understanding as working to appreciate and multiply "plurality" and, hence, as absolutely and essentially antitotalitarian in spirit even as it strives to understand, but never to condone, totalitarianism and to become reconciled to a world in which totalitarianism not only is possible but actually happened.

A case could be made that Socratic thinking pursues understanding, because it is focused on the question of meaning, but the emphasis on a harmony with myself is hard to put together with Arendt's comments on understanding. I guess we could say that the reconciliation with oneself that such a harmony offers is the other side of the coin of the reconciliation with the world that understanding achieves. I prefer to emphasize that, at least, Socratic thinking is as committed to the protection and fostering of plurality as is the kind of thinking that produces understanding:

> [T]he specifically human actualization of consciousness in the thinking dialogue between me and myself suggests that difference and otherness, which are such outstanding characteristics of the world of appearances as it is given to man for his habitat among a plurality of things, are the very conditions for the existence of man's mental ego as well, for this ego actually exists only in duality. And this ego—the I-am-I—experiences difference in identity precisely when it is not related to things that appear but only related to itself. . . . What thinking actualizes in its unending process is difference, given as a mere fact . . . in consciousness; only in this humanized form does consciousness then become the outstanding characteristic of somebody who is a man and neither a god nor an animal. . . . [T]he Socratic two-in-one heals the solitariness of thought; its inherent duality points to the infinite plurality which is the law of the earth. (*T*, 187)

Socratic thinking, in its encounter with the difference "inherent" *within* identity, discovers a duality that is analogous to, that "points to," the plurality of the outer world that is experienced by common sense and with which understanding attempts to come to terms.

Here Arendt is striving, I believe, to reconcile one of the perplexing dualities her own train of thought has produced. On the one hand, we have her insistence on the primary reality of appearances, her attempt to persuade modern humans, who search for certain knowledge in the reaches behind or beyond appearances, that such quests for unattainable truths are disastrous in the political realm of human being-together. She does not deny that certain scientific laws have proved pragmatically useful, but she is convinced that such knowledge (of actors' hearts and of the unambiguously proper course to pursue) has no place in politics. We have only concrete deeds to go by, and on that basis we come to know actors' identity, to judge their actions, and to figure out how to live and act with them. To ask for more than what appearances can yield is to try to replace the contingency of events in human affairs with a certainty that would kill freedom. We must be reconciled to appearances, to the world given to us by "common sense, this sixth sense that fits our five senses into a common world" (*T*, 81), and it is precisely in this sharing of a common world (and in our acting to maintain it) that we manage to have a public realm of being-with-others.

On the other hand, into this common world enters "man's faculty of thought and need of reason, which determine him to remove himself from considerable periods from it [the common world]" (*T*, 81). By insisting that thinking, even as it forsakes appearance, by its own distinctive route brings us to an experience of duality that points toward plurality, Arendt seems to be trying to limit the damage that might ensue from "the intramural warfare between thought and common sense" (80). And when she links thinking to understanding, she even more explicitly leads thinking's withdrawal—its spectatorship of, as opposed to common sense's immersion in, the world of appearances—to a final resting place that insures that thinking's conclusion—its reconciliation to what is—will not threaten common sense's way of being-in-the-world. Having introduced thinking, judging, understanding, and common sense as different ways of relating to the world, Arendt then seems to minimize the differences between them by having them all reach a rather similar experience of plurality at the end of the day. In this respect, none of the mental or perceptual faculties differs all that greatly from action, which both responds to and produces plurality. We might object that surely only action produces plurality, except that Socratic thinking quite clearly produces the distinctive self of the thinker who stands apart from the crowd; and we will see that judging produces "opinions," which are a crucial marker of the distinctive identity of those who engage in political debate. Arendt's account of the "faculties" at times suggests a conflict between them, an "intramural warfare," and certainly suggests crucial distinctions between them, but those conflicts dissipate, and even the sense of how the distinctions work and why they are crucial fades in the face of the relation of each to a fundamental acknowledgment of and reconciliation with plurality.

Judging

At the end of the volume *Thinking*, Arendt offers a plausible way of configuring the relation between the mental faculties thinking, willing, and judging:

> If we wish to placate our common sense, so decisively offended by the need of reason to pursue its purposeless quest for meaning, it is tempting to justify this need solely on the grounds that thinking is an indispensable preparation for deciding what shall be and for evaluating what is no more. Since the past, being past, becomes subject to our judgment, judgment, in turn, would be a mere preparation for willing. This is undeniably the perspective, and, within limits, the legitimate perspective of man insofar as he is an acting being.
>
> But this last attempt to defend the thinking activity against the reproach of being impractical and useless does not work. The decision the will arrives at can never be derived from the mechanics of desire or the deliberations of the intellect that may precede it. The will is either an organ of free spontaneity that interrupts all causal chains of motivation that would bind it or it is nothing but an illusion. (*T*, 213)

Determined to protect (at all costs) the freedom of action, Arendt must sever the will from all *necessary* connection to either desire or reason. No causal chain from desire nor any logical progression from ideas or beliefs determines the decision put into action by the will: "[T]he will acts like a 'kind of *coup d'état*,' as Bergson once said" (213). This severance of the will from the other mental faculties makes it difficult to see, at first, just what is left for judging to do. Judgment, as Arendt indicates, is usually seen as a process by which the lessons of past experience are brought to bear on present circumstances to decide what course of action to pursue in the future. The trick of judgment is usually seen as residing in the delicate problem of figuring out which lessons of the past are truly relevant to the novel situation in which I currently find myself. Judgment is the way that philosophers of action indicate that the self does not come to the present with a blank slate but carries into the present a whole history, which includes habits, predilections, prejudices, knowledge, and (most likely) an ongoing set of projects and plans. The self comes to the present with an agenda and a fund of skills and knowledge; judgment comes into play in the determination of how to act and react to present circumstances in ways that further that agenda and utilize those skills and knowledge. Theorists of judgment along these lines (the American pragmatist philosopher John Dewey is a good example) often stress the importance of imagination in this process, because the process requires discerning analogies between situations (those of one's past and the one now encountered) that are both similar and dissimilar. Just as a metaphor (comparing my love to a red, red rose, for example) depends on highlighting certain similarities between the two things compared, even while retaining a sense of the differences that remain (the metaphor doesn't lead me to water my love every second day), effective judgment relies on keeping in view both the similarities and the differences between the past and present if I am to take effective and appropriate action.

Arendt, however, grants this view of judgment only a limited legitimacy. Like Kant, she consistently takes autonomy as a sine qua non of freedom, and in *The Life of the Mind* that means that each of the mental faculties is portrayed as operating in isolation from the others. Thinking pursues its purposeless activity apart from the pressures of reality or of others, answerable only to its own desire for inner harmony. Willing is "free spontaneity" that exceeds any directives stemming from desire or intellect. Even judging, which (as we shall see) involves the self more intimately with others than does thinking or willing, gains much of its importance because it affords humans as individuals and as a species "an autonomy" that underwrites "a possible independence of things as they are or as they have come into being": "If judgment is our faculty for dealing with the past, the historian is the inquiring man who by relating to it sits in judgment over it" (*T*, 216). Humans are not the mere playthings of events or of history, because they possess this ability to step aside from it and to judge it— an ability crucial for the freedom that Arendt champions against any vision of the necessity of history, most notably Hegel's picture of history as an inevitable progress that plays itself out through unwitting human puppets.

If Arendt left it at that, we would see thinking providing freedom via withdrawal from the world of common sense and the common mores of one's society; willing providing freedom via its sheer arbitrary willfulness; and judging providing freedom via the adoption of a perspective apart from the sheer process of one event after another. But, in fact, she doesn't leave it at that—not surprisingly, as such an account of freedom would be completely individualistic. Judging is so important because it brings into Arendt's later work the intersubjective bases of freedom that are central to her political theorizing. And where the intersubjective is involved—our relations to our fellow human beings—the question of morality is raised. Just as thinking turns out to have a moral by-product, judging, we are told, "is of some relevance to a whole set of problems of theory and practice and to all attempts to arrive at a halfway plausible theory of ethics" (*T*, 216). Arendt's account of judgment (incomplete though it is) is her attempt to construct a moral philosophy (to use a grand term) adequate to the unprecedented modern experience of the evil perpetrated by totalitarianism and represented by the "thoughtless" Eichmann, who changed his moral beliefs as he might change his table manners.

But if Arendt's account of evil is distinctive, so is her notion of ethics. One puzzle of Arendt's view of judging is that she uncouples it from the influence over decision making that it is granted in the usual accounts (such as Dewey's). She seems to point judging away from an encounter with the present that is oriented toward deciding how to act in the future. Instead, judging, in her account, involves an evaluation of the past, of what has been done. Such a focus on the past, at first glance, deprives judging of any ethical import. Isn't ethics about deciding what to do? But Arendt's judging is more like a court case oriented toward making a pronouncement of innocence or guilt. She is much more focused on this judgment of innocence or guilt than on deciding what future actions are appropriate in light of the court's findings. How can that determination itself be "ethical," irrespective of how it influences future actions on the part of the prosecutor, the defendant, the judge, the jury, or the spectators? The answer, I think, is twofold. First, just as thinking has a moral by-product simply because the activity itself is undergone, so Arendt believes that the process of judging in and of itself involves a certain way of being in the world and of being with others that is ethical—that is, it is antithetical to the kind of evil done by the Nazis or by Stalin. We should recognize that this is a recurrent strain in Arendt's work: the experience of action, the experience of freedom, the experience of being a member of a fully functioning polis, the experience of thinking, the experience of judging—all are transformative (and, we might add, recursive) in that they place selves in new relations to themselves and to others, awakening or activating new possibilities whose full desirability can only now be recognized and built upon.

Second, judging, like understanding, fosters "reconciliation"; and if, as I have been arguing, reconciliation means, first and foremost, an acceptance, even love, of the world's irreducible "plurality," then reconciliation is itself ethical. Arendtian ethics is concerned not so much with questions of what to do as with creating a certain way of being in the world, a certain way of being with others. If judging is the most "political" of our faculties, that is because it is the faculty most oriented toward others, and it is the most ethical precisely because this experience of orienting our thoughts toward others promotes a way of existing with others that distances us from the evil of denying others a place in the world alongside and in relation to us. Radical evil "is an attack upon human diversity as such" (*EJ*, 268–69), and the path Arendt is pursuing is that thoughtfulness itself (Socratic thinking and "political thinking," or judging), as an activity, involves us with and relates us to that diversity in a way that would prevent our attacking it.

Judgment in Kant comes into play only in relation to aesthetic questions (Is the object beautiful or ugly?), not in relation to ethical questions (Is this action right or wrong?). Kant believed that the "categorical imperative" (I should perform only those actions which I could also willingly allow all other human beings to perform) provided a general law that covers all particular choices about what to do. Moral decisions involve simply applying the law given to the self by its own reason, because Kant believes we involve ourselves in a self-contradiction if we allow ourselves to do something we would forbid others to do. In the *Critique of Judgment* (often called the "third critique," because it follows *The Critique of Pure Reason*, which deals with knowledge, and *The Critique of Practical Reason*, which deals with morality), Kant gives the term "determinative judgment" to the mental operation required by morality, in which we decide how a particular instance relates to the given, general law. Determinative judgment "is only subsumptive. The law is marked out for it a priori, and hence it does not need to devise a law of its own so that it can subsume the particular . . . under the universal" (Kant [1791] 1987, 19). Thus, the general law tells me that lies are bad (if everyone lied, we wouldn't be able to communicate), and morality consists in recognizing that this particular instance is an example of lying and hence is subject to the general law. Arendt is impressed with the categorical imperative and does not leave it behind, as we shall see in her qualified use of the Kantian principle of "publicity," which follows rather directly from the categorical imperative.

But Arendt is even more impressed by Kant's recognition that in aesthetics, determinative judgments are not possible. There is no way to formulate a general law of beauty in the way he thinks we can for morality. An attempt to state a general law of beauty along the lines of the example of lies quickly reveals the problem. To say all paintings are beautiful makes no sense, so judgments of aesthetic value can't proceed by saying that because this is a painting, therefore it must be beautiful. And even if we could find a painting that we all agreed is beautiful and that thus could serve as a standard by which to judge other paintings, we could not expect those other paintings to be beautiful in exactly the same way. We are looking for beautiful paintings, not for a copy of the one painting we have agreed is beautiful. The point is that different things are beautiful in their own distinctive ways and, furthermore, that an object's beauty is often partly a product of its novelty, of its presenting a new facet of or perspective on being, one never really highlighted before. There is no formula by which beautiful things can be produced, just as there is no way to predict ahead of time what will be recognized as beautiful. And certainly no formula could foresee the incredible range, the sheer diversity, of the beautiful things that will appear, either naturally or through the efforts of artists, in the future. Some new object will always come along that will transcend (or even violate) any general law of beauty that we articulate, yet that object will (in some cases) still be recognized as beautiful by many observers. In aesthetics, therefore, Kant says we must make "reflective judgments," which are "obliged to ascend from the particular . . . to the universal." No preexisting law guides such judgments— and Kant's *Critique of Judgment* aims to discover the "principle" that guides judgment in the absence of law ([1791] 1987, 19).

It is "reflective judgment" that Arendt means by judging. In fact, just to keep matters confusing, Arendt first turns to Kant's notion of judging to elucidate her notion of "understanding." Because the aesthetic presents us with the continually new, it is no surprise that Arendt, with her focus on the novelty of action, would be drawn to Kant's attempt to think through how we process an experience of the new. Toward the end of her 1954 essay on understanding, Arendt tells us that "our endeavoring to understand something which has ruined our categories of thought and our standards of judgment appears less frightening" when we recall that we are creatures "whose essence is beginning." She then describes understanding in a way that reproduces the Kantian distinction between determinative and reflective judgment: "Even though we have lost yardsticks by which to measure, and rules under which to subsume the particular," our natality suggests that we "may have enough of origin" within ourselves "to understand without preconceived categories and to judge without the set of customary rules which is morality" (*EU*, 321). Seen this way, "understanding becomes the other side of action, namely, that form of cognition . . . by which acting men . . . eventually can come to terms with what irrevocably happened and be reconciled with what unavoidably exists" (321–22).

By the time we get to *The Life of the Mind*, "understanding," as we have seen, seems a residual concept not very well integrated with Arendt's other thoughts on thinking, and her return to the intricacies of "reflective judgment" in *Lectures on Kant's Political Philosophy* drops almost entirely the issue of "reconciliation." The lectures are more concerned with an issue foreshadowed in some of the comments on judgment found in *Between Past and Future*: validity. In Kant, the question of validity arises from the distinction (in aesthetic matters) between saying, "I like it," and, "It's beautiful." The first statement merely indicates a personal preference for something and makes no claim for objective validity. It is perfectly possible to say, "It's beautiful, but I don't like it." But to say, "It's beautiful," is to make an objective claim about the quality of the object. Hence it makes no sense to say, "It's beautiful, but I don't think so." We are not compelled to like a beautiful thing, but to state that it is beautiful is to make a claim about its appearance for myself and for others. The puzzle for Kant is how we can make such an objective claim in the absence of a general law and how we could ever make such a claim "stick," how we could get others to agree with it. It is a puzzle indeed, since aesthetic judgments are notoriously controversial and apparently endlessly disputable—and disputed.

Arendt adds to our troubles by suggesting that moral judgments under modern conditions are precisely like aesthetic ones. When we declare nowadays that a particular action is wrong, we do so in the absence of any universal or even culture-wide law or rule to which all would subscribe, not to mention that we are confronted with actions that transcend prior expectations or prior laws. The breakdown of traditional moral commitments shared by virtue of obedience or adherence to religion, combined with the novelty of action, means that the possibility of determinative judgments in ethics—if they ever were possible—is now lost. In our time, certainly, ethical judgments seem as prone to endless dispute, as incapable of resolution, as aesthetic ones are.

The first thing Arendt derives from Kant is that these difficulties, these embarrassments, don't stop us from uttering judgments in a form that makes a claim to general validity. Sometimes I do say, "I think that is wrong," thus indicating a tentativeness, a doubt, an unwillingness to insist that others see as I do. But at other times I say, "That's wrong," and feel strongly that those who don't see it as wrong are misguided, have missed something crucial about the action I so name, or that they must be judged wrong themselves in their willful refusal to judge that action as wrong. Arendt has little patience with those who would respond to the difficulties afflicting judgment in our time by claiming we have no right to judge or that the better course is to avoid judging because its processes appear so fragile. When Gershom Scholem wrote to Arendt, in reference to *Eichmann in Jerusalem*, that "I do not believe that our generation is in a position to pass any kind of historical judgment [on the actions of those caught up in the Holocaust.] We lack the necessary perspective, which alone makes some sort of objectivity possible—and we cannot but lack it" (*JP*, 241), Arendt is clear in her reply that she thinks such avoidance of judgment is a mistake: "I do believe that we shall only come to terms with this past if we begin to judge and to be frank about it" (248). We are simply a prey to history, we cannot be free, unless we take the distance from events afforded us by our ability to re-present them to ourselves in imagination and think about them. Not to judge is one way of being thoughtless. We cannot and should not sidestep our inclination and responsibility to judge just because it has become increasingly difficult to offer clear and indisputable grounds for the validity of judgments.

Arendt also pushes hard at Kant's insight that judgment focuses on particulars. Judging is especially suited to the recognition and appreciation of plurality, because it sees things not as instances of a general law but in their particularity, in their full individuality and uniqueness. In her report on the Eichmann trial and in various comments in the ensuing controversy, Arendt stresses the (mostly positive) limitations encountered in a law court, where "the question of individual guilt or innocence, the act of meting out justice to both the defendant and the victim, are the only things at stake" (*EJ*, 298). Questions of collective responsibility, of general historical trends or causes, are useless to making a judgment in particular cases, because such "generalities" make "all cats grey and . . . all equally guilty":

> Another such escape from the area of ascertainable facts and personal responsibility are the countless theories, based on non-specific, abstract, hypothetical assumptions—from the *Zeitgeist* down to the Oedipal complex—which are so general that they explain and justify every event and deed: no alternative to what actually happened is ever considered and no person could have acted differently from the way he did act. (297)

Any such general explanation, just like any declaration about "the collective guilt of the German people" or the "collective innocence of the Jewish people" is "absurd. . . . All these clichés have in common [is] that they make judgment superfluous and that to utter them is devoid of all risk" (297). To judge is to make the difficult determination in this particular instance—Is this beautiful or ugly? Is this right or wrong?—without the benefit of general explanations or theories that can examine this case and all its details and can come to a decision about them. Judging returns us to the world itself in all its full and messy particularity. Judgments are utterly contingent, utterly related to the circumstances of this case, and thus have no general validity—which is not to say no objective validity. It is not that judgments are totally unguided by "principle." (As we might expect, however, Arendt is skeptical that "precedent," on which the law relies so heavily, is actually as useful as judges insist [see 273].) Arendt is ringingly clear that "the purpose of a trial is to render justice, and nothing else" (252). But the principle of rendering justice offers little concrete guidance. Mostly it just returns us to the responsibility to see this case in its particularity and to make a judgment about it: "[T]he law's main business [is] to weigh the charges brought against the accused, to render judgment, and to mete out due punishment"; "Justice . . . is a matter of judgment, and about nothing does public opinion everywhere seem to be in happier agreement than that no one has the right to judge somebody else" (253).

Contrary to that "public opinion," Arendt believes we have not only the "right," but also, and more importantly, the *responsibility* to judge others, keeping in mind the "risk" involved. For if judging is characterized by its attention to particularity, the activity of judging is a crucial way that we create our own individuality. In this way, judging is similar to action; it is an identity-constituting activity. Our judgments are peculiar, particular, to ourselves; what I judge differentiates me from others who form different judgments. The product of a judgment is an "opinion" (just as the court renders an "opinion" in a case). Here lies the basis of the distinction Arendt makes between "opinion" and "interest." An "interest" (as the term is used in classical economics, adopted by Marx, and retained by Arendt) derives from my social position. If I am a state employee, I have an interest in preserving at least my part of the state and thus am not likely to support a political party pledged to cutting taxes and shrinking the state. An interest does not differentiate me from all others; it places me in sympathy with others in positions similar to my own, and in conflict with those whose positions dictate interests that threaten my interest. Interests, because they are not distinctive, are easily represented by one person who stands for the group, presenting its case in public debate. An "opinion," in Arendt's usage, is what I as an individual bring to public debate and for public consideration. An opinion is what allows me to participate in public, political interchanges as a distinctive voice. Only I can articulate my opinion in that interchange, not some representative. If the product of judging is an opinion, then judging provides me with the material that allows me to take my place, to make my presence felt, in the give-and-take that constitutes such a large part of democratic politics. Opinions are distinctive, both because they attend to the particulars of individual cases and because they are the judgments made by particular individuals in response to those cases. Obviously, this understanding of opinion flies in the face of any attempt to use "public opinion," the generalized opinion of the multitude, as a crucial datum in political debates. What Arendt undertakes in describing judging, then, is to describe the process by which opinions are formed and how they are brought into the public arena and make their claim to a validity others should acknowledge.

The analogy to Arendtian action will once again prove useful as I turn now to consider the specifics of the process of judging. Agonistic action reveals our unique identity, but that revelation (to oneself and to others) is utterly dependent on the witnessing of our actions by others in a public space of appearances. Hence, individual identity is created though competition with others with whom, on another level, we "act in concert." In a similar fashion, the formation of opinion through the process of judging moves toward attaining the desired validity by my taking into account the possible views of others in my own silent, personal deliberations. (Arendt follows Kant very closely here, although we should note that she works from four or five pages in Kant's *Critique of Judgment* that many previous commentators overlooked.) Here is one of Arendt's earliest, most provocative, and most memorable descriptions of the "enlarged" thinking that takes the standpoints of others into account:

> Political thought is representative. I form an opinion by considering a given issue from different standpoints, by making present to my mind the standpoints of those who are absent; that is, I represent them. This process of representation does not blindly adopt the actual world view of those who stand somewhere else, and hence look upon the world from a different perspective; this is a question neither of empathy, as though I tried to be or to feel like somebody else, nor of counting noses and joining a majority but of being and thinking in my own identity where actually I am not. The more people's standpoints I have present in my mind while I am pondering a given issue, and the better I can imagine how I would feel and think if I were in their place, the stronger will be my capacity for representative thinking and the more valid my final conclusions, my opinion. (It is this capacity for an "enlarged" mentality that enables men to judge; as such, it was discovered by Kant in the first part of his *Critique of Judgment*, though he did not recognize the political and moral implications of his discovery.) (*BPF*, 241)

No one would claim that Arendt is crystal clear here. As is true so often, she is more clear in designating what she does *not* mean than in specifying what she does. It is a question "of being and thinking in my own identity where actually I am not"—a beautiful, haunting phrase, but what can it possibly mean? The key to the position Arendt is groping toward becomes, in *Lectures on Kant*, "communicability." Taking a "linguistic turn" that is new to her thought, Arendt raises (briefly in *Thinking* and more fully in the Kant lectures) the issue of how I *represent* my identity to myself and others.[3] Arendt's position appears to be that my identity cannot exist—for myself or for others—unless it is "communicable," unless it takes a form that allows for its public appearance (we are back to the primary reality of appearances). Hence, "opinion" is "representative" in another sense: it represents me to

myself and to others. A process of translation, from ineffable inner experience to what can appear to others, is necessary for identity to become real. Only by taking into account where others stand and how I
might make something communicable to them can I hope they will see
the validity of my view. Even more fundamentally, only by taking
them into account can I expect them to see or hear me at all. To talk of
"being and thinking in my own identity where actually I am not"
points to this fundamental displacement of a solitary self by this infu-
sion of others into the process of forming an identity. "Kant is
aware," Arendt tells us, "that he disagrees with most thinkers in asserting that thinking, though a solitary business, depends on others to
be possible at all" (*LK*, 40). Arendt builds on this point to insist once
again (although in a manner rather different from the similar insistence
in *The Human Condition*) that the achievement of identity depends
on others to be possible at all.

This dependence is described in a passage that both recalls *The
Human Condition* (especially its consideration of the public space of
appearances that is necessary for action to take place) and departs
from the earlier work by distinguishing sharply between actors and
spectators:

> The condition *sine qua non* for the existence of beautiful objects is
> communicability; the judgment of the spectator creates the space
> without which no objects could appear at all. The public realm is
> constituted by the critics and spectators, not by the actors or makers.
> And this critic and spectator sits in every actor and fabricator; with-
> out the critical, judging faculty the doer or maker would be so iso-
> lated from the spectator that he would not even be perceived. Or,
> to put it another way, still in Kantian terms: the very originality of
> the artist (or the very novelty of the actor) depends on his making
> himself understood by those who are not artists. (*LK*, 63)

Keeping in mind that Arendt is elucidating Kant here, we can still note
that the stress on *communicability* shifts the creation of the public
sphere from actors acting in concert to the "judgment of the spectators." The actor and her action "[cannot] even be perceived" unless
they are presented in communicable ways; genius is the ability to render novelty in such a way that it can be understood, which means
that novelty must (by analogy or metaphor) always refer back to
the known, even while pushing forward the borders of expression.
The actor is able to accomplish this feat because a spectator lodges

in the actor's self as well. The spectator function is the presence of others' standpoints within me. The point of "enlarged thinking" is that the actor, in thought, already considers her actions and her ideas in the light of others' standpoints. Only through this process can difference (individual uniqueness) be perceived. The absolute singularity of identity becomes public, becomes available to others and to myself, only when the requirements of the spectator within the self and the spectators outside the self motivate the movement toward communicability. In this sense, the spectators create the public realm. For this reason, Kant insists that genius (originality, uniqueness) must bow to "taste" (the general norms of communal perception). Genius that ignores taste cannot be seen, cannot be public.

Political thinking or judgment thus turns out to be "representative" in still another sense. In Kant, a judgment of beauty is a three-step process. First, I see something and immediately respond by either liking or not liking it. (Apathy, of course, is a third possibility.) This "it pleases or displeases me" is not sufficient to call something beautiful (or, we can add for Arendt, to call something right). In the second step, I must judge the appropriateness of my immediate liking or disliking by submitting it to the imagined viewpoints of others. (This is "representative" in one sense already discussed.) This imaginative process leads me to an opinion I can assert with the confidence that it is not mere prejudice or unconsidered gut reaction. The third step is the communication of that opinion to others. Now I must be "representative" in another way. I must successfully represent my views in the language of the tribe in such a way that I can be understood. If we translate this process to the Arendtian model of action, it suggests that Arendtian ethics involves both an examination of my inclinations according to others' possible viewpoints before acting, *and* a recognition that my actions can create my identity in the world only if they take a form that can be understood by others. The stress in *The Human Condition* on "word and deed," on action as a kind of speech, has now become a stress on "communicability," on representing myself to others in ways they can comprehend. Language, we might say, is as primary a mode of appearance in human societies as are appearances registered by the senses. (Of course, language is registered by the senses, but the processing of these sensual impressions requires, in addition, the possession of specific cultural codes. The speaker of English and the speaker of German can see the same small, furry animal, but they cannot process the heard sound "dog" the same way.)

Arendt's account of judging, then, is partly an account of the requirements of appearance. To appear at all, it is not enough for humans to be physically present to one another. They must also represent to one another—in word and deed—who they are and what they think. In this way, the interiority experienced in thinking proper becomes public—and only in becoming public can it serve as one component that constitutes my identity. Given this emphasis on communicability, Arendt uses Kant's reliance on the *sensus communis* in the *Critique of Judgment* to expand her own understanding of the term. In *Thinking*, "common sense, the *sensus communis*, is a kind of sixth sense needed to keep my five senses together and guarantee that it is the same object that I see, touch, taste, smell, and hear. . . . This same sense, a mysterious 'sixth sense' because it cannot be localized as a bodily organ, fits the sensations of my strictly private five senses . . . into a common world shared by others" (*T*, 50). In *Lectures on Kant*, *sensus communis* refers to "an extra sense—like an extra metal capability . . . —that fits us into a community." At stake now is not a common world of objects, but relations of connection among humans: "The *sensus communis* is the specifically human sense because communication, i.e. speech, depends on it" (70). "Taste [which for Kant is what one acquires through repeated exercises of judgment] is this 'community sense' . . . [insofar as] 'taste is . . . the faculty of judging . . . the communicability of feelings'" (71–72). Arendt further quotes Kant, with her own clarifying additions in brackets: "We could even define taste as the faculty of judging of that which makes generally communicable . . . our feeling [like sensation] in a given representation [not perception]" (72). The *sensus communis* is experienced as this need to represent ourselves to the spectator within (in the process of enlarged thinking) and without (in the process of publicly expressing my opinion). Only in this way can we achieve that "sociability" that Kant identifies as "the highest end intended for man" (73).

If opinion is what I bring to public debate (and if "debate constitutes the very essence of political life" [*BPF*, 241]), does judging have any role to play in the adjudication among various, even conflicting, opinions within the debate? In her fullest discussion of judging prior to the Kant lectures (in the essay "The Crisis in Culture," included in

Between Past and Future), Arendt ties judgment's "validity" to the "potential agreement" it will elicit from others when communicated:

> The power of judgment rests on a potential agreement with others, and the thinking process which is active in judging something is not, like the thought process of pure reasoning, a dialogue between me and myself, but finds itself always and primarily, even if I am quite alone in making up my mind, in an anticipated communication with others with whom I must finally come to some agreement. From this potential agreement judgment derives its specific validity. (220)

This passage suggests that judgment finds its completion, even its "validity," in "agreement," as if I can know that my "enlarged thinking" has been successful only if, when I present my conclusions to others, they agree with me. But surely this is an impossible criterion to fulfill (even if we forget Arendt's statement that matters of decidable truth or fact are not political matters). If opinions are distinctive—unique to each political participant—and debate is ongoing and endless, then surely not every opinion can win the agreement of all other participants in the debate. The striking phrase for me in the passage just quoted is "others with whom I must finally come to some agreement." What is the sense and force of this "must"? With what others must I come to agreement—and what kind of agreement?

I suspect that what is troubling Arendt here is the possibility of sociability itself. We must come to some kind of agreement if we are to manage to live together at all. Recall her continued appeals to some kind of contract, some form of mutual promise, at the founding of a polity. In one sense, Arendt's ethics is very simple: we must find a way to live together because this world is occupied by humans in the plural, not by me alone. Evil, practiced with stunning frequency and chilling thoroughness in this century, is trying to eradicate that condition of plurality. Eichmann participated in something unprecedented, a "new crime" that can only be accurately named a "crime against humanity," since it was "an attack upon human diversity as such" (*EJ*, 268–69). I find myself in a world with others with whom I must come to some kind of agreement, some kind of modus vivendi that allows all of us to exist (and to be free) at the same time in this world. Judging seems crucial to Arendt because it incorporates into its very processes this acknowledgment of the existence of others. It takes others into account in forming its opinions.

But those opinions are distinctive. So how can I expect agreement from others? Wouldn't I have to abandon my opinion (at least some of the time) to agree with others? Surely I can't demand that they agree with me while I don't agree with them? And if one important function of opinion is to represent my identity, "agreement" seems the wrong word altogether. I don't "agree" with someone else's identity. I acknowledge and respond to it; I judge it and then respect, admire, or criticize it; but I don't "agree" with it.

In the Kant lectures, Arendt shifts the test of validity from agreement to communicability. She realizes that, especially under modern conditions, the *sensus communis*, the ties of community, cannot rest on shared beliefs or opinions. We might say (and once again Kant's aesthetics provides a precedent for the distinction used) that it is not the *content* of opinions but the *form* they take that establishes, maintains, and safeguards community (the continued interaction and interrelatedness among distinct individuals): "The validity of these judgments never has the validity of cognitive or scientific propositions. . . . [O]ne can never compel anyone to agree with one's judgments . . . ; one can only 'woo' or 'court' the agreement of everyone else" (*LK*, 72). To engage in this "wooing," one must put one's opinions in a form that is communicable. To successfully put opinions in that form requires the process of "enlarged thinking" and the translation into language that Arendt has described; and the very effort to shape one's thinking in a way that can be brought into debate evidences the fundamental ethical acknowledgment that I live with others and want to be in communication, in relation, with them. The definition of a political community, a populated public realm, then, would rest not on whom I agree with but on whom I keep talking to.

The public realm dissolves when I retreat into private and intimate spaces where I do not shape my ideas and feelings so that they are communicable to relative strangers, to nonintimates. Even though Arendt believes that all humans need such private spaces, she wants us to have public spaces as well, because all those who are my contemporaries cannot be my intimates and because different things can be accomplished, different satisfactions achieved, in public than can be achieved in private. The public realm also dissolves if talk cedes to violence and to other noncommunicative ways of relating to the other. We do not have community when "wooing" the agreement of others yields to compelling their obedience. And, oddly enough (but happily, if we truly cherish plurality), this suggests that sociability rests on wooing an agreement that would be fatal to the community if it were ever fully achieved. If we all agreed, what would there be to talk about? What would there be to encourage us to get our feelings and ideas into communicable form? What other viewpoints would there be for me to take into account to enlarge my thought? If plurality is threatening to us (and, clearly, on some level it is), it is also enticing. It pulls us out of ourselves and into the world, a world we can come to love precisely because it is ever changing and continually surprising and challenging us.

I assume the reader recognizes that this way of understanding the "validity" of judgments parallels fairly closely Arendt's take on action. In both cases, distinctive individual identity is achieved through interaction with others—others whose difference from me places me in an agonistic, even antagonistic, relation to them, but with whom I must also remain in relation and with whom I must communicate and interact if we are to create a public realm in which I can have an identity. I want merely to indicate briefly two consequences of this parallel. First, to stress the "form" of communicability over the "substance" of actual agreements is to risk, once again, the charge that Arendtian politics is "contentless." It is certainly worth considering whether it is really possible to have an ongoing community in the absence of all substantive agreements. At first blush, the notion seems absurd. Just think of all the agreements—to stop on red, go on green; to pay a minimum hourly wage to all workers; to spell "dog" *d-o-g*—that make various interactions within our society possible. Certainly, any one of these substantive agreements might, at some time or another, become a matter of heated dispute and might fall apart. But isn't the same true of formal agreements? I won't pursue these questions here, because I don't have an answer for them. My suspicion is that the distinction between formal and substantive, although it roughly designates agreements of different types and hence is useful, will not serve to identify one type as containing all the agreements necessary to holding a community together and the other type as containing all the agreements that could be dispensed with. My sense is that some minimal number or level of agreements is necessary for a society not to break out into civil war, and that the mix of types of agreement in that number is not as important as that that number is beyond some sort of minimal threshold. But how one could go about identifying that threshold, or even proving that some such threshold exists and is pertinent to the question being raised (e.g., What keeps a community from dissolving?), has me stumped.

The second consequence, and one that has irked some commentators on Arendt, is that judgment (as she describes it) leaves us with distinctive opinions and no way to move to some kind of adjudication about the worthiness of such opinions relative to one another. Isn't one problem of political life how to judge among the various competing opinions that are publicly aired? And isn't another problem to decide how to act after hearing all the opinions? Does judgment have no role to play as we come to take a vote at the end of the debate? It's all well and good to say that the debate is endless, but as a matter of practical consideration, we do limit debate, then take a vote, and then act on specific matters. Beyond urging us to make debate as "representative" as possible (and thus implicitly calling for "participatory" democracy because my opinions cannot be represented by another for me), Arendtian judgment has little contribution to make to the actual decisions of political bodies. To some writers this simply means that she has delivered us over to the cacophony that is political debate, without helping us think about how that debate can be transformed into a basis for collective action. In other words, democracy itself can be thought of as a process by which to attain closure in a debate where unanimity is not achieved; the agreement that the majority will rule gets us from multiple opinions to collective action. Judgment has a role to play in this process (in many accounts of democracy) in that it is during the debate preceding the vote (which identifies the position that the majority endorses) when different opinions each "woo" the agreement of the other(s). Each party to the debate then makes a judgment among the various positions articulated and votes accordingly. Judgment in Arendt, however, is utterly divorced from such public or collective decision making (just as her accounts of democracy almost never include references to voting).

Finally, we should note that Arendt closes the Kant lectures by striving to heal the rift between spectator and actor that her reflections on Kant appear to have opened. Her solution involves adopting tenets of Kant's humanism as well as his reliance on the notions of an "original compact" (*LK*, 74) and the categorical imperative. If we follow Kant in seeing "sociability as the very origin, not the goal of man's humanity, . . . the very essence of men insofar as they are of this world only" (73–74), then actor and spectator both are fundamentally guided by the "principle" of establishing and maintaining relatedness. The "original compact" is what first created relatedness; and the, "as it were, categorical imperative for action" can be stated as follows: "Always act . . . [so that] the original compact can be actualized." It is "at this point that actor and spectator become united; the maxim of the actor and the maxim of the spectator, the 'standard,' according to which the spectator judges the spectacle of the world, become one" (75). Irrespective of whether we think this appeal to "an essence" of humanity is plausible, the thrust of Arendt's description of that "political thinking" which manifests itself in "judging" is clear: against the attempted destruction of sociability (human relatedness) and plurality by totalitarianism, judging incorporates the other within the self and produces opinions that both make me distinctive and position me to communicate that distinction to others in a public forum.

Storytelling

The lecture notes on Kant also connect with an issue that runs like a red thread throughout Arendt's work, hard to miss yet never woven into a full piece of cloth: how to speak of action in such a way as to foster understanding. The unprecedented experience of totalitarianism and the novelty of action challenge our capacity to comprehend. We have already seen how Arendt is suspicious of "causal" accounts, which try to comprehend an event by showing how it is the logical or inevitable consequence of what came before it in time. We have also seen how she scorns "general" explanations, such as national character or zeitgeist; such explanations, like causal ones, do not take into account the basic contingent fact that neither all Germans nor all Jews acted the same way. And, finally, there is Arendt's desire to avoid polemic or "indoctrination." The historian's task is not to explain (since explanations hide the unique quality of the event), nor to forgive or condemn, nor to provide some kind of lesson or knowledge "with which to settle our arguments" (*EU*, 308). The historian—at least the kind of historian Arendt aspires to be—aims to promote understanding.

I have already touched on understanding and its attempt to activate the multiple meaning of things. "Meaning" for Arendt is not so much an answer to the question, Why? as it is the production or unfolding of significance. She is not addressing the question, What is the meaning of this? so much as the question, What is the meaning of life? The aim is to reconcile us to this life, to give us resources to go on. And for this task, stories are best suited: "No philosophy, no analysis, no aphorism, be it ever so profound, can compare in intensity and richness of meaning with a narrated story" (*MDT*, 22).

In contrast to the "explanations" sought by social scientists who are enamored with the model of the "hard" sciences, "understanding is closely related to the faculty of imagination" (*EU*, 404). The unprecedented experience of totalitarianism presented Arendt with various stylistic and methodological difficulties when she came to write about it. In a reply to Eric Voegelin's criticism of *The Origins of Totalitarianism*, Arendt declares that "the problem of style is a problem of adequacy and response" and, more provocatively, that an "'objective'" description of the concentration camps would be tantamount "to condon[ing] them" (404): "The natural human reaction to such conditions is one of anger and indignation because these conditions are against the dignity of man. If I describe these conditions without permitting my indignation to interfere, I have lifted this particular phenomenon out of its context in human society and have thereby robbed it of part of its nature, deprived it of one of its important qualities" (403). The complaint against the "objective" social scientific method, then, is that it reduces the event's full meaning by lifting it out of context and that this lifting is done to show how the event is an instance of a general law or trend. (The social scientist is a practitioner of determinative judgments as Kant describes them.) Arendt wants a method that moves in exactly the opposite direction, toward the fullest possible description of the informing context and toward an emphasis on the *particularity* of the event described.

Kantian reflective judgment can help in two ways. First, as we have seen, such judgment "deals with particulars" (*T*, 215). I need not reiterate this point except to stress that contexts (the historical circumstances in which a thing, person, or event is embedded) are also particular. That is, contexts particularize meaning; the same object can take on very different meanings in different contexts. Generalizations almost always depend on "abstracting" things from their contexts, so that social scientists who isolate the thing "in itself" from its context are (somewhat paradoxically) less attentive to particularity than are more narrative historians who try to understand the thing by including an account of all its surroundings.

Second, in dealing with the history of our own century, Arendt recognizes that one's own experiences are part of that context. Her "reflections" on "the problem of understanding" and on the problem of an "adequate" style were "originally caused by the special nature of my subject, and the personal experience which is necessarily involved in a historical investigation that employs imagination consciously as an important tool of cognition" (*EU*, 404). Arendt denies (in the essay "The Concept of History," an important source for considering her methodological commitments, included in *Between Past and Future*) that "objectivity" based on "the 'extinction of self'" can be achieved. Nature and history do not speak of their own accord: "[T]he confusion in the issue of 'objectivity' was to assume that there could be answers without questions and results independent of a question-asking being." In other words, all human reports about natural or historical events always emanate from a point of view. There is no "pure vision" (*BPF*, 49). Thus, the solution to partiality, to bias, is not "objectivity," not the denial of all experiential content and any other kind of input from the observer/reporter's side. Rather, Arendt aims at what Lisa Disch has strikingly called "situated impartiality" (1993, 666). Through the process of judgment, the self does not move out of the world altogether but supplements her own view, her own experiences, by taking others' views into account. Arendt's description of this process in "The Concept of History" makes the link to "understanding" explicit while clearly anticipating the Kant lectures: "[T]he Greek learned to exchange his own viewpoint, his own 'opinion'—the way the world appeared and opened up to him . . . —with those of his fellow citizens. Greeks learned to *understand*— . . . to look upon the same world from one another's standpoint, to see the same in very different and frequently opposing aspects" (*BPF*, 51). Arendt offers Homer as the prime example of this "impartiality" (51) and Thucydides as the prime example of this revisionist version of "objectivity" (52). Our thoughts arise "out of incidents of living experience and must remain bound to them as the only guideposts by which to take [their] bearings" (14). We cannot leave those experiences behind and occupy some point of unembodied knowledge that is not limited by the partiality of our standpoint. But that partiality can be tempered by the process of judgment, which "enlarges" my standpoint by taking others' standpoints into account.

Arendt offers examples and stories as two (related) ways that this taking of others' viewpoints into account can be concretely realized. Thinking of the problem in spatial terms can help dramatize what Arendt is after here. I stand in a particular place; the issue is not so much to move me from that place as to enlarge that place so that it accommodates the experience, ideas, beliefs, and opinions of others. How can I "judge" my experiences and beliefs in light of the experiences and beliefs of others—and how can I know that I have actually managed to encounter those others? Clearly, an act of imagination is required, an enlargement of my place to imaginatively include elements of others' experiences. What could stimulate such an imaginative leap? Arendt tells us that Kant offers two solutions: the first is the categorical imperative arising out of the "original compact" of sociability; the second (and "far more valuable") is "exemplary validity" (*LK*, 76). Validity enters here because it is a question of what "standard" I will measure (judge) my own viewpoint against, what articulation of some external view will garner my attention and respect so that I will feel that my own view is answerable to it. In other words, validity is a question of what other standpoints will impress me as worthy, so that I will be moved to question and revise my own viewpoint in relation to their views. Examples are crucial to Arendt because they can stand in for the general maxims that we moderns no longer possess. The example, unlike the categorical imperative or any other general law, places a concrete particular in front of me ("'example' comes from *eximere*, 'to single out some particular'" [77]) as an instance of the quality I wish to praise or condemn: "This exemplar is and remains a particular that in its very particularity reveals the generality that otherwise could not be defined. Courage is *like* Achilles" (77). Arendt prefers the specificity and the texture that the example of Achilles offers, to the more vacuous terms of a dictionary (or conduct book) definition of courage. The example shows me courage in action, courage in context.

Even more crucially perhaps, Arendt tells us that the example is a suitable form of persuasion in that realm of opinion, of nontruths, which constitutes the subject matter of the public, political debate: "That all men are created equal is not self-evident nor can it be proved. We hold this opinion because freedom is possible only among equals, and we believe that the joys and gratifications of free company are to be preferred to the doubtful pleasures of holding domination." But, in spite of the bold claim of the Declaration of Independence, "these are matters of opinion and not of truth. . . . Their validity depends upon free agreement and consent; they are arrived at by discursive, representative thinking; and they are communicated by means of persuasion and discussion" (*BPF*, 247). I cannot compel others to believe that all humans are created equal or to act upon that belief. But I can "teach by example" (247), acting out of that belief myself so that my life demonstrates the full consequences of holding and living by that opinion. Hence, Arendt turns to Socrates as the "model" of thinking at the end of *Thinking*. Not only does his example flesh out more of what thinking entails than a more abstract description could, but his example is exemplary: it offers an image of a possible life that we might wish not so much to emulate as to be worthy of. In the absence of general maxims, the example embodies another standard, another way of being in the world, against which we can judge our own lives. Arendt articulates this notion of judging one's own viewpoint against the example of others in her reference to "choosing one's company": "[O]ur decisions about right and wrong will depend upon our choice of company, with whom we wish to spend our lives. And this company [in turn] is chosen through thinking in examples, in examples of persons dead or alive, and in examples of incidents, past and present" (*LK*, 113).[4] To choose my company is to choose the concrete others whom I see as exemplary and to consider how I, in my own unique circumstances, might act in ways that would win recognition, even acclaim, from these exemplars. What would it mean to be publicly open to the scrutiny of Socrates—or to some other figure I respect highly? How could I live up to his example? With her bias toward the concrete and the particular, Arendt thinks that such considerations, such an orientation to moral exemplars, is more likely to be the source of our moral decisions than are abstract calculations about the relation of this deed to some general law, or the potential consequences of this deed on my own and others' future well-being. Examples are public embodiments, public articulations, of commitments. I not only hold this opinion, I live by it. Arendtian morality, we might say, depends on our viewing other examples and judging ourselves by them, *and* in living my own life in public view with the knowledge that that life might itself be seen as an example by others, an example (for better or worse) of what it means (in the Arendtian sense of manifesting or unfolding possibilities) to live out of the opinions and identity that are distinctively mine.

Because examples are generated in the living out of a life, they are intimately connected to stories. Socrates while alive is an example, not a story. But once his life is past, the example he offers can be presented only in story. We have seen already that Arendt believes that humans act (in part) because they desire to be remembered and that action "'produces' stories" (*HC*, 184): "*Who* somebody is or was we can know only by knowing the story of which he is himself the hero" (186). The actor, then, "[e]ven Achilles, . . . remains dependent upon the storyteller, poet, or historian, without whom everything he did remains futile" (194). Those about whom stories are told are those who are remembered; the rest pass into oblivion.

But it is not just remembrance that stories provide; they are also repositories of meaning: "[T]he story . . . begins and establishes itself as soon as the fleeting moment of the deed is past. The trouble is that whatever the character and content of the subsequent story may be, . . . its [the deed's] full meaning can reveal itself only when it is ended" (*HC*, 192). Thus, the repetition of deed in the words of the story also adds something: the revelation of meaning. Arendt's fullest meditations on the nature of this repetition can be found in her 1959 Lessing Prize speech and her essay on Isak Dinesen (both found in *Men in Dark Times*), as well as in some brief comments on Dinesen in the essay "Truth and Politics" (collected in *Between Past and Future*). It is in the "repetition" of storytelling, in which "events . . . are experienced a second time in the form of suffering by memory operating retrospectively and perceptively," that "action . . . establishes its meaning and that permanent significance which then enters into history" (*MDT*, 21). This point might seem self-evident. History does not exist until a deed is narrated; there is no history except the human deeds and events that are remembered in words or in other publicly perceivable monuments. But Arendt is adding that because every storytelling comes from a "situated" viewpoint, the story also fashions a "meaning," a "significance," for the tale it tells. Such meaning is not definitive; there is never any "last word," any final "mastering" of the past. Any event can be renarrated from another point of view, its meaning being understood differently in this new rendering (repetition) of familiar material. (Think of the many different versions of the Kennedy assassination that our culture has narrated, from the Warren Report to Don DeLillo's and Norman Mailer's books on the subject to Oliver Stone's film, to cite just a few.)

> Insofar as any "mastering" of the past is possible, it consists in relat-
> ing what has happened; but such narration, too, which shapes his-
> tory, solves no problems and assuages no suffering; it does not master
> anything once and for all. Rather, as long as the meaning of events
> remains alive—and this meaning can persist for very long periods of
> time—"mastering of the past" can take the form of ever-recurrent
> narration. The poet in a very general sense and the historian in a
> very special sense have the task of setting the process of narration in
> motion and involving us in it. (21)

Other accounts of the same event might configure its meaning differently; but only some configuring of that meaning allows the past to
become history, allows it to become a meaningful example or instance
to which we, in the present, stand in relation.

If we cannot expect "mastery" to follow from this repetition in
stories, we can expect intensity. Only a meaningful world, a world *full*
of meaning, calls to all our potential involvement in, and love for, this
world and this life: "Without repeating life in imagination you can
never be fully alive. . . . Be loyal to life, don't create fiction but accept
what life is giving you, showing yourself worthy of whatever it may be
by recollecting and pondering over it, thus repeating it in imagination;
this is the way to remain alive" (*MDT*, 97). Not surprisingly, that stories make us more alive moves Arendt back toward the goal of "reconciliation" that underwrites her concept of "understanding": "The
political function of the storyteller—historian or novelist—is to teach
acceptance of things as they are. Out of this acceptance . . . arises the
faculty of judgment—that again, in Isak Dinesen's words[,] . . . 'is
what is named the day of judgment'" (*BPF*, 262). (Arendt goes on to
say that "these politically relevant functions are performed from outside the political realm" [262], a point to which I will return in the
conclusion of this chapter.) An alternative formulation of this same
point may make it easier to grasp the connections among storytelling,
meaning, reconciliation, and judgment that Arendt is suggesting: "It is
true that storytelling reveals meaning without the error of defining it,
that it brings about consent and reconciliation with things as they really are, and that we may even trust it to contain eventually by implication that last word we expect from 'the day of judgment'" (*MDT*,
105).

I can only gloss this rather obscure passage by saying that storytelling opens up meaning in ways that multiply significance and resist

closure. Such storytelling highlights possibility—especially the possibility of novel action—against determination or predetermination. The uncharted, infinite horizon of possibility, the conditions of natality and plurality, reconcile us to the world. But we should not mistake a refusal to "define" meaning in any determinate or univocal way with a refusal to present some definite meaning as possible, as articulated in this story. If stories look toward some "last word," it is because they offer definite "opinions" even as they do not make any claim to definitive "truth." And we might also suspect that the "last word" in Arendt, the word that stories and judgments continually rediscover and honor, is the embracing of the sheer plurality of this world. This, as I have already argued, is the ethical significance of the activity of judging in Arendt: judging, in its very modus operandi, acknowledges and accepts plurality. Storytelling is the way that judgments about the past are best articulated, because stories also acknowledge and activate plurality through the opening of possible meanings.

Because judgments and stories neither convey truth nor impart information, they are not so much something that can be taught as something that should be experienced. Arendt quotes Kant: "[J]udgment is a peculiar talent which can be practiced only, and cannot be taught" (*LK*, 84). The opening up of meaning and the formation of an opinion about an event that does not fit preexisting general laws or expectations are "experience[s] in thinking," and they "can be won, like all experiences in doing something, only through practice, through exercises" (*BPF*, 14). Arendt wants her own writings to function this way. They are aimed not at imparting information nor at getting the passive reader to accept the "truth" or "force" of Arendt's positions; rather, she writes in the preface to *Between Past and Future*, her essays' "only aim is to gain experience in *how* to think; they do not contain prescriptions on what to think or which truths to hold" (14). As Melvyn Hill puts it, "Hannah Arendt does not so much tell us what to think or what to do, as she offers an example of how we might engage in thinking given the conditions of our world" (Hill, x).

It seems fitting to close with an example this discussion of Arendt's notion of storytelling and of her own ambition to move others to the *practice* of thinking. In *Eichmann in Jerusalem*, Arendt narrates a "dramatic moment" in the trial, a "few minutes" during which "a hush settled over the courtroom" (*EJ*, 230, 231). Certainly, Arendt's story of these few minutes stands out as one of the most moving and passionate moments in her own text: "[I]n those two minutes, which were like a sudden burst of light in the midst of impenetrable, unfathomable darkness, a single thought stood out clearly, irrefutably, beyond question—how utterly different everything would be today in this courtroom, in Israel, in Germany, in all of Europe, and perhaps in all countries of the world, if only more such stories could have been told" (231). The story recalls the deeds of Anton Schmidt, a sergeant in the German army, who "helped the Jewish partisans [in Poland] by supplying them with forged papers and military trucks . . . for five months, from October, 1941, to March, 1942," at which time he "was arrested and executed" (230). Other examples of non-Jews helping Jews were described during Eichmann's trial, "[b]ut this mention of Schmidt was the first and last time that any such story was told of a German" (231).

The absolute centrality of storytelling to Arendt's understanding of how we can manage to "go on" after the experience of totalitarianism and the Holocaust becomes evident in what she tells us the story of Schmidt accomplishes:

> It is true that totalitarian domination tried to establish these holes of oblivion into which all deeds, good and evil, would disappear, but the Nazis' feverish attempts . . . to let their opponents "disappear in silent anonymity" were in vain. The holes of oblivion do not exist. Nothing human is that perfect, and there are simply too many people in the world to make oblivion possible. One man will always be left alive to tell the story. Hence, nothing can ever be "practically useless," at least, not in the long run. It would be of great practical usefulness for Germany today, not merely for her prestige abroad but for her sadly confused inner condition, if there were more such stories to be told. For the lesson of such stories is simple and within everybody's grasp. Politically speaking, it is that under conditions of terror most people will comply but *some people will not,* just as the lesson of the countries to which the Final Solution was proposed is that "it could happen" in most places but *it did not happen everywhere.* Humanly speaking, no more is required, and no more can be reasonably asked, for this planet to remain a place fit for human habitation. (*EJ,* 233)

I feel like asking for a pause—especially to let that last sentence sink in. This story of the German sergeant, if it reminds us that evil is not inevitable, that even totalitarianism and terror cannot wipe goodness off the earth nor obliterate the memory of those good deeds, is all we need to be reconciled to this world. We cannot "reasonably" ask for more than the possibility of goodness and the certainty ("one man will always be left alive to tell the story") that it will be remembered in story.

Can a story bear this much weight? Perhaps not. Perhaps, even if we are moved, we will say that we need more to be convinced that life after Auschwitz can be affirmed. It is typical of Arendt both that she rejects cynicism, nihilism, and despair (her works try to make "love of this world" central to our lives and possible under the dispiriting conditions of modernity) *and* that she offers no metaphysical, transcendental, or ironclad solution to the problem of evil. All we have are our human resources, our human responses, our human knowledge and memories. Evil happens. Evil is human, too—even banally so—completely ordinary in its ever presence. We cannot be inoculated against evil once and for all. The world is saved only in the daily actions of those who love it and who work mightily to create and preserve it in concert with their fellow human beings. Confronted with the organized evil of totalitarianism, these human resources often seem hardly up to the task of preserving a world we could want to inhabit. Individual actions like Anton Schmidt's seem ineffectual, even pointless.

For Arendt, however, it is only on the level of individual deeds that resistance to evil (especially totalitarian evil) can be enacted, because it is precisely the generalizing and abstracting forces of modernity that are the sources of evil in our time. Against everything that would subsume the individual within the mass, that would render individual differences and individual existence "superfluous" and would obliterate the memory of individual deeds, stands the exemplary deed and the story that retells it. Against evil stands the "solitary" act of thinking, in which the thinker conducts a dialogue with herself and feels answerable to her own internal standards. Against evil stands the "more political" act of judgment, in which the individual takes others into account but still takes up the individual responsibility to form an "opinion," to refuse to take at face value what the world presents before considering its worthiness to be called "beautiful" or "right" in reference to the "standards" and "examples" that one chooses as one's company in making these determinations.

And, finally, there are deeds of resistance undertaken in those moments of extremity when one must fight force with force. At such moments, Arendt tells us, one's "care for the world" must take "precedence" over one's "care for the self." I must abandon my concern for self-preservation and/or self-righteousness, for the demands of the moment: "Though it is true that, by resisting evil, you are likely to be involved in evil, your care for the world takes precedence in politics over your care for yourself—whether this self is your body or your soul. (Machiavelli's: 'I love my native city more than my soul' is only a variation of: I love the world and its future more than my life or my self.)" (*LK*, 50). A love of this world that exceeds one's love of oneself may be, in drastic times, the only resource against the world-obliterating designs of evil. No wonder Anton Schmidt is such an exemplary hero, such a crucially important figure, for Arendt. And it is also no wonder that the horror she cannot bear to contemplate is that such deeds could be performed and yet never find their storyteller. When there is no one left alive to tell the tale of goodness as exemplar and the tale of evil with indignation, then this world will have been truly and utterly lost to humans.

Conclusion: Are We Being Political Yet?

That Arendt identifies the "political function" of the storyteller *and* says that this function is "performed from outside the political realm" (*BPF*, 262) highlights the difficulties raised for readers of her later works. The mental activities of thinking and judging, like her ethical musings, are undertaken with constant reference to the political, but they themselves are not quite political. Thus, her work still seems utterly oriented toward the political, but now it also seems to be considering activities that are apart from the political—and that stand in an uncertain relation to it. The banal evil that Arendt wants to combat is the antithesis of politics as she understands that term, but evil operates in the very space where politics should be—but is not—in a totalitarian or (to a lesser extent) mass society. If totalitarianism or the bureaucratic "rule by Nobody" (*OV*, 137) has replaced politics, is there a place outside politics from which politics can be revived?

In looking to thinking, judging, and storytelling, Arendt is (to some extent) pondering what the intellectual can do to stand against the perversion of the political in the twentieth century. She states in the 1972 colloquium transcribed in Hill, "I, by nature, am not an actor" (306), but one who, as a thinker and writer, has "spoken out of the experience of thinking" (305) and thus has had so much to say about action because "I had this advantage to look at something from outside" (306). Her final works explore the resources of this "outside" and their "politically relevant functions" (*BPF*, 262). The intellectual and the storyteller are not actors but spectators, who are not engaged in the concerted creation of identity and the public space of appearances in the present. Against the heroic, courageous, and world-creating action of political agents (which makes her account of politics so inspiring), Arendt makes very modest claims for what the thinker and writer might accomplish. Challenged in the 1972 colloquium to show how her work advances her (or anyone else's) political commitments and attempts to solve pressing social problems, Arendt replies: "I cannot tell you black on white—and would hate to do it— what the consequences of this kind of thought which I try, not to indoctrinate, but to rouse or to awaken in my students, are, in actual politics. . . . But one thing I would hope: that certain extreme things which are the actual consequence of non-thinking . . . will not be capable [of arising]" if her students adopt the practice of "think[ing] 'critically'"(Hill, 309; brackets in original). The political "relevance" of thinking and judging is not direct and certainly does not translate into any determinate political position on either the left or the right.

Arendt's political theory, we might say, presents her utopian vision of the world at its fullest. Her account of thinking, on the other hand, presents her minimalist account of a place to start if we are looking to prevent evil and its destruction of a world that "lies between" humans. And just as Kant needed judging to create a bridge between the first and second critiques, a way (to put it roughly) to get from fact to value so that we may find this a world we can live in, given our commitments; so Arendt needs judging to get from thinking to politics. That she uses judging as this bridge reinforces the fundamental intersubjective basis of Arendtian politics, the fact that the bottom line of her politics is that I live with others in a world that I create with them. This premise is so crucial that Arendt comes to equate the acknowledgment of it with a reconciliation with reality and with having more than halfway won the battle of preserving politics.

Although the later works are absolutely faithful to the way Arendt describes politics throughout her career, they add an ethical vision that recognizes that her politics implies a moral commitment to plurality and an ontological commitment to that plurality's manifestation in the multiple appearances of this world. From thinking's withdrawal from the world of appearances, we move to judging, which is a kind of halfway house, one where I am still solitary, still a spectator, still on the outside of the political, but where I am already engaging with others (whose viewpoints I consider) and with appearances (which I judge). There is nothing in Arendt to say that I think first, then judge, then act (will). These activities can occur in any particular order. She thus indicates that we are not political all of the time—and that to demand direct political consequences from the activities of the intellectual is inappropriate. We are political, however, when we are being-for-others and being-for-the-world. But even thinking, which is most fully for-myself and not for-others, is potentially "politically relevant." We should not, therefore, regard whether an activity is "political" or not as the litmus test of its worthiness. Rather, we should recognize that there is a plurality of activities, each with its own rationale and legitimacy, each enabling and establishing a certain relation to the world. Such activities are politically significant and oppose evil to the extent that they acknowledge the experience of plurality and strive to embrace and broaden the possibilities (including risks and anxieties, as well as exhilarating change and intensity) that plurality affords.

4
Arendt Now

To write about what Arendt means to us and has to offer us *now* is to suppose that there is some way to define our present moment. For a short time in the 1960s, at the height of the Civil Rights and student movements and at the beginning of contemporary feminism, and then again in the early to middle 1980s, in the articulation of and debate about the term "postmodernism," our era seemed to have a readily identifiable focus, a set of discernible concerns and conflicts. But the 1990s, like the 1970s, appear more diffuse, a decade of drifting defined mostly by the qualifier "after": after Communism in Europe, after the boom 1980s in America, after feminism, after postmodernism. We are slouching toward the millennium, the utopian promise of 1989 having yielded little but political chaos and economic hardship in the former Soviet Union and its satellites, while the Western democracies experience the unraveling of the welfare state consensus that prevailed from 1930 to 1980. Deprived of the grand apocalyptic narrative provided by the cold war, the social democracies of the West find themselves increasingly unable to foot the bills for the services promised to the elderly, the sick, the poor, and the ordinary workers. The gap in the West between the haves and the have-nots is wider than at any time since 1945, partly as a result of a "global economy" in which unskilled and semiskilled jobs have moved from Western countries to more impoverished lands where much lower wages prevail, or are performed domestically by imported "immigrant" workers. This economic transformation, coupled with demographic changes that include aging populations and large influxes of immigrants from nonwhite portions of the world, has rendered conflicts of resource allocation and distribution more virulent than at any time in recent memory. Meanwhile, the apparently interminable internecine violence in Africa, the Middle East, and Eastern Europe offers an image of the direction in which Western conflicts could lead—and of a general impotence to find ways for people to live together in peace. Out from under the shadow of the atom bomb (at least for the moment), none of these problems carries the threat of obliterating human life; they are more like AIDS—dangerous, deadly, and ever present as they prove resistant to all our best efforts to control or eliminate them.

Diffuse times have their advantages, if we can avoid low-energy depression or despair. When the stakes don't seem quite so high, when we are not in a permanent crisis mode, there is more opportunity for reflection and experimentation. On the domestic American scene, I think we can see this reflective mode at work both in politics and in the academy. My sense of things will inevitably strike some as naive or just willfully blind. Certainly, much has been written of the polarization of American politics, with elites of all stripes (but particularly liberal to leftist elites) bemoaning the Republican Right's pandering to populist passions that include racism, xenophobia, homophobia, and paranoid suspicion of the government. I know that Rush Limbaugh, Pat Buchanan, and Newt Gingrich are valuable rallying points for a Left that needs to organize its forces, but I think we seriously misread the current political landscape if we take that trio as emblematic of our time. Yes, there is a growing sense that a number of our institutions are dysfunctional (to use the day's jargon)—a conviction that has led to wholesale denunciations of the government on the extreme Right, and (much more significantly) to the cynicism-laden apathy that leads many Americans to resolutely refuse to pay any attention to politicians, elections, and/or public debates. (I would caution, however, that any reading of citizen apathy needs to recognize that for the millions of Americans who work long hours for minimal pay, daily survival is so constant a struggle that the time and energy needed to attend to political matters simply are not available.) Although the recognition that much has gone wrong with our political infrastructure is a factor in the political ills we currently suffer, it has also been a source of creative thinking about issues ranging from tax reform to campaign financing to proportional representation to the creation of new political parties. Admittedly, actual change has proved hard to come by. But along with the contentious heat currently emanating from our gridlocked government, there has been some serious thinking going on. I still have hope that, just as the Progressive Era eventually led to the significant reforms of 1912–19 (direct election of senators, the income tax, the vote for women), so our times are the foreground for significant interventions in the forms and practices of American democracy.

On the academic front, I see a retreat (on both sides) from the more hysterical and apocalyptic claim that postmodern theory meant the end of Western civilization as we knew it. One side feared that death while the other tried to hasten it along, but both believed nothing less was at stake than modernity itself, the whole way Western life (at both the societal and the individual levels) has been organized and experienced for the past four hundred years. The stakes seem much less high today. For one thing, the 1989 fall of the Soviet empire has made it clear that the West, for better or worse, is the bloodied warrior left standing after the self-destructive cold war, when the Soviets spent themselves into bankruptcy in the arms and space races. (The United States flirted with doing the same during the 1980s, but we had the unarmed Germans and Japanese on hand to buy up our debt.)[1] On the more positive side of the ledger, the admirable and heroic actions of Russian and East European dissidents suggested that there was much more life left in certain Western, liberal notions, such as rights, personal integrity, courage, and civil society, than postmodern theory had allowed. At the same time, adherents of the so-called new social movements in the West (feminism, gay rights, and ethnic or racial rights), which had been inspired by and, to a certain extent, had aligned themselves with postmodern theory, began to worry about issues of agency and commitment that the new theory seemed to ignore or to slight. The result has been, in the 1990s, a renewed interest in a more open-minded encounter with the liberal tradition, where contempt for all things liberal is replaced with a consideration of what might prove useful in current circumstances. (It doesn't hurt that right-wing Republicans have tried to make the label "liberal" deadly for any mainstream politician. If Ronald Reagan and Newt Gingrich hate liberals that much, there must be more to like in the term than we previously thought.) One symptom of the shift in theory since the 1980s has been the explosion of work in ethics among social, political, and literary theorists. This interest in ethics reflects an attempt to reformulate notions of agency, responsibility, belief, and commitment in light of postmodern theories that questioned the ability of selves to stand apart from linguistic and ideological structures or forces. For many (among whom I count myself), the intellectual task of our time is to think through postmodern theory, acknowledging its seriousness and cogency, to arrive at a rearticulated sense of which facets of modernity (as embodied in both its sociopolitical and its intellectual legacies) we wish to retain (even in altered forms) and which we should jettison.

I can make this formulation of our fin de millénaire task sound less academic if I insist that the questioning of modernity occasioned by postmodern theory hardly relies on a familiarity with the work of Jacques Derrida, Michel Foucault, or Catharine MacKinnon. When the American Right sees a whole way of life as threatened by non-English-speaking immigrants and the banning of prayer from public schools, we don't need postmodern theory to tell us that the ability of pluralistic democracies to actually live with "difference" is at stake. No one today imagines that we have achieved "the end of ideology" (the title of Daniel Bell's famous 1960 book) or that modernity has been experienced or accepted by all as an unmixed blessing. Challenges to the fruits of modernity are highly visible today, posed by a wide range of social actors, from proponents of "creationism" to the most fervent ethnic separatists to activists who protest against the environmental and human costs of the global economy. We live every day with what modernity has wrought and, for a variety of reasons, in today's world modernity seems less a fate we must suffer than a historical legacy with which we must come to terms. We have the task of renewing those parts of the legacy that still seem to enable us to live for ourselves and with others in ways that we can affirm, and rescripting that legacy where it betrays our convictions about what is right and what is desirable. Of course, there is ongoing disagreement about which parts of the legacy are useful and which harmful.

That Arendt can help us think about modernity and our relationship to it is, I hope, obvious to all who have read the first three chapters of this book. Here, in this final chapter, I will confine myself to two issues: how Arendt's understanding of the political expands the meaning of democracy, thus indicating political needs and desires that confound the usual issues adopted as the platforms of Left and Right

in our day; and how Arendt's ontological stress on appearances, epistemological reliance on examples and storytelling, and political theory
of action in concert offer resources to efforts to construct an ethics in
the wake of postmodern theory.

What I will not do in this chapter is consider the ways that other
recent writers have found Arendt's work helpful in their engagement
with a wide variety of contemporary issues. There has been a lively
discussion of Arendt's work among feminists, an active enlistment of
Arendt in the debate between Habermas and the poststructuralists
(with proponents on both sides viewing Arendt as their ally), and continual references to Arendt among those working on topics ranging
from democratic theory to nationalism to racism to human rights. I
have listed some of this contemporary work, with short descriptions,
under the heading "For Further Reading" at the end of this book. My
decision not to engage with other commentators on Arendt is partly
practical (there is so much work out there that I would feel compelled
to respond to) and partly deliberate policy: the goal of this book is to
engage with Arendt, and the first thing I want to accomplish is to send
readers to (or back to) Arendt's own writings.

The Meaning of Democracy

The years 1989–90 saw the founding of a startling number of new nations in what had been the Soviet Union and its Eastern European
satellites. While economists (sometimes hired by the new governments
as consultants) sketched what it meant to move from a "command" to
a "market" economy, political theorists considered how to move from
one-party states to democracies. Progress on both fronts has been
slow. The benefits of Western-style economics and politics have hardly
proved obvious to the people of Eastern Europe, a fact that should be
seen not as evidence of "their" backwardness so much as an indication that "our" institutions and values could use some revision. In any
case, both the hopes and the disappointments that have followed the
exhilarating years 1989–90 have occasioned new attention to the
forms, limitations, and goals of democracy. And even before 1989, in
works such as Ernesto Laclau and Chantal Mouffe's much discussed
Hegemony and Socialist Strategy (1985), there was a growing sense
that questions of democracy raised issues that the Left's traditional
focus on economic goods and class struggles missed. Because democ-

racy in and of itself is a good, people will take to the streets (or perform other, less dramatic actions) to obtain or protect it. In the contemporary effort to articulate why democracy can mean so much to us, Arendt can be a great help.

In titling this section "The Meaning of Democracy," I am using "meaning" in the Arendtian sense. What strikes me as most valuable in Arendt's political theory is the way she opens up and expands our conception of what politics might include. At first it may seem odd to call Arendtian politics expansive, as she takes such pains to tell us what is *not* political. But her vision is expansive when we focus on the *experience* of politics. What Arendt highlights for us is the distinctive experience of appearing in public. Politics in our time has dwindled down to issues of allocation of resources and of protection or expansion of rights. We tend to define the political in terms of content. If something is an issue of public resources or of the interface between government and the nongovernmental (be it a corporation or a self), we consider it political. Thus, the political has shrunk to the interactions between political institutions and selves who live primarily apart from those institutions.[2] Those interactions are usually, if not painful, at least burdensome. We go to the state when we feel entitled to something (from good roads to unemployment benefits to protection from criminals) or when we feel our rights have been violated (either by some branch of the government or by some other social actor). Government provides services and a "safety net" for its taxpayers. Apart from issues of rights, the relation of such a government to its citizens is little different than the relationship of a department store to its customers. Citizens will vote into power the party that most efficiently delivers the goods at the least cost. Political arguments will be about which services the government should provide and how it should pay the costs of providing those services. Certain conservative politicians in contemporary America not only see nothing wrong with this model of the state, but even believe that if we could just get everyone to view the state in this way, we would be better off. (This variety of contemporary conservatism is sometimes called neoliberalism, a label that accurately sums up the sources of its ideas in the "classical liberal" political economists, most notably Adam Smith.) Once we think of taxpayers as customers, we will recognize that efficiency and good service are what we should demand of our government; and once we consistently make these demands, we will get better government.

If the past thirty-plus years of social unrest have taught us any-thing, it is that citizens do not relate to governments as customers do to department stores. Even the most business-oriented neoliberal must face the fact that his supporters include another type of conservative (sometimes called a "social" or "cultural conservative"), one for whom "values" issues, such as school prayer, abortion, and drug use, are more important than economic issues or even the amount he pays in taxes. To a certain extent, these cultural conservatives are actually protesting the social disruptions that come in the wake of the kind of modern economic practices that the neoliberals espouse. Of course, this potential fundamental conflict between the two largest groups in the Republican Party has been mostly papered over thus far, despite Pat Buchanan's efforts. The Republican Party over the past thirty years has consistently used values issues to win elections, although it has done little to advance its "cultural agenda" once in office. There is an obvious fissure, an inconsistency, in Republican attitudes toward gov-ernment, one most dramatically revealed by Ronald Reagan's running up the deficit while preaching the goal of smaller government. Repub-licans want to shrink the government insofar as it regulates business and redistributes wealth through welfare, Medicaid, and other social programs, but they (for the most part) want to expand the govern-ment insofar as it regulates individuals' deviant behavior (however de-fined) and provides for national defense. On the Right, only a libertar-ian position is consistent, an anarchic individualism that follows to its logical consequences Thoreau's dictum that the best government is the one that governs least, calling for no public schools, no farm subsi-dies, no national parks, and no standing army beyond what is needed for protection from criminals.

The Democrats are no more consistent. They want a powerful government to counterbalance the large power that corporations pos-sess in a modern economy, but they want a minimalist government when it comes to value concerns, which they hold to be matters of personal, private decision. (The consistent position on the Left—a mirror image of libertarianism—is a socialism that advocates the state ownership and management of everything—a position about as at-tractive as its counterpart.) One way to make this point about incon-sistency is to say that although Democrats have inherited the "liberal" label, in fact Democrats and Republicans have divided up what was once a much more consistent liberal political philosophy. Republicans have adopted the laissez-faire part of liberalism in relation to economic matters, whereas Democrats have adopted the laissez-faire part of liberalism in regard to personal behavior. Each side thus gets to accuse the other of violating rights. Democrats see Republicans as violating rights to privacy as well as encroaching on the rights that protect citizens in criminal and civil court proceedings. Republicans see Democrats as violating the rights of property owners and other economic agents. These differences have been complicated by the growth of the welfare state in the twentieth century, which has added a new role to government. Since its advent, the government has been seen as responsible not just for the protection of its citizens (both the protection of their rights and the protection of their life and property from the aggression of other citizens or other nations) but also for providing a minimum sustenance for those citizens. "Liberal" has become the term that designates those who wish to maintain, even expand, governmental involvement in sustenance (involving the government not just in providing food and housing for the poor, but also in finding jobs for those needing them and securing health care and retirement benefits for all workers), whereas "conservative" designates those who would limit the sustenance function of government and focus on its protection function. I agree with Richard Rorty's statement (1995) that the fundamental political divide of our time is whether we think the government should be oriented to serving the needs of its poorest citizens or whether it should be oriented to protecting the property and opportunities of its most prosperous citizens. Of course, there is a moral position buried not too far below this political divide—a moral position about the causes (and about who is to blame) for poverty amid plenty in a wealthy country such as ours, which has the highest rate of indigent children among all industrial nations.

My point is not that a consistent attitude toward the state is desirable or necessary. The point is that Left and Right, as currently understood, designate what one wants the state to do and not to do. Our entire conception of politics has shrunk to this focus on citizens' relation to the state. And it is precisely here that Arendtian politics is expansive. From Arendt's point of view, politics, as currently practiced, infantilizes citizens. We act as if all power is vested in the state, to whom we must appeal, begging for its largesse or notice or remediation of wrongs. It is no surprise that citizens so disempowered come to resent politicians as privileged, out of touch, and ignorant or contemptuous of the real needs of the citizenry. The very imbalance of power between the government and its people almost inevitably breeds resentment.

Arendt points us in an entirely different direction, away from government toward what is sometimes called "civil society." This term indicates spaces of public involvement (i.e., interaction with nonfamilial others in a space outside the home) that are (at most) only indirectly linked to the state. Although I have to be somewhat unfaithful to her work to make this argument, much in Arendt calls us to focus on the various public spaces in which people act together to achieve some collective goal. Take, for example, an AIDS action group. Such a group might engage in a wide range of activities: fund-raising to help AIDS patients pay medical expenses; arranging home and hospital visits to the sick; running meetings for people who are HIV positive and/ or for their relatives, friends, and lovers; and using various means (from demonstrations to lobbying to getting involved in electoral politics) to influence the government's actions. Arendt's work leads us to emphasize that such an AIDS action group creates a public space in which the various people involved work together in ways that provide them an identity within a community that recognizes and values actions that accord with its values (humane, helpful, and effective responses to the suffering of those with AIDS).

It may seem strange to say that such work can be its own reward—and certainly we do not want to belittle the good (helping people with AIDS) that the work aims for. But Arendt leads us to see that what people do together has the added benefit of creating their togetherness, of placing them in relation to one another in a public space that gives them a way of having identities vis-à-vis one another. One great problem of our political, economic, and social theories has been that they have few ways of talking about this good—the good of togetherness, of sociality itself. It is often lamented that modernity, with its large cities and large corporations and large bureaucracies (including, but not limited to, government), destroys the communities of yesteryear. What Arendt indicates is that our notion of community has been both too place-bound (stuck on the image of a shared place, some lost village) and too all-encompassing (as if one belonged to only one community and that others who also belonged to that community were members of it alone). A community exists wherever there is collective action—action that creates the space in which it unfolds, that shapes the identity I possess vis-à-vis these specific others in this specific space, and that reveals new possibilities and new identities even as it moves toward its stated purpose (which also might change as we go along). An AIDS action group is not a community because it shares a place; it is a community because these people act in concert. And the people involved in an AIDS group act in concert with a different set of people when engaged in other activities. At any time, I might be a participant in any number of such collective actions, be a member of any number of communities, although, given the modern bias against the public, it is no surprise that many possible tasks for collective action have been alienated from the citizenry and delegated to the government. I could be the member of many communities, but most likely I am not if I live in 1998. This is what contemporary writers are bemoaning when they talk of the decline of civic or civil society—the absence of public spaces apart from the government, spaces like the ones created out of necessity by the Eastern European dissidents, who shaped what might seem a contradiction in terms: an underground public culture. What is needed are sources of connection, interaction, and interrelatedness among citizens apart from the state—but also apart from the intimacies of private life.

We are not talking about family relations here, and not even about friendships, but about public relations among relative (not total) strangers who act together in a publicly visible space. I am tempted to go so far as to say that what defines such work as publicly visible is that it is addressed to the polity as a whole. That is, my friendships are my private affair, and I don't expect the world to take any notice of them one way or another. But my AIDS activism has an element that is meant to be seen and judged by others, that is meant to communicate what I regard as proper ways to respond to AIDS, and to garner others' response to the fact of AIDS. It seems to me that Arendtian ethics helps us here—and serves somewhat to fill out her sometimes overly restrictive view of politics. Action in the public sphere is exemplary, communicative; it sends a message about what can be done and calls on others in the polity (either other citizens or other institutions, including the government) to judge my actions in relation to the situation to which I, with others, am responding. The creation of public spaces through collective action, then, need not result in a multitude of isolated spaces, because the spaces' openness to view renders them examples of possible action for the others who are spectators.

In other words, Arendt points us to a different way to think of democracy. It is not the election of government officials that is crucial, but the proliferation of public spaces in which people work together as partners in collectively reaching (or at least forwarding) some goal and gain an identity through that activity. In this way, citizens are empowered, not infantilized. The focus is on citizens' activities in a multitude of spaces (and on membership in multiple spaces as well), not on the government's monopoly of all things "political." Democracy does not delineate the citizens' relation to the state, but instead indicates an ideal for the citizens' relations to one another. The way to judge a democracy is not by some poll that tells us the president's approval rating, but by the quality of the public relationships it fosters. A various, lively, contentious, invigorating, and challenging public life is what we look to democracy to achieve. Perhaps the closest I've come to this experience in my own life is in teaching a good class at the university—a class in which passionate engagement with the subject matter grows week by week because I am startled, provoked, and transformed by the opinions expressed by other members of the class and thus am moved to articulate my own ideas, both to sort out for myself what I really believe and to influence the other members of the class, as I have come to care about what they think as well.

It might seem inappropriate to use the word "democracy" to describe such interactions. But several considerations suggest that "democracy" is the right word after all. For starters, Arendt would insist that the success of such actions in concert (as measured by the quality of the interactions and the ability to sustain the public space over time) is absolutely dependent on equality among the participants. Such equality does not mean no division of labor, no recognition of expertise. In the example of the university class, to recognize that the teacher knows more about the subject matter and has the responsibility to guide the discussion need not be fatal to a fully democratic interaction. But it will be fatal if disparities in knowledge and experience are seen as rendering some opinions less valid than others. All opinions will be tested through their reception by the others in the class. Students will learn to think through their opinions more thoroughly before articulating them, by experiencing how opinions are taken up by others in discussion. Thus, the very experience of discussion will lead us to consider others' possible reactions before speaking out. But the fact that all opinions will be judged, that not all opinions will end up proving equally fruitful or interesting, means that no opinion, prior to its being worked through by the group, is ruled unworthy of serious consideration. The kind of class I am describing is impossible if the professor's knowledge is deemed to render her or his opinions more worthy than the students'. In situations where that premise rules, the result is never discussion but only the professor's articulation of knowledge that students are expected to imbibe.

My intention is not to declare lecture classes evil; they are just undemocratic. My example is chosen to illustrate how essential equality is to interactions that Arendt would call democratic, not to argue that all classes—or all human interactions—should be democratic. Arendt herself would have thought democracy inappropriate in the classroom, insofar as knowledge, not opinion, is the material to be communicated. Pushing democracy in the way I have been doing here inevitably raises the question of how much (that is, what sectors) of our public life should be democratic? "Democratic," in Arendt's sense, is an adjective that can be applied to any public sphere of activity in which participants are equal, in which their actions reveal their identity, and in which the activities of all the participants create and maintain the very space and the interrelations required for that activity to occur.

If we accept an understanding of democracy along these lines, the terms of "Left" and "Right" shift dramatically. (Arendt herself said that she "couldn't care less" about the distinction between Left and Right, because she did not believe "that the real questions of this century will get any kind of illumination" by figuring out whether someone's work is conservative, liberal, socialist, or something else. She acknowledges that "the left think that I am a conservative, and the conservatives sometimes think I am left or I am a maverick or God knows what" [Hill, 333–34].) Instead of focusing on what the government should or should not do, the issue now becomes what spheres of interrelatedness should or should not be democratic. The infantilization of citizens in politics parallels their infantilization in the workplace. Using the word "management" to refer to our business enterprises' upper echelons is revealing. Workers, like citizens, are all too often viewed as unruly and untrustworthy; they need to be carefully managed if one hopes to extract work—or votes—from them. The contempt for the voter and the worker is plain to see in contemporary politics and industrial relations.

In the workplace, that contempt has recently been expressed economically as well as in employee-employer relations. The growing gap between management's megasalaries and the shrinking purchasing power of worker salaries indicates that political inequality is usually expressed as economic inequality—and vice versa. There is no way to completely disentangle the two, even if they are theoretically distinct—a point Arendt failed to see. (The gap in pay levels for men and women who do the exact same job offers a pointed illustration of the fact that in our society, an unrelated kind of inequality plays itself out in economic inequality, even though the market, in theory, should be "blind" to gender—or other—differences.) This persistence of what we might call "economic symbolization" (the economic rendering of noneconomic inequalities), coupled with the disadvantages that burden the less well-off when entering any public sphere, means that Left and Right will continue to be defined by the Left's insistence that economic factors play a role in *all* sociopolitical interactions and the Right's equally adamant insistence that the market is not influenced by sociopolitical factors and that things like "family values" and racial prejudice have no economic causes, components, or ramifications.

But a focus on democracy in the Arendtian sense does shift the characteristics of Left and Right, because the issue becomes not economic redistribution so much as equality of participation. To use an old-fashioned word, the issue is dignity more than money. Or, it is an issue of money only insofar as money signifies social worth. What Arendt claimed, and what many events over the past thirty years confirm, is that identity—being able to act freely out of one's convictions and aims in ways that others respond to, that have an impact on the world—is at stake in politics as much as, if not more, than economic concerns are. To take a trivial, but telling, example, think how often people protest a decision not primarily because they disagree with it, but because they were not consulted as the decision was being made. People are able to go along with all kinds of policies they oppose, so long as they are involved, are given a choice to voice their objections, and have the sense that those objections were truly heard and considered. In such circumstances, it seems that what people most want is to be acknowledged as parties to the interaction, participants whose right to "have an input" is recognized. It is the participation itself that is at stake and is as satisfying as the actual outcome. In other words, the symbolics of the process are often (although not always) more important than the substantive decisions made. (It is an interesting question, although one I cannot pursue here, just how much adoption of democratic processes would influence the substantive decisions made. Some theorists of democracy write as if being more democratic would necessarily result in the kinds of social policies they favor. I suspect the connection would hardly be so automatic. But just what the connection would be is difficult to predict. For Arendt, the benefits of the process itself make the question of its concrete, substantive results of little interest.)

My argument pushes us toward seeing Arendt as advocating what Cornel West calls "a culture of creative democracy" (1989, 239). Democracy comes to seem "cultural" when it is viewed as setting the terms for all public interactions among citizens, instead of just designating a set of governmental institutions, regular elections, and a bill of rights. A democratic culture is one in which the public possibilities for equal participation in collective processes and action are multiplied, and in which citizens are empowered precisely because these public possibilities for equal interaction are generated by their own activities, not mandated or supervised by the state.

What could foster such a democratic culture? The past thirty years offer two great examples: the activities of the Eastern European dissidents and of the new social movements. In both cases, citizens have rediscovered what Arendt believed all revolutionaries experience: a sense of their own capabilities apart from official political institutions. In the case of both the dissidents and feminists (to use just one example of a new social movement), there was a fundamental protest against various state actions and an attempt to change the state. To that extent, dissidents and feminists were locked into the citizen-state relationship that dominates modern politics. But in both cases the protesters did not wait for the state to change before changing their own lives and the conditions under which they lived. While working to change the state's violation of rights of free speech and assembly, dissidents published their work in various underground formats and met in various ways. Similarly, feminists in this country created the kinds of institutions—women's health clinics, shelters for battered women—that they wanted the state to provide and/or support. In the process, the very identities of the dissident and feminist became a way of being-in-the-world.

The discovery of how fulfilling it is to achieve a public identity, combined with the urge to have that identity acknowledged as valid and valuable by the body politic, has generated the "identity politics" of our day. The phrase covers a wide variety of phenomena, a fact that should make us hesitant about any wholesale embrace or denunciation of identity politics. From an Arendtian perspective, citizens should not think of their identities as preformed, as faits accomplis, that the state or polity must acknowledge. Identity in Arendt is always in process, and that process itself is public and political. Identity, then, is not the source of my demands on the polity. Rather, my demand on the polity is that I get to have an identity, that I get to be an individual amid others. Thus, to the extent that "identity politics" in this country has been a protest against invisibility—against being denied participation on the basis of prejudicial notions of what people of "that" sort (black, gay, woman) are "like"—Arendt (I think) would be sympathetic.

It seems equally clear to me that Arendt would oppose any "essentializing" of identity—either in seeing identity as "fixed" rather than ever changing or in seeing all people of one "kind" as essentially like one another and essentially different from all others of different "kinds." (I should add that "identity politics" is continually accused of such simple-minded essentialism, but it is hard to find many spokespersons for the essentialist position. Nevertheless, the ethnic violence in Bosnia and Africa in the past few years demonstrates that we should take the danger represented by essentialism very seriously indeed.) A democratic culture involves being open to change in myself, taking the risk that in my interaction with others, my identity (my beliefs, my goals, my orientation to the world) will be transformed more than theirs. Only when I am open to being stimulated, made uncomfortable, provoked, and delighted by others is democracy possible. That openness has to go two ways. Anyone who comes to the interaction convinced that identity is not fluid and is not formed in that interaction but is, rather, the product of pre- or nonpolitical (in the Arendtian sense) sources (such as biological sex or ethnic heritage), threatens the reciprocal plasticity that is crucial to democracy. Where the risk of interaction is not equal, I am not really taking the other as an equal. Instead, I believe in my heart of hearts that I have already achieved the "right" identity and that now it is just a case of getting that benighted other to see the light.

Arendt, however, is not an advocate of continual transformation. She wants the relative fixity that the word "identity" provides, a middle ground between an inborn essential "nature" and the dizzying parade of ever-new selves that some postmodern theories seem to offer. Her attraction to storytelling and narrative and her emphasis (in her ethics) on responsibility attest to her belief that we carry our identities through time, that the changes we undergo do not entail becoming new selves in each moment. For this reason, I think she would be sympathetic to the idea that gender and race and sexual preference and economic status are markers of identity whose significance might change over time but that also signify important circumstantial conditions that influence the choices I make and the actions I undertake. In other words, action always takes place in front of and with others, but it also takes place in circumstances in which physical and social facts play a role in defining the range of possibilities. There is no absolute freedom. Circumstances limit what is possible, and surely we promote freedom if we identify that some circumstances (such as being a woman) limit some people's freedom relative to other people's. Because Arendtian democracy relies so heavily on equality, identifying social sources of inequality is crucial to achieving that democracy.

It's harder to know how Arendt would react to the celebratory side of identity politics. If the years prior to 1989 in Eastern Europe highlighted the joys of public action apart from the state, the years since 1989 have brought home the chaos of ethnic particularism. One characteristic way to respond to social sources of inequality, to a society's refusal of equality to a marked group, is to develop a compensating sense of that group's superiority, of its not wanting to interact with other kinds of people anyway: we wouldn't play with you even if you did invite us to. But we certainly shouldn't reduce all celebrations of individual or group identity to some kind of pathological compensation for injuries received. Surely there is a positive role to be played by some affirmation of who one is and becomes, and of each public space's particularity, the way that it distinctively enables a way of our being together. The problem is, how do we endorse and encourage plurality without breaking down the polity into multiple hostile camps? The simple answer, I guess, is that if we really cherished plurality, we wouldn't want to be a member of a camp defined by its homogeneity. But that answer is simplistic, because it doesn't suggest how difficult it is to describe or achieve a balance between being at home with one's identity (i.e., accepting responsibility for that identity as mine and deriving some satisfaction from its being mine) and viewing that identity as one among many others, with no more fundamental right to exist than any other and no more fundamental claim to being right. What the Arendtian emphasis on plurality reminds us is that, for a democratic culture, a positive cherishing of difference is as crucial as a fundamental equality. The trick no one seems to have mastered thus far is how to have differences that do not translate into inequalities. And we can't even get the opportunity to attempt that trick, if difference generates only a murderous passion to eliminate the other.

I prefer considering Arendt's viewpoint on democracy expansive, as a way to reorient what we look to democracy to accomplish and enable, because I think it undeniable that she does not offer anything remotely resembling a comprehensive theory of democracy. Clearly, such was not her intent. Arendt's aim was to present a theory of the political, of what it means for humans to relate to one another and to act with one another in public. As a result, she has little to say about many issues that must concern any theorist of democracy, including the institutional forms and basic rights that would foster equality and open debate, and the various devices (including taking a vote) by which democracy attempts to alleviate (and even resolve) conflicts. Her work can seem rather thin if we expect it to address the various ways that contemporary societies manage to structure, reproduce, and signify inequality. But if we attend to her focus on what we should look to the political to enable and on the quality of the relationships between people in public, her writings can provide a change in perspective that renders a familiar landscape breathtakingly new yet still recognizable. She points us toward aspirations that we only barely knew we had, to reasons we cherish and honor democracy that we never knew how to articulate.

A Democratic Ethos

The dictionary defines "ethos" as "the characteristic and distinguishing attitudes, habits, beliefs, etc. of an individual or of a group," a definition that follows fairly directly from the Greek *ēthos*, which means disposition or character. Tobin Siebers has argued, however, that *ēthos* as "character" is a fifth-century B.C. usage that developed from the Homeric use of the word to mean "'the place where animals are usually found.' *Ēthos* is a word about a 'place,' a 'haunt,' or a 'habitat' that becomes habitual and eventually characteristic of its inhabitants"

(1992, 63). By extension, ethics can thus be understood not simply to encompass the formation and judgment of character, but also to include the production of a place that characters can inhabit. To put it in even more strongly Arendtian terms, ethics must build on the intimate connection of character to place. Only where we create a certain kind of place can a certain kind of person emerge. The "we" here comprises humans acting in concert, and the place Arendt would like to see us create is a democratic polity. Putting it this way highlights that Arendt's emphasis on place, on the public space of appearances, is physical but not territorial. We need to appear physically to and with one another, but because that physical appearing exists only while the performance is "on," there is no commitment to holding the space of appearances as exclusively ours or as exclusively available for only one type of performance. The "place" of any activity is where it is physically manifested this time.

The advantage of Siebers's recovery of the Homeric significance of "ethos" is that it highlights the situated and communal elements in the formation of character (the last being the traditional concern of ethics). It is in Arendt's conjunction of place and community that I want to locate her contribution to the project of fostering a democratic culture. To say that Arendt urges us to cherish difference already suggests a strong ethical commitment at the base of her political vision. What concerns me here is not the content so much as the form of her ethics. The content is, I trust, clear by now: an emphasis on the primacy of freedom, with plurality as the existential condition within which free agents are called to act; natality as the name given to action's irreducible originality; and equality as the political condition required for action to be free in a world we occupy with others on whom we are dependent. The product of free action is identity, which both gives each individual a sense of making a difference in the world by virtue of her existence and actions, and reproduces the very plurality that is the condition within which all action takes place.

The problem Arendt faced in presenting this ethical vision is the same one facing all nonfoundationalist ethics. A nonfoundationalist ethics is one that does not rely on any source of authority or compulsion external to humans to ground its guidelines for action. Neither the voice of God nor the nature of the universe can be taken as the source of moral law in such a view. Instead, humans are the source of all definitions of the good, and the problem is to see how humanly produced understandings of the good could ever acquire any power to convince others. What makes a humanly created law legitimate? By what authority could any human ever presume to tell another human how to act? A nonfoundationalist ethics tries to answer these questions without falling into complete relativism (every individual simply decides for herself what is right and wrong and has no way to influence those who hold different views) or into the pronouncement that everything is an effect of power (what is understood as right at any given time is the definition of right imposed by the most powerful on everyone else). Philosophical ethics traditionally tries to find compelling arguments to explain why people *ought* to act in the ways the philosopher wishes to recommend. Mere exhortation is not considered enough—but ethics seems more and more like disguised pleading if we deny any suprahuman grounding to moral injunctions.

There are four characteristic ways to make nonfoundationalist ethical arguments. To a certain extent, Arendt employs each of the four. She is hardly completely consistent or systematic in the kinds of arguments she uses; she deploys a variety of ways to convince her readers of her views on democracy and other issues. I will quickly characterize these four familiar ways here, then move on to a fifth way that has seemed fruitful to a number of contemporary writers and to which I think Arendt can make a significant contribution.

First, we have consequentialist arguments. Given a range of choices, the consequentialist argues that our decision should be based on the action that we believe will have the best results. The problem the consequentialist faces is the difficulty in measuring "best" (is it the result that best furthers my aims? the result that best serves the needs of my immediate community? or the result that best serves the needs of all humanity?) and our limited ability to predict consequences. These problems are not necessarily fatal to the consequentialist position, provided that it acknowledges that all actors are fallible and thus argues only that looking to consequences offers our best possible—though hardly a perfect—guide. Still, the consequentialist position leads to problems in judging actions. Are we to judge others solely by the results of their acts? Such an exclusive focus violates the usual sense that motives are a significant factor in deciding whether an act is praiseworthy or not. We are more likely to admire the person who donates $10,000 out of an income of $100,000 to AIDS research than the person who gives $2 million (of his $50 million) to have a hospital wing bearing his name built for AIDS patients. Presumably, the larger gift does more good (has better consequences), but that fact is not the only relative one we consider when judging the two actions.

Even worse is the suspicion that the consequentialist position is circular, since everything follows from the definition of what is best. Take the example of buying a car. I can spend $20,000 to buy a car with a catalytic converter and a six-cylinder engine that gets twenty miles per gallon; I can spend $8,000 and get an old Toyota that gets thirty miles per gallon but has no protection against air pollution; or I can spend $35,000 and get one of the experimental electric cars now available. If I define "best" solely by what is most financially advantageous to me, then I am unlikely to buy the electric car. If, as is most likely the case, I recognize the pull of two competing goods—not bankrupting myself and not contributing overly much to air pollution—I will try to choose the best compromise. The consequentialist position offers no guidelines for what I should define as best or how to weigh one good against another. As a result, this position is sometimes presented (especially in the social sciences) as a neutral description of what humans do when they act "rationally" in making choices, given preexisting preferences the observer does not question. But this position quickly becomes prescriptive when it urges humans to act rationally, since they quite obviously do not always make choices in the way the consequentialist thinks they do (should). Beyond offering a restricted definition of what counts as rational, however, the consequentialist position affords the moral theorist no way to intervene in what this or that agent values. The choice of values remains an individual matter—or, all too often, a kind of black hole in these kinds of theories. Where people get their own personal definitions of what's best is a mystery, the consequentialist says, but give me that definition and I can tell you what will (or at least should) follow. The individualist bias of this account leaves little to say about the social and cultural factors that influence the acquisition of values, and even less to say about the way ethics might intervene in the formation and transformation of values. All these criticisms being registered, however, it still makes sense to say that a consideration of consequences does play a role in our decisions about what to do and in our judgments of our own and others' actions. We have already seen how incredibly difficult it is not to point to beneficial consequences when one wishes to recommend a course of action to someone else, so that even an anticonsequentialist as resolute as Arendt still slides into arguing that her form of politics is justified by the fact that it results in freedom.

The second ethical position identifies certain components of the ethical circumstances in which humans find themselves and then draws conclusions about how humans should act. This position flirts with foundationalism, because it usually tries to denote universal facts about being human. The problem is that many humans act as if those facts are not facts—or as if those facts do not apply to them. For example, take the claim that we are dependent upon others to have an identity. Such a claim has fairly obvious consequences about how we should interact with our fellow human beings; the problem is that many people do not act as if they are dependent on others, and many of these people would explicitly deny the fact of such dependence. The ethicist who follows this strategy must first convince the reader that the hitherto unrecognized existential condition describes the reader's situation and then must convince the reader that certain beliefs, values, and actions would place her in an appropriate relation to those conditions. This position, then, tends to link ethics to knowledge. If we would just get a clear view of our situation in the world and with others as it really is, then right action would be easier to discern and to undertake.

The third position is Kantian. Here the ethicist focuses on insuring that each individual autonomously gives the law, the command, to herself. Only such autonomous self-legislation protects human freedom and guarantees that ethics is nonfoundational in the sense that neither an external authority nor external circumstances dictate my values or my actions to me. I give the law to myself, out of my own capabilities as a rational being. My values and my actions are self-generated, and I am motivated primarily by that cornerstone of rationality, the interdiction against self-contradiction. Because my dignity, autonomy, and freedom rest on my being a rational creature, my ethics will judge my beliefs and potential actions in light of their rationality, which rules out any self-contradictory beliefs or actions. And as Kant believes that reason is essentially the same in every rational being, all humans who legislate to themselves rationally will formulate the same law—the categorical imperative. It's a neat solution to the fear of relativism; every single person gets to create his or her own values, but all persons just happen to form the same ones. The only problem, of course, is that we hardly experience such unanimity of values in our actual interactions with others.

The fourth position, in different variants, is the one most commonly found in postmodern theory. Here culture, or one's social milieu, is seen as the source of one's beliefs and values, with society also possessing the means of enforcing those values (through both legal sanctions and less formal sanctions, such as social disapproval). "Social constructivist" theories of this sort vary in the degree of individual autonomy that they admit, but they are generally deterministic and endorse some version of cultural relativism. Along with the difficulty of explaining how the same culture produces individuals who are noticeably different, such theories are also bedeviled by the question of how an individual within a culture could ever judge its values and actions. Arendt is clearly struggling with both these issues in the Eichmann report; she does not accept that individuals are the product solely of social forces, and she does not accept that individuals possess no standards that allow them to judge their own society. Recent versions of social constructivist theories (especially as expressed in theories of ideology) almost always claim that any given society is riven by internal divisions and contradictions that afford individuals some vantage points and some choices within the social terrain, even as such theories deny that the individual could ever occupy a position outside that terrain. The specter of totalitarianism looms large here, since it is exactly the aim of totalitarianism to annihilate all such divisions and contradictions and thus to render all citizens docile followers of the prevailing ideology. The other ethical dilemma consistently raised by social constructivism is how anyone outside a particular culture could have the means to judge that culture's practices. If, as the anthropologist Marshall Sahlins puts it, "different cultures, different rationalities" (1995, 14), then how could a person from one culture ever understand or criticize a person from another? When Arendt talks of people changing their morals as they would their table manners, she is facing the possibility that social context could be all-powerful in the matter of ethics. Such is the "central moral, legal, and political phenomenon of our century" (*EJ*, 148)—a phenomenon Arendt wants to oppose, not to accept as the inevitable fact of how values are produced. In accepting the notion of "crimes against humanity" (255), Arendt insists that there is something that transcends any particular culture and can serve as a standard against which to judge actions (such as Eichmann's) within it. Members of that culture *and* observers from outside it can invoke that standard.

I hope the reader can see that Arendt occupies each of the first three ethical positions at different times. Nevertheless, I suggest that, despite her attempt to find a universal standard by which to judge Eichmann, she is primarily a social constructivist. She offers beneficial consequences to justify her political vision. And, like the consequentialist, even though she realizes that not everyone values freedom (many value "life" more than freedom), Arendt has little to say about why we should value freedom highly. She simply tells us the Greeks valued freedom and describes for us the world that results when humans act on that value. Also, Arendt's rejection of consequentialism on the individual level masks somewhat her acceptance of it on a collective level. She argues strenuously that individuals cannot sensibly base their reasons to act on consequences, because they manifestly cannot control those consequences. But collective action, in her account, does reliably produce the desired consequences. The polis, in her view, almost inevitably follows from action in concert, although as a by-product not directly aimed for. She does not imagine any nasty surprises here, such as action in concert that ends up producing less desirable modes of being together. The irony of unintended consequences is fairly strictly circumscribed in Arendt.

The second strategy is the one most characteristic of Arendt. Her argument, basically, is that humans are social animals, born into a world where each person lives with and is dependent upon others, and that this fact has implications for our choice of actions. Her work illustrates that the dependence on others goes deeper than we might realize. The very thing we think most fully our own—our individual uniqueness, our identity—can come into existence only through interaction with others. If Arendt can get us to accept the full extent of our sociality, then the definition of action as appropriate or inappropriate follows. And this intimate connection of humanness to sociality, to being with plural others, justifies identifying certain actions as "crimes against humanity." The tricky part here is the force accorded to the fundamental fact. The fundamental facts in Arendt are plurality, natality, interrelatedness (sociality), and the appearances given to us by our senses. A hard-line realist would say that these facts simply place us in a situation in which certain actions will have disastrous results whereas other actions will have neutral or beneficial results. The facts place us under nonreformable constraints. An example is someone who appeals to the fact that humans must breathe to argue that if we pollute the air past a certain point, the death of the species will inevitably follow.

But Arendt is not a hard-line realist. She recognizes that humans continually modify, redefine, and otherwise transform existential conditions and limits. So, we might pollute the air past that certain point yet also develop another way of delivering oxygen to the body to compensate. Thus, although plurality, natality, sociality, and appearances are fundamental conditions of human life for Arendt, there are forms of life that ignore or transform those conditions. These alternative forms of life are not impossible, but they are, for the most part, monstrous in Arendt's view. Not just totalitarianism but even the *vita contemplativa* (if pursued exclusively, to the neglect of common sense and of relations to others) strikes Arendt as the perverse refusal to acknowledge and be "reconciled" to fundamental conditions. That such refusals are both possible and fairly widespread means that purely existential arguments won't work, although at times Arendt relies on just such arguments. In other words, she is caught between arguing that the consequences are better if we act to foster plurality and arguing that because plurality is a basic fact of the human condition, only action that accepts that fact can be successful, or even sustained, in the long run.

I call attention to this confusion in Arendt, this inability to decide between two very different kinds of arguments, not because I want to belittle her work but because I believe that most efforts to construct a nonfoundationalist ethics fall into the same logical bind. Since neither the facts from which action starts nor the consequences it generates are secure enough to be regarded as a foundation, ethical arguments swing from one to the other in the effort to produce some "hold" on the reader's commitments. To what can I appeal in the effort to change another's beliefs, another's bases of action, or another's standards or modes of judgment? Do I base my own commitments and judgments on anything that deserves to be called more than mysterious preference, individual or cultural prejudice, or the fickle and arbitrary whim of the moment? No very satisfying answer to these questions is, as far as I know, currently available or in the offing. And it may be—just as it is in the search for a "safeguard" against evil—that we are asking the wrong question. There is no general formula, no cut-and-dried criterion, by which an opinion on an ethical question can be judged applicable to all. Rather, opinions about ethical matters are like all opinions in Arendt, aired and contested in public discussions in which sometimes some minds are changed but in which there are never any absolutely compelling arguments to be had.

The Kantian answer to the preceding two questions is Reason. But just as the postmodern critique of realism has deprived the first two ethical positions of their anchors in consequence and existential conditions, so that same postmodernism has relentlessly criticized the pretensions of reason. The book *Thinking* gives us the Arendt who tries to find an ethical base in a fairly traditional version of reason—one that focuses on the thinker's autonomy and on her desire to avoid self-contradiction. Postmodern theory questions the very image of being present to oneself in consciousness that underlies "thinking" as Arendt describes it, while also worrying about our seemingly endless capacity for self-delusion. How can I ever know when I am being rational? Finally—and most crucially—postmodernism has shown that the standard of rationality has consistently been used to legitimate my beliefs and to denigrate and/or exclude others' beliefs: I am rational, but you are not. Reason is something that, in theory, every human possesses; in practice, however, reason is the term used to separate some values as moral, approved, and human, from the "irrational" beliefs of others who court subhumanness in their inability or refusal to act "rationally."

It is right here—where we face the problems that afflict the standard ways to gain an ethical purchase over those whose values we wish to influence—that I think Arendt's work provides threads that might lead us out of the labyrinth. The key, I think, is to shift the focus from the *bases* of values and actions to the *process* of action and to what that process produces (the world, relations to others, and identity). Instead of looking back at how values were formed or what motives or beliefs stood behind my action, we need to look forward to what my action creates, what it brings into being. Admittedly, such an emphasis seems consequentialist, but I hope its rather different inflection will become clear as I proceed.

In the wake of postmodernism, certain writers—notably Judith Butler (1990), who builds on Jacques Derrida's notion of "iteration" and "citation" and on various writers' emphasis on "practice"—have turned to the "performative" as a way to think about agency, that is, about how individuals act and how those actions "signify" (both for the actor and for others). Not surprisingly, commentators on Arendt (Bonnie Honig [1993] and Frederick M. Dolan [1994], for example) have pursued the question of how her theory of action relates to various models of the performative. To be schematic about it, a performative theory of action focuses on the way an action creates the very thing to which it seems to refer. The term "performative" comes from J. L. Austin (1965), a British philosopher of the 1950s. Austin contrasted the sentence "The book is on the desk" with a sentence such as "I promise to bring the book to you on Saturday." The first sentence describes a state of affairs in the world that preexists the statement; before I said a word, the book was on the desk. But the sentence in which I make a promise creates a state of affairs in the world; before the statement was uttered, there was no promise, no relation between me and you, that entailed my undertaking to bring you the book on Saturday; the state of affairs and the utterance came into existence together. A theory of action that focuses on the performative argues that action neither reflects a preexisting identity nor simply reproduces a preexisting state of affairs, but creates identity or alters states of affairs.

In Judith Butler's work, the performative functions simultaneously as an account of social constructivism and an account of the way individual differences are produced within the same cultural setting. There are cultural models and ideals for various possible identities; for example, there is a storehouse of cultural images of what it means to be a girl, of what the "proper" way to be a girl is. But the identity of "girl" exists only as it is acted out by the numerous individuals to whom that label is attached. In these millions of enacted repetitions of "girl," variations inevitably are produced. Such variations may ultimately shift the prevailing cultural definition, or (more likely) they may cause an individual girl to feel anxious about her deviance from the cultural norm. Butler's hope—and her ethics, it would seem— is that the recognition (in theory) of the inevitability of deviance, coupled with the proliferation (in practice) of deviant performances (especially those that parody the current images of the "proper"), might lessen the stranglehold that cultural norms have on our actions. Freedom from the false guilt (and the more material social liabilities) of deviance, freedom to act in ways less dictated by preexisting cultural forms, is the goal.

The version of the performative that we can derive from Arendt has a rather different focus—one that emphasizes not the liberation of the individual from social constraints but the production of a social space by action. Recall that Arendt believes that actions create relations among people, and from this point of view we can see that Butler's notion of the performative is bound to seem solipsistic. In Arendt, relatedness is not a burden but something we are striving to produce. We might say that Arendt's relation to social constructivism is to find some way to affirm it. Rather than imagining the social as inevitably the source of oppressive power, Arendt thinks about how the social is something we collectively produce, something that enables actions and reveals identities we can delight in. Despite the worries evidenced in the Eichmann case, Arendt, it seems to me, is a social constructivist. But because she believes that power can rest in individuals acting in concert, her social constructivism does not focus on power invested in ideology or state apparatuses or insidious surveillance or disciplinary practices. Her account of totalitarianism fully recognizes that such alienation of power from the people and its redirection into dominating social forms is possible, but she wants to maintain a description (at least) of a way in which power does not have to work that way, of the democratic alternative. Power can designate our ability to create social forms that, in turn, influence the production of our identities— an ability that can lead to a polity we can affirm as our own and as what we desire.

The Arendtian performative is what I would call "projective." The best description I know of this projective performance comes from William James's essay "The Will to Believe." James considers the action of someone who is falling in love with another person but does not know if the feeling is reciprocated. By acting on the belief that you do or can come to love me, James argues, I am much more likely to generate the very state of affairs that I desire: "The previous faith on my part of your liking's existence is in such cases what makes your liking come. But if I stand aloof, and refuse to budge an inch until I have objective evidence, until you shall have done something apt, . . . ten to one liking never comes" (1954, 104). The point is that my action *appears* in the world and calls forth certain responses from others. There is no certainty, because my action can elicit a wide variety of responses. But I cannot get the particular response I am hoping for if I do nothing at all. Thus, the action is "projective"; it is performed in the hope of establishing a certain relation to another. But it is not a relation I can establish unilaterally. My action is a gambit that will fall flat unless the other takes it up and responds in such a way that a new entity—our love—comes into existence in the world.

Arendt's description of the American revolutionaries' act of founding a republic is similar. When the framers of the Constitution wrote, "We, the people of the United States," their utterance was a performative in the strictest J. L. Austinian sense. The United States did not exist before that utterance—and Arendt's point is that the United States could not exist solely on the basis of that utterance. Only when the people whom the Constitution describes as "the people of the United States" respond in a way that acknowledges that this phrase applies to them and that they will undertake to be "the people" so designated, does the new entity come into existence. The very possibility of the founding act depends on this audacious stepping out into the dark; and the success of the act—as well as, crucially, the legitimacy of what it produces—depends on how it is taken up by the others before whom it is performed and to whom it is addressed. The founders' action brings a new thing into the world, but only when that action is taken up by the audience, which accepts the relationship between actor and audience that the action projects. In this sense, the action is a "promise," a statement about the public space that will be created and the actions it will make possible if the relationship offered by the statement is taken up by its auditors. The mutual promises that Arendt sees at the origin of the polity in *On Revolution* are perfect examples of the performative.

The use of examples and the importance of stories in Arendt's ethics work in similar ways. If we consider how the ethicist could convince anyone to question or change his or her values, we should not look for irrefutable arguments or for rational demonstrations that this value or that action is inconsistent or self-contradictory. Instead, we can only "woo" the agreement of others with what we value by providing illustrations of the qualities and actions we admire, or stories that portray the kinds of lives made possible by adherence to those values. Ethics is not a matter of knowledge or truth or logic; it is a matter of projective instances, of concrete particulars that offer themselves as possible examples. An example's fate, like the fate of the founding fathers' proclamation, depends on how it is taken up by the audience. The actor and the storyteller alike can only do their routine,

striving for excellence and distinction in what they do. The rest is out
of their control—which doesn't mean they do not care about the audience's response. I can be deeply invested in trying to sway my audience, trying to influence how they conduct their lives. But I understand
that only leaving all power in their hands protects their freedom. As a
teacher, I aspire to change my students' lives. I want them to be transformed by what they learn and experience in my classroom. But a
transformation adopted because they want to curry favor with me
would travesty the effect I hope to have on them. Like love, ethical
agreement is something I can solicit, but if I receive it on demand, if it
is not freely offered by the other, it is worthless.

We can see now how recalling the Homeric use of *ēthos* as place
helps clarify Arendt's ethics. The projective performative calls into
being a community, projects relations of interinvolvement, in which I
stage myself as an example both because I want the esteem of these
others and because I wish to influence their actions. (Of course, others
are also acting in ways they hope will win my esteem and garner my
agreement or emulation.) It is in the quality of this being-together, the
quality of this place where we act for and in front of one another, that
the possibility of ethics (the formation of character) resides. Thus, as
with judgment, it is in the *process* (the projective action that calls others into relation with me so that a public space emerges in our meeting
place) as much as, if not more than, in the *content* of the action that
ethics resides. My feeling of connection, of being in communication,
with others is what stimulates my desire to *appear* in ways that others
can admire and that I can affirm.

The ethical, then, is fully political for Arendt; the ethical comes
into existence only in that public space of appearances that action in
concert produces. But this does not mean that ethics and politics are
exactly the same thing in Arendt. What ethics highlights is that things
can be otherwise. Humans can act in ways that do not produce or foster the ethos of democracy. Other places—such as the "hell" of the
concentration camps (see "The Image of Hell," *EU*, 197–205)—can
result from human activities. Political theory tells us what can happen
when people act in concert in certain ways. Ethics speaks to the quality of what that action can create, to the risks that projective action
entails (such an action is admirable, in part, because it can fail), and
to the fact that other choices of how to be in the world are available
to humans. Ethics, in other words, looks to examples of how people

have lived together and, in Arendt's case, tries to woo us to a vision of a democratic, pluralistic polity as the world we could most willingly inhabit.

One final word on the way that ethics, epistemology, and ontology are entwined in Arendt: it seems to me that her ontology works in ways strikingly similar to her ethics. The world, in Arendt's ontology, is profoundly political, in her sense, because it is intersubjectively produced in public. But I think we can go further and say that the world of appearances is projectively produced. Reality changes as a result of action for Arendt. But such changes cannot be unilateral. The real is what appears to many selves. Transformative action does not produce real changes until those changes are taken up (recognized) by others. The creation of a world of common sense, then, is a political undertaking, a somewhat willful acceptance or affirmation of the world I can share with others through visibility and communicability. We might say that my acceptance of this common world is one form of my acceptance that I live with others. Such acceptance is not inevitable; the rejection of common sense is fairly common. And Arendt is very clear that there are no absolutely conclusive arguments against solipsism and skepticism. The epistemological positions that each of us perceives his own reality and that the world of appearances is an illusion cannot be overturned by philosophical means (see *LK*, 32–33). The world of common sense is one we have to choose (to will)—just as we have to choose to act in ways that cherish the human condition of plurality. Arendt's ontology, then, is imbued with the ethical and with ethos. How we act in the world is not just an embodiment of our character but also the creation of the very place in which that embodiment gets to be displayed. How I orient myself to reality and to others, how I *place* myself in relation to the not-me, is quite literally world-enhancing or world-destroying. We are called to act in ways that projectively call into being a world we can inhabit with others and can love. As the singer Van Morrison has it in "Glad Tidings," "It gratifies when you see it materialize, right in front of your eyes, by surprise."

Notes

1. Origins: Arendt's Life and Coming to Terms with Totalitarianism

1. Biographical information used in this chapter is derived primarily from Elisabeth Young-Bruehl's fine biography of Arendt (1982). Additional information comes from Derwent May (1986); from *Hannah Arendt/Karl Jaspers Correspondence, 1926–1969*, edited by Lotte Kohler and Hans Saner; and from the interview with Arendt entitled "What Remains? The Language Remains," reprinted in *Essays in Understanding, 1930–1954*, ed. Jerome Kohn.

2. For another important discussion by Arendt of the legal, nonnatural basis of rights, see *On Revolution*, 108–9 and 148–49.

3. For a sensationalistic account of the Heidegger-Arendt relationship, see Elzbieta Ettinger (1995). Young-Bruehl, esp. chapters 2 and 6, is probably a more trustworthy guide. See Alan Ryan (1996) for a judicious review of the Ettinger volume, and Hannah Pitkin (1995) for a sensible brief discussion of Arendt's postwar view of Heidegger. The most extended treatment of the intellectual relation between Arendt's and Heidegger's work can be found in Dana Villa (1996).

4. In "A Reply to Eric Voegelin" (reprinted in *Essays in Understanding*), Arendt tries to clarify her methodology in *The Origins of Totalitarianism*:

> What I did . . . was to discover the chief elements of totalitarianism and to analyze them in historical terms, tracing these elements back in history as far as I deemed proper and necessary. That is, I did not write a history of totalitarianism but an analysis in terms of history; I did not write a history of anti-Semitism or imperialism, but analyzed the element of Jew-hatred and the element of expansion insofar as these elements were still clearly visible and played a decisive role in the totalitarian phenomenon itself. The book, therefore, does not deal with the "origins" of totalitarianism— as its title unfortunately claims—but gives an historical account of the elements which crystallized into totalitarianism; this account is followed by an analysis of the elemental structure of totalitarian movements and domination itself. (*EU*, 402–3).

5. Alexis de Tocqueville and Georg Simmel are the two earlier social theorists whose work adumbrates Arendt's concern about the replacement of concrete webs of relationship by an "abstract" relation to distanced and large bureaucracies, be they connected with the state or with big business.

6. Although marked by its insistence that Stalin's Soviet Union is totalitarian, *The Origins of Totalitarianism* is Arendt's most Marxist book. It owes three central ideas to Marxism: the connection of imperialism to overproduction, the tendency to read modern history in relation to the activities of the bourgeoisie, and the insistence that the aspirations and actions of that bourgeoisie are primarily "social" (as Arendt will later come to use that term), meaning concerned primarily with economic gain rather than with strictly political achievements. I will have more to say about Arendt's critique of Marxism in chapter 2, but we can note that her interest in racism and nationalism in *Origins* already suggests important motives apart from economic interest and, thus, a move away from the Marxist matrix that still dominates her thinking in this, her first "political" work.

2. Politics as Identity-Disclosing Action

1. For clarity's sake, let me state that I follow what has become fairly standard usage in employing the term "modernity" to designate the era of Western history from 1500 to the present, "modernism" to designate the arts from (approximately) 1890 to 1945, and "postmodernism" to refer to developments in the arts and in the criticism of them (loosely called "theory") since 1945. For a fuller explanation of this usage, see John McGowan (1991), chapter 1.

2. Michel Foucault's *The Order of Things* (1973) offers an extended analysis of the modern predilection to find truth in the depths. One primary example is Freudian psychoanalysis, in which a complex interpretation of surfaces (such as symptoms or the "manifest" dream content) is required before the deep, unconscious reality can be uncovered. Arendt's insistence on appearance as reality offers one way of understanding her complete lack of interest in psychoanalysis. I think it fair to say that Arendt does not believe in the existence of the unconscious.

3. *The Human Condition* also introduces another form of activity that is not encompassed by the triad of labor, work, and action: the activity of thought. Thought is characteristic of the *vita contemplativa*, as contrasted to the other three activities, which constitute the *vita activa*, the subject of Arendt's book. (*The Human Condition* was originally titled *The Vita Activa*.) To a certain extent, Arendt's book is meant to reverse—or at least to trouble—the Platonic and Christian valuation of the contemplative life as superior to the life of action. However, Arendt also closes her book by quoting Cato's description of the thinker as "never . . . more active than when he does nothing, never . . . less alone than when he is by himself" (*HC*, 325). The relevance of thinking to the political, scanted in *The Human Condition*, increasingly comes to obsess Arendt in the years following her characterization of Eichmann as "thoughtless." Chapter 3 will take up the place of "thinking" in Arendt's conception of political action.

4. The American Revolution, along with the spontaneous action taken by the people in the early days of other revolutions, does provide an alternative understanding of the political and a model for how it might be institutionalized. It is this "lost treasure" of the "revolutionary tradition" (*OR*, 215) that *On Revolution* tries to recapture in the face of the dominance of the French Revolution for modern political thought. I discuss this aspect of Arendt on revolution in the penultimate section of this chapter.

5. I have elsewhere tried to untangle Arendt's complex views on violence (see McGowan [1997]).

6. Arendt identifies these underlying desires as "principles," but she insists that such principles "do not operate within the self as motives do" but have instead a "universal" validity "not bound to any particular person or to any particular group" (*BPF*,

152). I must confess that beyond recognizing that she is using "principle" to identify the orientation that guides actions, I find this facet of her theory of action obscure. See *BPF*, 152–53, and *EU*, 329–33, for her most extended discussions of "principle."

7. In a formal game, this is the point when the power of the referee comes into play. His or her interpretation of the rule goes—and play continues. In a similar fashion, judicial courts are positioned to interpret the rules in a constitutional democracy. Arendt, as we shall see, is very much in favor of constitutions but has almost nothing to say about "judicial review" of laws or, even more generally, about the use of courts in "civil" matters. Almost all her interest in the courts focuses on the criminal side. I think this is because her emphasis on participatory democracy sees debates about interpretation and applicability of rules as part of the stuff of politics itself and thus as not to be handed over to the jurisdiction of courts elaborately separated from the give-and-take of political debate.

8. Michael Walzer, in his influential *Spheres of Justice* (1983), argues that such a separation of spheres of activity is the hallmark of liberalism. If we accept Walzer's somewhat idiosyncratic definition of liberalism, Arendt is, to this extent, a liberal, which is a way of saying that she is a fairly straightforward follower of Kant and his demarcation of separate spheres of human activity and cognition. Seen from this angle, Arendt's separation of the political from matters of "life" could be read as in line with the liberal attempt (in its "classical" eighteenth- and nineteenth-century forms) to insulate economic activities from political "interference." The crucial difference, however, is that Arendt values the political and scorns the economic, whereas classical liberals do just the opposite.

9. Robert Nozick's *State, Anarchy, and Utopia* (1974) has been the most influential and most comprehensive recent articulation of this "minimalist" politics.

10. For other influential discussions of the modern hostility to politics, see Chantal Mouffe (1993), Benjamin Barber (1984), and Sheldon Wolin (1960).

3. Understanding and Judging the Reality of Evil

1. See Stephen Leonard (1997) for a particularly powerful version of this argument.

2. It is worth keeping in mind the phrases "to keep . . . company" and "*has* to come to some kind of agreement," because very similar phrases recur in Arendt's discussions of judging, although in the former case the references are to harmony with others (although not necessarily *all* others), not to harmony with only oneself.

3. The "linguistic turn" refers to philosophy's predilection (after World War II) to rethink many traditional philosophical issues as matters of our languages and how we use them. Ludwig Wittgenstein's *Philosophical Investigations* (1953) is often cited as precipitating this "turn." Arendt, I think, is influenced by Wittgenstein in focusing on "communicability" and the representation of identity to others. Not only is *The Life of the Mind* strewn with references to Wittgenstein, a thinker absent from all her other texts, but also Arendt's view seems closely parallel to Wittgenstein's "private language argument," which holds that selves would have no way to experience their own selfhood without the categories provided by public, intersubjective language.

4. I have taken this passage from Ronald Beiner's "Interpretive Essay" in Arendt's *Lectures on Kant's Political Philosophy*. He is quoting from the last, and still unpublished (although it is to be included in the promised second volume of *Essays in Understanding*), lecture in the course "Some Questions of Moral Philosophy" taught by Arendt at the New School in 1965.

4. Arendt Now

1. One economic lesson of the past fifty years, which the Right in this country has managed to miss altogether, is that prosperity goes to the nations that are not burdened with huge "defense" costs. The German and Japanese "miracles" are largely due to the greatest gift we bestowed on those nations after World War II: strict exclusion from military buildups.

2. We should recognize that the powerful feminist slogan "The personal is political" not only questions how the lines are drawn between public and private in contemporary societies, but also (and perhaps even more crucially) moves us away from a *content*-oriented definition of the political to a *process* model. Much feminist theory has highlighted the processes—legal, social, institutional—through which the definitions of "public" and "private" are created and enforced. In this way, feminism has been a major impetus toward rethinking the "meaning of democracy"—and thus influences the way I am approaching Arendt's relation to our contemporary concerns. We read Arendt now in light of how she helps us to rethink democracy because of developments in feminism and in certain segments of the Left, and because of events in Eastern Europe and the rise of the new social movements.

References

Austin, J. L. (1965). *How to Do Things with Words*. Cambridge: Harvard University Press.

Barber, Benjamin (1984). *Strong Democracy*. Berkeley: University of California Press.

Benhabib, Seyla (1996). *The Reluctant Modernism of Hannah Arendt*. Thousand Oaks, Calif.: Sage Publications.

Bernstein, J. M. (1992). *The Fate of Art*. University Park: Pennsylvania State University Press.

Bourdieu, Pierre (1984). *Distinction: A Social Critique of the Judgment of Taste*. Translated by Richard Nice. Cambridge: Harvard University Press.

Butler, Judith (1990). *Gender Trouble*. New York: Routledge.

Calhoun, Craig, and John McGowan, eds. (1997). *Hannah Arendt and the Meaning of Politics*. Minneapolis: University of Minnesota Press.

Disch, Lisa (1993). "More Truth than Fact: Storytelling as Critical Understanding in the Writings of Hannah Arendt." *Political Theory* 21, no. 4: 665–94.

Dolan, Frederick M. (1994). *Allegories of America*. Ithaca: Cornell University Press.

Eagleton, Terry (1991). *The Ideology of the Aesthetic*. New York: Blackwell.

Ettinger, Elzbieta (1995). *Hannah Arendt/Martin Heidegger*. New Haven: Yale University Press.

Foucault, Michel (1973). *The Order of Things*. New York: Vintage Books.

——— (1979). *Discipline and Punish*. Translated by Alan Sheridan. New York: Vintage Books.

Habermas, Jürgen (1983). "Hannah Arendt: On the Concept of Power." In *Philosophical-Political Profiles*. Cambridge: MIT Press, 171–88.

Honig, Bonnie (1993). *Political Theory and the Displacement of Politics*. Ithaca: Cornell University Press.

James, William (1954). "The Will to Believe." In *Essays in Pragmatism*. New York: Hafner Publishing.

Kant, Immanuel ([1791] 1987). *Critique of Judgment*. Translated by Werner S. Pluhar. Indianapolis: Hackett Publishing.

Lasch, Christopher (1979). *The Culture of Narcissism*. New York: Norton.

Leonard, Stephen (1997). "Evil, Violence, Thinking, Judgment: Working in the Breach of Politics." In Calhoun and McGowan, 323–37.

May, Derwent (1986). *Hannah Arendt*. New York: Penguin Books.

McGowan, John (1991). *Postmodernism and Its Critics.* Ithaca: Cornell University Press.
———— (1997). "Must Politics Be Violent? Arendt's Utopian Vision." In Calhoun and McGowan, 263–96.
Mouffe, Chantal (1993). *The Return of the Political.* London: Verso.
Nozick, Robert (1974). *State, Anarchy, and Utopia.* New York: Basic Books.
Pitkin, Hanna (1981). "Justice: On Relating Private and Public." *Political Theory 9,* no. 3: 327–52.
———— (1995). "Conformism, Housekeeping, and the Attack of the Blob: The Origins of Hannah Arendt's Concept of the Social." In *Feminist Interpretations of Hannah Arendt,* edited by Bonnie Honig. University Park: Pennsylvania State University Press, 51–81.
Rorty, Richard (1995). "Demonizing the Academy." *Harper's,* January, 13–17.
Ryan, Alan (1996). "Dangerous Liaisons." Review of *Hannah Arendt/Martin Heidegger,* by Elzbieta Ettinger. *New York Review of Books,* January 11, 22–26.
Sahlins, Marshall (1995). *How "Natives" Think, about Captain Cook, for Example.* Chicago: University of Chicago Press.
Siebers, Tobin (1992). *Morals and Stories.* New York: Columbia University Press.
Villa, Dana R. (1996). *Arendt and Heidegger: The Fate of the Political.* Princeton: Princeton University Press.
Walzer, Michael (1983). *Spheres of Justice.* New York: Basic Books.
West, Cornel (1989). *The American Evasion of Philosophy: A Genealogy of Pragmatism.* Madison: University of Wisconsin Press.
Wittgenstein, Ludwig (1953). *Philosophical Investigations.* New York: Macmillan.
Wolin, Sheldon (1960). *Politics and Vision.* Boston: Little, Brown.

For Further Reading

The past five years have seen the publication of Arendt's correspondences with Karl Jaspers (see "A Note on Usage and References" for bibliographic information) and with Mary McCarthy (*Between Friends: The Correspondence of Hannah Arendt and Mary McCarthy, 1949–75*, ed. Carol Brightman [San Diego: Harcourt Brace, 1995]). Her doctoral dissertation has also been published in English under the title *Love and St. Augustine* (Chicago: University of Chicago Press, 1996), and her essays on American politics in the 1960s are collected in *Crises of the Republic* (San Diego: Harcourt Brace, 1972).

The two best recent comprehensive overviews of Arendt's work are Margaret Canovan, *Hannah Arendt: A Reinterpretation of Her Political Thought* (Cambridge: Cambridge University Press, 1992); and Seyla Benhabib, *The Reluctant Modernism of Hannah Arendt* (Thousand Oaks, Calif.: Sage Publications, 1996). A group of younger scholars have produced a number of fine studies that use Arendt's work as a lens through which to revise, extend, and otherwise enter into a dialogue with postmodern and feminist theory. Recommended are Susan Bickford, *The Dissonance of Democracy* (Ithaca: Cornell University Press, 1996); Lisa Jane Disch, *Hannah Arendt and the Limits of Philosophy* (Ithaca: Cornell University Press, 1994); Frederick M. Dolan, *Allegories of America* (Ithaca: Cornell University Press, 1994); Bonnie Honig, *Political Theory and the Displacement of Politics* (Ithaca: Cornell University Press, 1993); and Dana R. Villa, *Arendt and Heidegger: The Fate of the Political* (Princeton: Princeton University Press, 1996).

Richard J. Bernstein's *Hannah Arendt and the Jewish Question*

(Cambridge: MIT Press, 1996) starts with the Varnhagen biography and considers Arendt's responses to the Holocaust and the Eichmann trial. Lewis P. Hinchman and Sandra K. Hinchman have collected a number of the classic essays on Arendt (including the two by Jürgen Habermas and Hanna Pitkin that I refer to in my text) in *Hannah Arendt: Critical Essays* (Albany: State University of New York Press, 1994). *Feminist Interpretations of Hannah Arendt*, edited by Bonnie Honig (University Park: Pennsylvania State University Press, 1995), offers a wide range of feminist responses to Arendt's work, with essays by fourteen contributors. Finally, two very recent collections of essays offer a good introduction to the current ways that Arendt is invoked in postmodern work in politics, ethics, and, more loosely, "theory": *Hannah Arendt and the Meaning of Politics*, edited by Craig Calhoun and John McGowan (Minneapolis: University of Minnesota Press, 1997); and *Hannah Arendt: Twenty Years Later*, edited by Larry May and Jerome Kohn (Cambridge: MIT Press, 1996).

Index

Achilles, 140, 142

action, 11, 14, 19, 29, 42, 43, 59, 62, 71–72, 97, 101, 128–29; and appearances, 106; and consequences, 74–75; and control, 67–68; as distinct from work, 44–45; and freedom, 16, 60–61, 65–66, 70, 120; in front of others, 41, 111, 130–31, 159–60, 165; and identity, 63–67, 80, 135, 164; and judging, 120–21, 125; and the new, 27, 37, 55–56, 81, 114, 124–25; as noninstrumental, 44–45; and the political, 23, 34, 38, 47, 54, 69–70, 82, 83–84, 88–89, 94–95, 148–49, 154, 167, 174–75, 179; and relatedness, 176–78; and thinking, 110, 113–14, 115, 119

Adams, John, 81

Adorno, Theodor, 109

aesthetics, 61, 99, 123–24, 125

agonistic interaction, 65, 69, 71–72, 73, 128–29, 135. *See also* contestation

agreement: in collective activities, 73; in judgment, 125, 133, 177–78; in a polity, 76, 89, 133–36; in thinking, 114–15; and validity, 141

American founding fathers, 34, 43, 81, 87–88, 90, 177

American Revolution, 50

anomie, 59

anti-Semitism, 4, 6, 20. *See also* racism

appearances: and action in public, 62–63, 66, 106–8, 111, 155, 176; and judgment, 149; and language, 131–32;

and morality, 102–5, 107, 178; and the political, 106; the reality of, 14, 38–39, 71, 100–102, 109, 118–19, 154, 172–73, 179; thinking's withdrawal from, 110–11. *See also* space of appearances

Arendt, Hannah: arrest by Nazis, 3; childhood, 1–2; early political activities, 2–3; early years in New York, 6–7; escape from Europe to America, 5; first marriage, 2; later years in New York, 13; reaction to learning about the Holocaust, 7–8; relation to Zionism, 2–4; second marriage, 5. *See also* Eichmann controversy; specific titles of Arendt's works

Arendt, Martha, 1, 2, 3, 5

Arendt, Paul, 1

Aristotle, 115

Augustine, 29, 30, 55, 105

Auschwitz, 7, 146

Austin, J. L., 175, 177

authority, 168; and constitutions, 88; modern decline of, 36, 58–59

Beiner, Ronald, 13, 98

Bell, Daniel, 153

Benjamin, Walter, 5, 13

Bentham, Jeremy, 46

Bergson, Henri, 101, 120

Bernstein, J. M., 62

Bernstein, Richard J., 187–88

Between Past and Future, 9, 58, 125, 133, 139, 144

Bickford, Susan, 187
Blücher, Heinrich, 5
Blumenfeld, Karl, 2, 3
the body, 42
Bourdieu, Pierre, 58, 62
the bourgeoisie, 31, 56, 94; in modern
    Europe, 20–22, 23
Brecht, Bertolt, 3
Buchanan, Patrick, 151, 156
bureaucracy, 19–20, 54
Butler, Judith, 174, 175, 176

Camus, Albert, 117
capitalism, 20; global, 59, 150–51; and
    rise of the social in modernity, 54–56
citizenship, 14, 16, 93–95; in constitu-
    tional democracy, 89–90, 161; and
    ethnicity, 4–5; in participatory democ-
    racy, 162–63; and rights, 6, 24, 25–26
civil rights movement, 54, 89, 150
civil society, 152, 158, 159. *See also*
    public sphere
Classical Greece, 34–35, 38, 50, 52, 63,
    65, 94, 139
common sense, 40, 56–58, 100, 111, 112,
    119, 120, 179; *sensus communis* in
    Kant, 132, 134
communicability, 129–32, 135, 179; and
    public appearance, 133–34, 159
community, 158–59, 178
Conrad, Joseph, 52
conservatism, 85–86, 153, 155–56, 157,
    161–62
constitutions, 24, 25, 81, 82, 87–89, 91
contestation: of public/private divide,
    76–77; as sign of vital polity, 20, 86.
    See also agonistic interaction
contingency, 68–69, 70, 89, 101, 104–5,
    119, 137; and judgment, 127
Copernicus, 57
councils, 83–85, 91
courage, 65, 70, 152
crimes against humanity, 9, 10, 30–31,
    171–72
Crises of the Republic, 13, 54

Darwin, Charles, 53
DeLillo, Don, 142
democracy, 15, 16, 36, 54, 79, 81, 83,
    136, 154–55, 160–61, 164–66,
    178–79; Arendt's critique of Western

democracies, 81–82, 84–85; in con-
    temporary West, 150–52, 153; and
    freedom, 93–94; and local associa-
    tions, 91–92; and participation,
    87–88, 91–92, 94, 162–63, 167, 176;
    and role of experts, 86–87
Democratic Party, 156–57
Derrida, Jacques, 153, 174
Descartes, René, 57, 112
Dewey, John, 121, 122
Dinesen, Isak, 13, 142, 143
Disch, Lisa, 139, 187
disinterestedness, 61, 62, 77, 78, 110
Dolan, Frederick M., 175, 187
domination, 70, 82, 86, 140
Duns Scotus, 101
Durkheim, Emile, 59

Eagleton, Terry, 62
economic individualism, 16–17, 94; and
    collapse of living communities, 19–20
economic welfare, 49–50, 76, 85, 162.
    See also poverty
Eichmann, Adolf, 9, 10, 25, 27, 96, 103,
    106, 108, 109, 116, 122, 133, 171, 172,
    176. *See also* Eichmann controversy
Eichmann controversy, 9–13, 14, 31, 96,
    97, 105, 126–27
Eichmann in Jerusalem, 9, 99, 104, 126,
    144
Engels, Friedrich, 51
Enlightenment rationality, 36; in Kantian
    morality, 170–71; postmodern critique
    of, 37, 174. *See also* instrumental
    reason
equality, 25, 26, 71, 73, 78–79, 88,
    160–61, 164, 165; and economic bar-
    riers to political participation, 50; as
    partial and situational, 77–78. *See
    also* inequality
Essays in Understanding, 8, 13
ethics. *See* morality
evil, 20, 26, 31, 33, 38, 97, 99–100, 107,
    133, 145, 146, 173; "banality of,"
    9–11, 96, 105, 147; and morality,
    103–5, 122; "radical," 6, 30–32, 104,
    123, 147; as real, 29, 100–102; resis-
    tance to, 147, 148–49; and thinking,
    109, 115–16
examples: and action in public, 159–60,
    177–79; as heuristic, 117; and learn-

ing, 144; and morality, 141–42, 146–47; and stories, 142–43; and understanding, 139–40; and validity, 140–41
existentialism, 24, 26, 68, 69, 70

federalism, 13, 87, 91; critique of, 92–93
feminism, 76, 150, 152, 163, 184
Ford, Ford Madox, 34
forgiveness, 32, 69–70
Foucault, Michel, 85, 86, 87, 153
freedom, 14, 16, 26–27, 42, 45, 47, 48, 49, 50, 52, 68, 70, 73–75, 84, 93–94, 97, 99, 101, 119, 120, 140, 162, 165, 167, 170, 172, 175, 178; Arendt's notion of, 19, 23, 41, 60–63, 65–66, 121; as distinct from strength, 44; and intersubjectivity, 122; as positive liberty, 26, 84; and thinking, 110. *See also* negative liberty
French Revolution, 49, 50
Freud, Sigmund, 31, 105
Frost, Robert, 112

Galileo, 56
Gingrich, Newt, 151, 152

Habermas, Jürgen, 89, 154, 188
Hegel, G. W. F., 43, 51, 55, 66–67, 105, 121
Heidegger, Martin, 2, 8–9, 98, 105, 109
Heller, Joseph, 71; *Catch-22*, 71, 78
Hill, Melvyn, 144, 147
history, 110, 142–43; and judgment, 126, 144; and necessity, 55–56, 121; and understanding, 137–39
Hitler, Adolf, 5, 19, 28, 107. *See also* Naziism
Hobbes, Thomas, 53, 94
Holocaust, 104, 109, 145; Arendt's first reaction to, 7–8; and the banality of evil, 10–11; and the Jewish councils, 11–12, 105; and judgment, 126; and understanding, 14, 96–97, 103, 117
Homer, 139, 167, 168
Honig, Bonnie, 175, 187, 188
Horkheimer, Max, 109
The Human Condition, 8, 9, 23, 41, 43, 45, 54, 56, 58, 63, 84, 113, 116–17, 130, 131
Husserl, Edmund, 8

identity, 14, 27, 39, 61, 162, 165; in consumer society, 53; and distinctiveness, 34, 41; as intersubjective, 17, 22–23, 26, 37, 80–81, 130–31, 170, 172; and judgment, 128, 129, 133–34; and political action, 16, 19, 24, 38, 53–54, 62–63, 66–68, 93, 94–95, 110, 163, 167; and social constructivism, 175–76
identity politics, 80–81, 164–66
ideology, 28, 46, 58, 59, 60, 153, 171, 176
imagination, 110, 111, 121, 126, 138, 140, 143
imperialism, 8, 15, 18–22
individualism: postmodern critique of, 37, 59
inequality, 67, 150, 162, 165, 166
instrumental reason, 46–47, 61, 63, 111, 112. *See also* Enlightenment reason
interests, 49, 82, 84–85, 94, 110, 128

James, William, 176
Jarrell, Randall, 7, 30
Jaspers, Karl, 2, 6, 8, 9, 13
Jefferson, Thomas, 81, 91, 92, 93, 94
Judaism: and assimilation, 4–5; and the Holocaust, 11–12; and the modern nation-state, 21–22, 23
judgment, 13, 33, 35, 66, 71, 76, 79, 95, 97, 98, 100, 106, 120, 171; and adjudication of disputes, 136; Arendt's notion of, 108, 116, 119, 120, 122–23, 139, 143–44; as "enlarged" thinking, 129–32, 140; and freedom, 121; and the Holocaust, 12, 32, 105, 106, 126; in Kant, 123–25; and morality, 116, 122–23, 126, 127–28, 141, 146, 168–69, 173–74, 178; and particulars, 126–28, 138–39, 140; and the political, 147–49; and sociality, 137; and validity, 132–33, 134–35
justice, 49, 75–76; in law courts, 127

Kafka, Franz, 7
Kant, Immanuel, 1, 2, 13, 30, 36, 44, 58, 97, 98, 99, 103, 105, 110, 112, 114, 115, 120, 123–32 passim, 134, 136, 138, 144, 148; *Critique of Judgment*, 58, 61, 123, 124, 128, 132; on judgment, 99, 123–25, 131–32, 144; on morality, 170–71, 174

Kierkegaard, Søren, 2
Kohn, Jerome, 13, 188

labor, 42, 45, 46, 47, 54, 56
Laclau, Ernesto, 154
Lasch, Christopher, 86, 87
law, 89–90, 127, 170; and legitimacy, 168, 177
Lectures on Kant's Political Philosophy, 13, 15, 98, 129, 132
liberalism, 24, 46, 48, 52, 82, 85, 153, 156–57; Arendt's relation to, 25, 81, 85–86, 94–95; and the private sphere, 40
Liebknecht, Karl, 2
life, 42, 67, 75, 78, 95, 172
The Life of the Mind, 9, 13, 14, 15, 31, 40, 97, 98, 99, 107, 110, 111, 112, 113, 120, 125, 132, 174
Limbaugh, Rush, 151
Locke, John, 24, 94
Love and St. Augustine, 14, 187
Luxemburg, Rosa, 2, 81

Machiavelli, Niccolo, 65, 81, 94, 147
MacKinnon, Catharine, 153
Macpherson, C. B., 94
Mailer, Norman, 142
Mao Zedong, 19
Marx, Karl, 43, 51, 55, 56, 85, 128
mass society, 8, 15–17, 39, 49, 60, 94, 146, 147
McCarthy, Eugene, 75
McCarthy, Mary, 7, 97
meaning, 14, 32, 33, 37, 53, 68, 70, 110–11, 113, 114, 117, 120, 137–38, 142–43, 144, 155
Men in Dark Times, 13, 142
Merleau-Ponty, Maurice, 102
Mill, John Stuart, 24, 94
modernity, 14, 16, 23, 36, 46, 62, 84, 146, 153; and anomie, 59; Arendt's critique of, 34–35, 38, 39–40, 45, 53, 60, 94–95, 118, 158; and decline of the public sphere, 40, 53–54, 112; and loss of common sense, 57–58; narratives of transition to, 55–56; postmodern critique of, 36–37, 152; and rise of the social, 47–49
Monroe, James, 81
Montaigne, Michel de, 94

Montesquieu, Charles, 90, 91, 94
morality, 13, 15, 99, 102–3, 125, 147, 149, 152–53, 165, 166–67; collapse of under the Nazis, 6, 10–11, 103–4, 105, 107; consequentialist, 168–70; and examples, 141–42, 159–60, 177–78; and intersubjectivity, 122, 148, 178–79; under modern conditions, 125–26, 154; and nonfoundationalism, 167–68, 170–74; and publicity, 103, 107; and social constructivism, 171–72; and thinking, 115–16; as way of being-in-the-world, 123, 133–34, 144, 146, 179
Mouffe, Chantal, 154

natality, 37, 55–56, 59, 67, 110, 114, 124–25, 144, 167, 172–73
nationalism, 14, 15, 20, 21, 56, 93, 154
nation-state, 4–5, 15, 18, 20–21, 48, 49. See also nationalism
Naziism, 3, 4, 5, 6, 8, 10, 11, 16, 37, 103, 105, 122, 145
necessity, 14, 42, 45, 50, 51, 52, 53, 73–74, 75, 95, 112
negative liberty, 24–25, 26, 74, 82, 84, 86, 110. See also freedom
Newton, Isaac, 56
New York intellectuals, 7
Nietzsche, Friedrich, 47, 52, 53, 72

objectivity: Arendt's critique of, 138–39
On Revolution, 9, 40, 43, 49, 52, 70, 81, 106, 113, 177
ontology, 14, 15, 67, 95, 172–73, 179; of appearances, 38–40, 43–44, 100–102, 105; and modern science, 57–58; and plurality, 30, 41–42, 70, 148–49; and public realm, 82; and thinking, 108–9; and totalitarianism, 26–29, 103
opinion, 84–85, 87, 112, 119, 136, 144, 174; and distinctive identity, 133–34, 141; and the political, 132–33, 137, 140–41, 160–61; as product of judgment, 128–29, 131; and representation, 129–30
The Origins of Totalitarianism, 6, 8, 9, 14, 15, 22, 23, 27, 33, 35, 56, 97, 138

performatives, 65–66, 71, 174–78
Pitkin, Hanna, 75, 188

plurality, 26–27, 37, 61, 62–63, 67, 70, 80, 93, 110, 117, 134–35, 137, 165–66, 167, 179; Arendt's notion of, 16, 19, 22–23, 30, 41, 107; conditions for flourishing of, 23–24, 38, 41, 118–19; and judgment, 126–27, 144; and morality, 123, 133–34, 148–49; as ontological fact, 29, 172–73
the political, 14, 15, 23, 32, 34, 45, 47–49, 60, 89; and acting in concert, 44, 68–70, 72–74, 88, 159; and appearances, 106; Arendt's notion of, 16, 19, 25, 29–30, 38–41, 61, 63, 65–66, 75, 78–79, 147–49, 155, 157–58, 160–61, 162, 166, 179; critique of Arendt's notion of, 74–77, 93–94; and evil, 107; and identity, 79–81; and judging, 123, 137, 146; in liberal thought, 24, 85–86; in *The Life of the Mind*, 99, 115, 116–17; limits of, 49–52; and plurality, 17, 19, 26–27, 41, 49, 133–34, 167; as product of action, 62, 83–84, 176; and public debate, 75, 84–85, 91–92, 128, 132, 136, 140–41; and public happiness, 85–86, 94; and remembrance, 43–44, 69, 142, 147; totalitarianism's destruction of, 6, 18, 19; and willing, 98; and work, 42–44
political parties, 84–85
Portmann, Adolf, 102
postmodernism, 36–37, 61–62, 77, 78, 80, 150, 152–53, 165, 171, 174–75
poverty, 48–52, 157. *See also* economic welfare
power, 18–19, 26, 28, 29, 75–76, 82, 168, 176; as cooperative action in concert, 70, 72–74, 76–77, 83, 88–89; as distinct from force, 44, 73, 76, 83; in Foucault, 86; multiplication of in democracy, 87, 90–92. *See also* domination
private enterprise, 48
private sphere, 39, 40, 42, 47–48, 57, 75–77, 84, 91, 93–94, 134, 159; and thinking, 107–8, 116–17. *See also* public sphere
promises, 69–70, 87–88, 133, 175, 177
property, 43, 57, 157
public sphere, 41, 47–48, 54–55, 65, 75–77, 80, 82, 106, 137, 158, 159,

160, 176; and morality, 103, 107, 124, 133–34, 141, 178–79; as space of appearances, 38–39, 94, 167. *See also* civil society

race, 15, 165; and nation, 4. *See also* racism
racism, 8, 14, 17–18, 20, 21, 22, 56, 83, 154, 162, 164. *See also* anti-Semitism
Rahel Varnhagen: The Life of a Jewish Woman, 4
Reagan, Ronald, 152, 156
reason. *See* Enlightenment rationality
recognition, 66–67, 71–72, 80, 101, 102, 122, 141, 162, 179
reconciliation, 32, 113–14, 123, 125, 138, 143–44, 146, 173
religion: modern decline of, 36, 58–59, 126
remembrance, 43, 66, 69, 141; and stories, 145–46, 147
republican form of government, 4–5, 13, 81, 91–92
Republican Party, 151, 156–57
rights, 5–6, 24–27, 30–31, 76, 82–83, 88–89, 152, 154, 155, 157
Roman Republic, 34–35, 65, 94
Rorty, Richard, 157
Russian Revolution, 49, 81

Sahlins, Marshall, 171
Sartre, Jean-Paul, 68, 69
Schmidt, Anton, 145, 146, 147
Scholem, Gershom, 12, 126
science: and modern forms of knowledge, 56–57
Smith, Adam, 36, 155
the social, 21, 23, 34, 38, 39, 75, 84–85; as administration, 51–52, 86–87; Arendt's notion of, 47–49, 63, 95; and capitalism, 55–56; and consumer society, 53, 55; and morality, 171–72
sociality, 88–90, 122, 133–34, 140, 148, 159, 172–73; and communicability, 132, 134; and democracy, 161; established through action, 68, 160, 176, 178–79; as fundamental good, 136–37, 158
society. *See* the social
Socrates, 97, 114–15, 116–19, 141, 142
space of appearances, 14, 60, 66, 69, 70,

72, 128, 130, 167, 178. *See also*
    public sphere
spectators, 66, 102, 111, 113, 119, 122,
    130–31, 132, 136–37, 148, 149, 159
speech, 63, 64, 131. *See also* performatives
Stalin, Josef, 5, 8, 19, 28, 37, 122
the state, 82, 85, 91, 92, 94, 128, 155,
    157–58, 160, 163, 176. *See also*
    nation-state
statelessness, 5–6, 24–26
Stern, Günther, 2–5 passim
Stone, Oliver, 142
storytelling, 33, 36, 66, 67, 68, 100, 139,
    165, 177–78; and the Eichmann trial,
    144–46; and examples, 140, 142; and
    love of the world, 147; and meaning,
    137–38, 142–44; and the political,
    147–48

terror, 6, 10, 20, 22, 28, 49, 50–51, 106,
    145
thinking, 13, 23, 33, 38, 97, 98, 99, 100,
    105; Arendt's notion of, 108–9,
    114–15, 118–19; and morality, 105,
    107, 109, 115–16, 123, 146; and oth-
    ers, 130; and the political, 112–13,
    115–16, 147–49; and understanding,
    110–11, 113–14, 117–18; and will-
    ing, 120, 121; and withdrawal from
    reality, 109–10
Thinking. See The Life of the Mind
Thomas Aquinas, Saint, 105
Thoreau, Henry David, 24, 156
thoughtlessness, 10, 11, 100, 108–9, 116,
    122, 126. *See also* thinking
Thucydides, 139
Tocqueville, Alexis de, 92
totalitarianism, 6, 8, 9, 10, 14, 15, 22,
    23, 35, 38, 49, 52, 60, 67, 69, 91, 92,
    99, 110, 113–14, 117, 122, 138, 145,
    146, 171, 173, 176; and banal evil,
    104, 147; and destruction of plurality,
    20, 24, 27, 29–31, 41, 137; and fabri-

cation of a fictional world, 22, 27–29;
    and hostility to politics, 16, 18, 19,
    26, 29–30; and obliteration of history,
    11, 145–46, 147; and radical evil,
    30–32
truth, 113; as inimical to politics, 75, 87,
    112, 118, 133, 140–41; and stories,
    144

understanding, 30–31, 137, 139–40;
    Arendt's notion of, 32–33, 99, 113–14,
    117, 124–25; and evil, 96, 99; and the
    Holocaust, 12, 14, 31–32, 113; and
    meaning, 110–11; and stories, 138,
    143; and thinking, 108, 110–11, 117,
    118–19
United States of America: as multi-ethnic
    state, 4–5

validity: and examples, 140–41; and
    judgment, 125–30, 133–35; and law,
    89–90; and truth, 112
Vietnam War, 13; protests against, 54
violence, 18, 19, 44, 51, 52, 54, 82, 134
virtuosity, 65–66, 75, 81
Voegelin, Eric, 138

Warren Report, 142
West, Cornel, 163
willing, 13, 96, 97, 98, 99, 120, 121, 179
Willing. See The Life of the Mind
Wittgenstein, Ludwig, 117
work, 42–43, 45–46, 47, 54, 56, 57; as
    contrasted to action, 44–45
the world, 14, 28–29, 30–31, 34, 61, 72,
    75, 93, 95, 105, 106, 117, 135, 176;
    Arendt's notion of, 16, 23, 26–27, 68,
    100–101, 179; and common sense,
    40, 56–57, 119; love of, 146–47, 179;
    and morality, 123

Zionism: Arendt's relation to, 2–5, 6–7

John McGowan is a professor of English and Comparative Literature at the University of North Carolina at Chapel Hill. He has taught at the University of Michigan and the University of Rochester and is the author of *Representation and Revelation: Victorian Realism from Carlyle to Yeats* (1986) and *Postmodernism and Its Critics* (1991), and coeditor, with Craig Calhoun, of *Hannah Arendt and the Meaning of Politics* (University of Minnesota Press, 1997).